RIGOROUS DAP
in the Early Years

RIGOROUS DAP in the Early Years

FROM THEORY TO PRACTICE

Christopher Pierce Brown, PhD, Beth Smith Feger, PhD,
and Brian Nelson Mowry, PhD

Redleaf Press®
www.redleafpress.org
800-423-8309

Published by Redleaf Press
10 Yorkton Court
St. Paul, MN 55117
www.redleafpress.org

First edition 2019
Cover design by Erin Kirk New
Cover photograph by WavebreakmediaMicro/stock.adobe.com
Interior design by Percolator
Typeset in Chronicle Text
Printed in the United States of America
25 24 23 22 21 20 19 18   1 2 3 4 5 6 7 8

Library of Congress Cataloging-in-Publication Data

Names: Brown, Christopher Pierce, author. | Feger, Beth Smith, author. | Mowry, Brian Nelson, author.
Title: Rigorous dap in the early years : from theory to practice / Christopher Pierce Brown, Beth Smith Feger, and Brian Nelson Mowry.
Description: St. Paul, MN : Redleaf Press, 2018. | Includes bibliographical references and index.
Identifiers: LCCN 2017035357 (print) | LCCN 2017056552 (ebook) | ISBN 9781605545585 (e-book) | ISBN 9781605545585 (pbk. : alk. paper)
Subjects: LCSH: Early childhood education.
Classification: LCC LB1139.23 (ebook) | LCC LB1139.23 .B75 2018 (print) | DDC 372.21—dc23
LC record available at https://lccn.loc.gov/2017035357

Printed on acid-free paper

To my family for challenging me to be a better person, educator, researcher, husband, and father —CPB

To all my teachers, especially Nathan, Jack, Jesse, and Michelle —BSF

To my wife, Lisa Katherine Mowry, my father, Dr. James Mowry, and my mother, Clara Mowry, all of whom are (and were) outstanding educators and the most important people in my life —BNM

Contents

Acknowledgments

From Christopher:

Professionally, I'd like to thank those who've provided with me the educational experiences that led me to think and write about the early education process in a more complex way: Dr. Peterman and Peters at Sewanee, Drs. Cahill, Theilheimer, Stile, and Ortiz at New Mexico State, and Drs. Graue, Bloch, Price, Ladson-Billings, Apple, O'Day, Gomez, Hess, Popkewitz, Reynolds, Hassett, and many more, including fellow students and friends, at the University of Wisconsin-Madison. To my colleagues at the University of Texas at Austin: thanks to Drs. Goldstein and Reifel for giving me a chance in academia, Drs. Adair and Nxumalo for being amazing colleagues in early childhood education, and to all the wonderful folks who I have the good fortune to work with at UT-Austin on a daily basis. Thanks to the groups of early childhood researchers and teacher educators at such organizations as the Early Education and Child Development and Critical Perspectives in Early Childhood SIGs of AERA, the National Association of Early Childhood Teacher Educators, and RECE for allowing me to share and develop my work across multiple venues and outlets. I also want to thank my former preschool and elementary school colleagues and the many students, be it young children and their families, preservice teachers, and doctoral students whom I've had the opportunity to work with over the years. Each of you has shaped me as an educator in ways you'll never know. I also want to the thank the Spencer Foundation's Small Grants program and UT-Austin's Special Research Grants program; both have provided me with funding over the years that led to the studies that impacted the development of this book. Finally, I want to thank all of the teachers, parents, administrators, policymakers, researchers, and others who have allowed me to study what it is they do. This book and my research in general would not be possible without their generosity of time in and/or opinion about educating young children.

Personally, I'd like to thank my parents, their partners, and my extended family for helping me become who I am today; my father for his unwavering support in my education and my mother for her belief in me. I'd also like to thank my wife, Michele, for her continued love and support over the past twenty-one years of marriage, and to our three daughters, Camille, Vivienne, and Lucille, for always reminding me what's important in life and the significance of early education in the lives of all children.

Finally, I'd like to thank Kara Lomen, formerly at Redleaf, for reaching out to me about the possibility of putting this book together. With the assistance of Laurie Buss Herrmann, she helped me develop an idea that emerge in articles I wrote with Brian and Beth into this book. I'd also like to thank Heidi Hogg and her colleagues at Redleaf for following through with this project, as well as Stephanie Schempp and Lindsey Smith for their insightful editing of our text.

Introduction

Every day as twenty-three four-year-old children arrive at Ms. Simpson's prekindergarten classroom, they complete the following tasks:

- *They put their jackets and backpacks away in their lockers.*
- *They walk into the classroom holding their homework folders and packed lunches. The folders contain homework, notes from families, and sign-up sheets for after-school programs or sports activities. They place their folders and lunches into two different baskets by the door.*
- *Next they check the welcome board that has a poll question on it. Today's question is "Do you like pizza?" posted next to a picture of a girl eating a slice of pepperoni pizza. The students put their magnetic name cards under the yes or no column.*
- *Learning centers in the classroom include a library, construction center, writer's corner, puzzles/games table that focuses on early math skills, and pretend and learn center, which is currently set up like a flower shop. The students go to the learning centers chart that's next to their daily schedule. A name card shows them where they will start their day. Additionally, every morning Ms. Simpson selects one student to write or draw the morning message at circle time. No matter what the student writes or draws, Ms. Simpson adds a dictated sentence from the student.*
- *Finally, students write their names on a sign-in sheet, which is a piece of large tablature paper numbered one through twenty-three. Positioned close to the door is the listening center, with a sign-in sheet. The order of students is determined by how their oak name tags appear in a names basket next to the sign-in sheet. Students can use their name tag as a model for writing their name on the paper. If students can't read the name of the student who is to follow them, they can ask Ms. Simpson for help.*

As students complete these tasks on a September morning, Ms. Simpson works with individual students at the sign-in area. While some students use the available models of their names, other students' fine-motor or cognitive skills aren't as developed. For these students, Ms. Simpson writes down their names, which they then trace over. Participating in this activity with her students gives Ms. Simpson a sense of her students' literacy skills. It also positions her near the door so she can say hello to arriving children and their families. By sitting here, she can remind students about what to do as they arrive. For example, when Javier comes into the classroom, she helps him locate his name on the center chart, and when he looks at the picture labeled Construction Center, he sees where he is to start his day.

Arrival time lasts about twenty minutes each morning. As the students engage in the centers, Ms. Simpson checks on what each child is doing. She walks over to check on Luis, an English language learner (ELL), who was selected to write the class morning message. He has drawn a stick figure but is struggling with what to write underneath it. Ms. Simpson gets down on her knees so her face is level with his. Then she asks in a warm voice for Luis to tell her about his picture so she can write the words for him to copy or trace. She says, "I noticed you have a person in your picture. Tell me about that person." He mumbles, "I'm playing outside," and Ms. Simpson responds, "Ooh, that sounds like fun. Can I write 'I'm playing outside' under your picture?" Luis says, "Uh-huh," and Ms. Simpson slowly repeats each word as she writes it out. As she leaves, she tells Luis he has a few more minutes to finish his message. She encourages Luis to remember to sign his name so his classmates will know the morning message is from him. Ms. Simpson and the children engage in these learning activities until the announcements begin.

This scenario shows some of many morning routines we've witnessed over the years at preschool, Head Start, pre-K, kindergarten, and other early childhood classrooms serving children ages three to eight. Although Ms. Simpson is not her real name, she is a very real person. In her classroom, the impact of increased academic expectations on children and teachers is clear. These four-year-old children have homework, they are expected to complete a series of academic routines as soon as they walk in the door, and many of their learning centers focus on academic skills. Your evaluation of Ms. Simpson as a teacher depends on the educational theories you believe in. Those who think children learn best when they can self-select their learning experiences (typically referred to as *child-directed learning*) will notice that Ms. Simpson's prekindergarteners have few opportunities to do so. Even at the learning centers, the children have little freedom to engage in activies beyond Ms. Simpson's prescribed expectations. Those who believe children learn best through direct instruction (often called *teacher-directed learning*) will notice that Ms. Simpson has time to work with only a few students beyond a superficial level.

We do not believe in choosing one form of instruction or set of practices over another to appropriately challenge each student. We put forward the idea that the right instructional strategy depends on the cultural, developmental, and linguistic talents of the children in the classroom, the content the teacher needs to cover, and the context of the classroom at that time. We provide this example of Ms. Simpson's classroom to illuminate the complexity of teaching young children in this current age of standardization, academic achievement, and limited resources. Ms. Simpson must arrange her day with twenty-three prekindergarteners in such a way that satisfies the demands of state policy makers, her school and district administrators, and her students and their families. It must also statisfy her professional vision of what the children in her classroom must do to develop the skills and knowledge needed to succeed.

Of the voices competing for Ms. Simpson's attention in her instructional decision-making, two are the loudest—state policy makers and her school and district administrators. These groups tend to focus on the children's academic success. Below, Ms. Simpson describes the pressure she faces:

> When I started teaching pre-K twenty years ago, the administrators said, "Oh, don't worry about the alphabet and numbers—it's not a big deal." Now if my students don't know all their letters and sounds by the time they finish pre-K, I am in trouble. That's the gamut that I've taught through. For my children to be ready for kindergarten, they now need to be reading.

Meeting the Changing Expectations in Early Education

This expectation for young children to be reading by the time they leave pre-K is disconcerting. But with the implementation of high-stakes, standards-based accountability reforms like the No Child Left Behind (NCLB) Act of 2001, such academic demands for young children have become more common. Teachers like Ms. Simpson feel every child must leave the classroom having mastered a predetermined set of specific academic skills. If they don't, educators fear being labeled as bad teachers by state policy makers, their administrators, or even children's families.

Ms. Simpson, like many other early childhood educators working in the United States, must reconcile what she knows about child development and learning with a mandated set of knowledge and skills her school administrators and state and federal policy makers think all children must acquire. Ms. Simpson has let those mandates dictate how she approaches her instruction and interactions with young children. Considering that Ms. Simpson's evaluation as a teacher is tied directly to which skills her students master, this appears to make sense. But it doesn't have to be this way.

In this book, we offer an alternative approach to teaching young children that takes into account both the required content, skills, and knowledge and how children learn best. We call this approach RIGOROUS DAP:

Reaching all children
Integrating content areas
Growing as a community
Offering choices
Revisiting new content
Offering challenges
Understanding each learner
Seeing the whole child

Differentiating instruction
Assessing constantly
Pushing every child forward

With these eleven principles that make up RIGOROUS DAP, early childhood educators can make instructional decisions that address children's developmental domains and what children need to know to succeed in school. Using this book, teachers can identify the rigor and appropriateness in their instructional decision-making—empowering them to help their children succeed. We believe that this process will equip and inspire teachers to make meaningful changes that satisfy the demands of those outside the classroom, meet the needs of the children in their classrooms, and align with their knowledge and beliefs about how children develop and learn.

Applying RIGOROUS DAP

To show how RIGOROUS DAP works as a whole, let's revisit Ms. Simpson's classroom. Ms. Simpson's routine is structured so each child can engage in developmentally appropriate learning activities. While the academic content covered in these routines is disjointed, children are offered several specific learning experiences that ask them to read, write their names, compose a morning message, and follow a specific sequence of events to prepare them for the day. All these tasks are intended to teach students the skills needed to succeed within the larger schooling system. Ms. Simpson attends to children's developmental needs by individualizing their sign-in experiences; name tags are available for children who need to look at an example, and Ms. Simpson helps students who struggle with fine-motor skills by letting them trace over her writing. She also supports ELLs by providing pictures of vocabulary words (for example, the picture of the girl eating pizza) to illustrate their meaning. Finally, children can engage with their classmates in a range of play-based centers that foster opportunities for social, emotional, physical, and academic learning.

Ms. Simpson engages with her students in a manner that values what they bring to the classroom. For instance, Ms. Simpson attempts to level the difference in power and knowledge about writing by asking Luis to tell her about the person he drew. She did not evaluate his work or question why he had not written any words. Instead, Ms. Simpson asks him if she can write words for him. She does so in a manner designed to strengthen her relationship with him. Also, by aiding Luis with this activity, Ms. Simpson shows him how he might extend his work by adding written language to his picture. Finally, by strategically positioning herself near the door, Ms. Simpson can welcome all families as they arrive at school. Through these interactions, Ms. Simpson's students and their families can see that she values them and supports their presence in the classroom.

WAYS TO IMPROVE PRACTICE

While there are many positives in Ms. Simpson's morning routine that are tied directly to our construct of RIGOROUS DAP, we've identified some areas for growth. One is the narrow nature of each of the daily tasks; much of the children's morning routine is based on ensuring the children develop and experience specific academic skills in literacy. Second, the structure of the routine isolates students from one another. They have no choice in deciding what they will do or whom they will be working with. While structure and teacher-led decision-making are needed at times, a morning routine is an easy place within the typical school day to allow children to have choice and voice in their learning. While the centers can offer children academic, social, emotional, and physical challenges in their learning, the repetitiveness of the other activities across a 180-day school year, such as the sign-in sheet, may not push every child forward in their learning. The routine itself does not offer Ms. Simpson's students the opportunity to grow as a community, either socially or culturally. For example, socially, many of the activities are set up to guide children to engage in individualized rather than community-based learning experiences. Furthermore, the activities are void of any references or experiences tied to the children's sociocultural backgrounds. For instance, Ms. Simpson decided the pretend and learn center should be a flower shop without asking her students how many had ever been inside one. Finally, if there were fewer students in Ms. Simpson's class, there would be more time for intentional teaching. But policy makers in Texas, where she works, did not mandate a teacher-to-student class size ratio. As such, Ms. Simpson has twenty-three students in her class. Such limited resources add to the challenge of engaging in RIGOROUS DAP.

How to Use This Book

To help you understand and use RIGOROUS DAP with your students, we examine in detail the eleven essential components of RIGOROUS DAP across the remainder of the book. We've constructed this text to assist practicing teachers and teachers-in-training in developing their understanding of how to engage in high-quality instruction with young children in this current age of standardization, academic achievement, and limited resources. In each chapter, we provide real-world examples from the preschool, prekindergarten, kindergarten, and elementary school teachers we've worked with over the years to explain and identify the essential components of RIGOROUS DAP.

In sum, the focus of this book is how you can recognize, create, and sustain RIGOROUS DAP classrooms. We provide you with a construct and acronym that offers eleven principles of instruction that will help you address your students' individual, sociocultural, and developmental needs while preparing for elementary school success. RIGOROUS DAP is designed to help you manage the pressures and demands that exist within this current age of standardization, academic achievement, and limited resources.

Remember, implementing RIGOROUS DAP is a journey, not a destination. As you embark on this journey, it is vital to inform preschool and elementary school colleagues, administrators, and families about the strengths each child possesses, as well as the importance of how teachers facilitate children's learning and development. Teachers should be able to confidently explain how the intentionality of their instruction offers children meaningful choices, opportunities to experiment with new ideas in a safe and comfortable setting, and time to revisit new knowledge and skills. When offering this explanation, stakeholders will understand how the academic rigor embedded in RIGOROUS DAP practices builds on children's skills and knowledge to further develop the areas needed to be successful now and throughout their academic careers.

1

Why RIGOROUS DAP Is Needed

Twice a day, children in Ms. Sanchez's full-day pre-K classroom at a public elementary school have free-play time. In the morning, they spend between sixty and ninety minutes in this activity, and in the afternoon, between fifteen and forty-five minutes. This instructional activity allows children to choose and engage in a range of self-directed learning activities affiliated with numerous learning centers. Ms. Sanchez's instructional goal is to offer children integrated learning experiences across all their developmental domains. Many of these centers (blocks, home, cars, puzzles, and computers) remain constant throughout the year. Others, such as the listening, reading, math, dress-up, science, and pretend and learn centers, evolve alongside the curriculum. For instance, in the fall the listening, reading, math, and science centers focused on the life cycles of plants, specifically pumpkins, beans, and corn. In the math center, children sorted, counted, made patterns, and so on with the three types of seeds. The pretend and learn center evolved from a forest (where the children helped wild animals prepare for winter) to a cave made of plastic held up by a fan at one end and an opening on the other. In the cave, the children pretended to be bears and bats hibernating and also learned about spelunking. This transition in centers from a fall forest to a winter cave helped the children understand the impact of the seasons on a range of animals.

During free-play time, children can choose to go to any center they want; each is labeled with both the center's name and a picture (for example, the block center has a photograph of blocks under it). None of the centers have a capacity limit. Rather, Ms. Sanchez asks the children to choose another activity when a center feels full. Some days a parent volunteer might be present during the morning session; he or she typically engages in an art-based activity or a game that addresses academic skills the children are learning. For example, the children once made maracas with

seeds, paper cups, toilet paper rolls, and tape, which they used during an improvised whole-group singing activity later that day. During the activity, Ms. Sanchez and the students sang and shook their maracas and bodies to represent the number of seeds she had in her hand. As she sang, "I've got one seed in my hand," the students shook their maracas and bodies one time. They repeated this pattern until they hit the number ten.

At some point during the morning session, either by choice or when Ms. Sanchez asks, the children are to complete what Ms. Sanchez calls their job. This job entails the children working with Ms. Sanchez either one at a time or in small groups to complete an academic activity. For instance, when examining pumpkin seeds, she worked with the children during morning free-play time to complete a sequencing activity. The activity asked the children to organize a series of pictures to demonstrate how a seed becomes a pumpkin. There were six images on a sheet to cut out and rearrange on a large piece of paper to represent the following life cycle sequence: a seed, a sprout, a vine and leaves popping out of the soil, a flower on the vine, a small pumpkin, and a large pumpkin. She used this activity to assess students' understanding of the life cycle of a pumpkin, which she recorded in her student-learning journal.

If she's not working in a small group assisting children in completing their jobs, Ms. Sanchez can be seen documenting student learning by taking photographs of children pulling seeds out of a pumpkin and looking at the seeds under a microscope. Often she engages with the children in their play. For instance, as the children examined the seeds under the microscope, she helped them split a seed in half to look at the seed coat and discuss how that coat protects and prepares the seed to become a plant. On another morning, she spent an hour with the children discussing and experimenting with different types of ramps they could build to allow cars to jump the longest distance possible. Then they measured and compared these distances with nonstandard objects. Their conversation covered such scientific and mathematical terminology as speed, length, slopes, force, motion, and gravity. After repeated use of these words within this center, she placed these words on the word wall located next to the writing center.

We purposely begin this chapter about the necessity of RIGOROUS DAP with the example of Ms. Sanchez engaging in what she termed free play with her students. We do so because it illuminates one of the central issues within early childhood education (ECE): how should early educators prepare young children for success in the elementary grades? A common response we've heard over the years in policy and administrative circles is that early childhood teachers need to engage in more rigorous instruction to prepare children for school success.

While such a statement sounds reasonable, it does not explain what rigorous practices look like with young children, and it assumes that up until this point, early educators have not been engaging in such practices. Furthermore, the term *rigor*, be it academic or instructional, has typically been tied to the notion of *more*. Meaning that children must possess more academic skills to be ready for school, and the only way to do that is to give them more content, more direct instruction, more seatwork, more homework, and so on.

We developed RIGOROUS DAP in response to these and similar troubling statements. In RIGOROUS DAP, rigor and developmentally appropriate practice go hand in hand. By engaging in these practices, early educators can make instructional decisions that address both the children in their classroom and what their students need to know to succeed in school. Moreover, we see this construct as a vehicle that can empower early childhood educators by helping them identify to others—whether parents, administrators, or even policy makers—the rigor and appropriateness in their instructional decision-making.

What Is RIGOROUS DAP?

RIGOROUS DAP is a set of instructional practices designed to assist early childhood educators make instructional decisions that provide children with multiple learning opportunities to gain the knowledge and skills needed for success in and out of elementary school. The construct itself comprises two parts: academic rigor and developmentally appropriate practices. An academically rigorous learning environment allows all children to learn at high levels through hands-on learning experiences that address the whole child. A developmentally appropriate early learning environment considers the children's cognitive, social, emotional, linguistic, and physical development, as well as the sociocultural worlds in which they live. This aspect of the construct points to the significance of learning being a whole child process that requires the child to engage with his mind, body, and heart as he learns to construct new knowledge with you and his classmates.

Teachers who engage in RIGOROUS DAP recognize that there is no one way to educate children. Instead, they create the conditions for all children to learn at high levels by providing them with multiple learning opportunities to gain the knowledge and skills needed for success in and out of elementary school. They also ensure these learning opportunities consider children's individual, sociocultural, linguistic, and developmental talents. As the school year progresses, teachers build on their content and increase their performance expectations. As teachers do this, they must provide appropriate levels of support to children through regular and consistent monitoring of their achievement across all developmental domains. The goal is for every child to have, or be on the trajectory to attain, the social, emotional, physical, and academic knowledge and skills necessary for success by the end of the school year.

RIGOROUS DAP AND MS. SANCHEZ

When Ms. Sanchez tells children's families or her administrators that her students engage in free play twice a day, it may sound to them as if she is simply letting children run wild in her classroom. This assumption misses the planning, purpose, and intention of her teaching within this instructional activity. To allow families and administrators to understand better, she must confidently explain that she intentionally designs, maintains, and amends an instructional period during her day that allows for self-directed learning, addresses ongoing skill development, offers multiple opportunities to engage with academic learning, requires social flexibility and adaptability, and fosters critical thinking. Using this language and terminology helps others understand how the intentionality of Ms. Sanchez's instruction is embedded in developmentally appropriate practices that prepare children for the rigor of elementary school. Her instruction builds on what her students already know and can do so they can further develop the skills and knowledge needed to be successful in kindergarten, in their community, and beyond.

Moreover, if Ms. Sanchez were to make use of our notion of RIGOROUS DAP to evaluate her teaching, she might see that she could improve her instruction by rethinking how she addresses the students' mandated job activity or her use of the term *free play*. For instance, framing how the students help the classroom function through the term *job* assumes the children must perform this activity for the teacher. However, renaming it a *learning opportunity* frames the activity in such a way that students can realize how it contributes to their academic development rather than how it pleases the teacher.

The same can be said for how Ms. Sanchez frames important instructional and learning time within her day as *free play*. Using a term like *purposeful play* does not take power out of the hands of children in choosing what they want to do, and instead, it demonstrates that what is occurring during this time is important and intentionally designed to support growth and learning. Ms. Sanchez might also reconsider the types of seeds the students are exploring as well as the types of animals that are preparing for winter so that they reflect students' immediate and cultural histories. For instance, the children could examine how animals in their local or regional area prepare for winter, or they could use seeds from plants or produce they have accessible in their school community or at home.

Still, Ms. Sanchez has invested a significant amount of time in planning, developing, and executing these learning activities for students. The goal for her, as well as any early educator, should be to demonstrate to herself, her students, the families she works with, and the larger learning community the intricacies of her teaching. Her acts in the example demonstrate how she strives to ensure she is offering her students meaningful choices, opportunities to experiment with new ideas in a safe and comfortable setting, and time to revisit new knowledge and skills, which are some of the central components that define RIGOROUS DAP. Engaging in these rigorous activities keep students interested, motivated, and engaged in their learning.

How the Need for RIGOROUS DAP Evolved

RIGOROUS DAP is a response to the changes that have occurred to publicly funded ECE in the United States as a result of increased standardization, which emphasizes improved academic achievement by all children while using limited governmental resources. Policy makers at all levels continue to push and promote ECE as a program that is designed to prepare children to achieve academically in elementary school, leading to the standardization of ECE programs. Thus, children are expected to obtain a specific set of knowledge and skills to achieve academically at high levels by the time they leave these programs (Bassok and Reardon 2013). This framing of ECE replaces the common knowledge of childhood development and learning with what they are to *know* (knowledge) and what they are to *do* (skills) (Brown 2007).

STARTING WITH HEAD START

The current push toward standardization and academic achievement in ECE is not a recent phenomenon. In fact, it has been going on since the 1960s with the establishment of the federal government's Head Start program. Part of the Johnson administration's War on Poverty, Head Start was created to address the problem of poverty through a two-generation approach that would remedy "the educational inequalities borne by impoverished children" (Zigler, Marsland, and Lord 2009, 23). To help stop poverty from being passed on from one generation to the next, the federal government decided to intervene and provide publicly funded early intervention programs that could help poor children be ready for school. Legislators believed that doing so would not only help ensure they were not lagging behind their more affluent peers when they started elementary school, but it would also put children on a trajectory where they could succeed in school and rise out of poverty.

The establishment of Head Start is significant for four reasons. First, policy makers framed publicly funded ECE in the United States as a tool for intervention rather than as a basic right for all children. Second, it established a system of education in which the children who participated in it were always deemed at risk for school success, and these children primarily come from low-income and nonwhite families. Third, at-risk children were to learn a specific set of skills and knowledge to be ready for school. Finally, the term *at risk* was and continues to be the marker that policy makers, as well as many members of the early childhood community, still use to define particular populations of students and their families. These four ideas still pervade the politics and policies of ECE in the United States.

The implementation of federally funded ECE programs was (and continues to be) controversial. Studies such as the Westinghouse Learning House's evaluation of Head Start suggested that IQ gains of students who participated in the program quickly faded once leaving Head Start, which raised concerns over the effectiveness of these government-funded programs (Vinovskis 2005). Many in ECE argued that students who participated in such programs were more successful academically and socially as they continued through school than similar students who did not receive these services. These assertions spawned the "return on investment" argument that underlies the current push for the expansion of ECE programs (Reynolds et al. 2001). These studies argue that every dollar invested in early childhood programs returns a particular dollar amount in savings (depending on the program). The researchers define savings as money saved from not having to spend additional funds on future social and educational services for the children who participated in the program. This argument shifts the premise for funding ECE programs: rather than being about breaking the cycle of poverty, the argument proposes that funding ECE programs will save taxpayers money (Heckman et al. 2010).

This struggle within Head Start exemplifies the tenuous notion in which policy makers and others think about ECE in the United States. Since access to these programs is not a basic right for all children, ECE stakeholders must justify their programs as worthy recipients of public funds. Such justification also depends on identifying populations of children and their families as deficient or at risk, which ultimately perpetuates rather than challenges the racist and classist policies and structures that create these disparities for families seeking or qualifying for publicly funded early education services (Polakow 2007). Last, they must also define ECE as something different from elementary and secondary education to protect the instructional practices that support the growth and development of young children.

INCREASED ACADEMIC ACHIEVEMENT EXPECTATIONS AND ECE

The waves of reform that led to the current standards-based accountability (SBA) movement, which emphasizes standardization, accountability, and academic achievement, further demonstrate this odd positioning of early childhood within discussions surrounding public education. The continued drive by policy makers in the United States to ensure high academic achievement not only escalated the academic demands placed on young children, but it framed school readiness as something that children need to possess when they enter elementary school. The Clinton administration's Goals 2000 legislation, which made its first goal that every child in the United States starting school would be ready to learn, exemplifies this point.

Within current discussions, most people think of school readiness in two distinct ways: either an empiricist understanding or an interactionist understanding (Meisels 1999).

FIGURE 1.1
An empiricist conception of school readiness

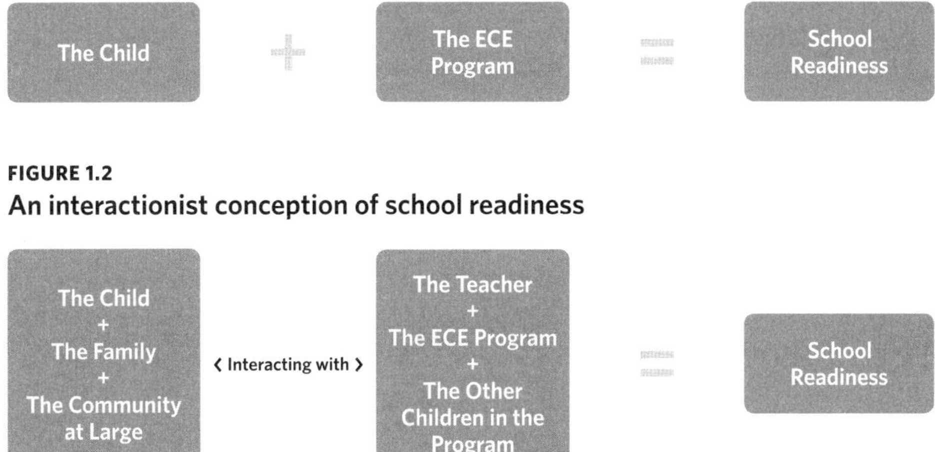

FIGURE 1.2
An interactionist conception of school readiness

Policy makers' reforms that focus on readying young children for elementary school through rigorous academic instruction tend to take an empiricist perspective. ECE advocates and organizations such as NAEYC promote an interactionist view of school readiness that takes into account the role of the child, family, teacher, school, and the community at large.

This distinction in how ECE stakeholders view school readiness is important. The empiricist perspective tends to put the responsibility for school readiness on the children, their families, or their early educators. To ensure children are ready for school, the expectations for them and the rigor of schooling often increase. Like most early educators, we struggle with this because we do not think of school readiness in a unidirectional fashion. Consequently, as policy makers' expectations for increased student achievement have continued to escalate, it is difficult for ECE stakeholders to respond in a manner that addressed policy makers' concerns while still respecting the complexity of children's development and learning.

NCLB AND ECE

Even with organizational responses from NAEYC and others that questioned policy makers' narrow focus on academic achievement, the enactment of No Child Left Behind (NCLB) only escalated the demands placed on public education systems. NCLB required public school teachers to demonstrate annual yearly performance gains in student achievement across the content areas of reading, math, and science. Additionally, the Bush administration's Good Start, Grow Smart (GSGS) initiative required the Head Start program to increase its focus on students' academic achievement as well as mandated that states receiving federal monies supporting preschool programs formulate early learning standards in prereading, language, and mathematics. Policy makers put these standards in place so the academic and social expectations of preschool programs aligned with their K–12 counterparts. Together these federal initiatives ensured that SBA reforms would continue to define the policies and practices for publicly funded ECE programs (Brown 2009a).

ACCOUNTABILITY SHOVEDOWN

Many within ECE in the United States worry that by framing ECE programs such as pre-K through their ability to improve the academic achievement of young children, policy makers are promoting "expedient solutions to complex problems" (Meisels 2007, 31). ECE advocates disagree with policy makers' belief that at-risk children need to be fixed through early learning programs that teach a specific set of skills and knowledge (Stipek 2006). This conception of ECE programs can limit children's learning experiences to those that can be tested on exams used either at kindergarten entry or in elementary school to measure their academic achievement.

Early educators working in public K–12 school systems also face what professor and researcher J. Amos Hatch calls "accountability shovedown." This term means that content and performance expectations, as well as the didactic instructional practices of older grades, have been shoved down by administrators and others into younger-grade classrooms. This shovedown frames learning as a lock-step process where student outcomes demonstrate the effectiveness of teachers. These expectations and policies have been shown to limit the instructional practices of teachers (Brown and Lan 2015), redefine the purpose of such programs as pre-K and K (Sherfinski 2013), and deemphasize the development of positive interaction between early educators, their programs, and the children and families they serve. This, in turn, affects children's readiness for school. For instance, researchers have found that prioritizing academic achievement in early childhood programs such as pre-K and kindergarten has led to teachers having "a lack of confidence" in what their students learn through self-initiated or play-based activities (Parker and Neuharth-Pritchett 2006, 76).

One of the primary goals behind this text, which advocates for RIGOROUS DAP, is to provide early educators with the confidence they need to engage in such play-based activities as demonstrated by Ms. Sanchez at the beginning of this chapter.

NAEYC'S POSITION STATEMENT

NAEYC revised its guidelines on developmentally appropriate practice in 2009. This revision noted that while high expectations for all children are required for teachers to be engaging in DAP, there are variations in their practices and the process of learning for children. According to Carol Copple and Sue Bredekamp (2009), teachers who engage in DAP use a wide range of instructional practices, including acknowledging what children do or say, encouraging persistence and effort, asking questions that provoke children's thinking, scaffolding children's learning, or making purposeful use of various learning formats. The third edition also further refined this understanding of appropriate practice by substituting the term "in contrast" for "inappropriate practices" (Copple and Bredekamp 2009, 149). NAEYC did this for two reasons. The first was to avoid a typology for DAP that automatically labels particular practices as appropriate or inappropriate without knowing the children and the particular program. The second was to help practitioners reflect on and understand how their "well-intentioned" practices may not "serve children well," which at their most extreme can be "dangerous or would cause children lasting damage" (149). For example, to ensure children are exposed to the content, knowledge, and skills needed for kindergarten, a pre-K teacher may schedule every moment of children's learning across the day, which gives children little time to interact socially and denies them an opportunity to make choices about their learning. This last point is significant and acknowledges the complexity of teaching children, particularly those who possess a range of linguistic and cultural talents.

Developmentally Appropriate Practice and Cultural and Linguistic Diversity

While DAP has typically provided educators with an instructional response to national, state, and local demands for standardization and increased student achievement, DAP doesn't always take into account children's diverse ways of knowing and learning. Furthermore, DAP does not specifically address the challenges high-stakes reforms create for ECE teachers.

Early educators need to pay attention to the power relations and shared constructs (race, class, and gender) in their classrooms to attend to each child's individual and sociocultural experiences. Researchers have shown that reforms that prioritize all children learning specific sets of academic knowledge and skills reduce the opportunity for teachers to incorporate culturally relevant practices into their instruction (Brown 2015; Castro et al. 2010). These reforms can also lead teachers to project a limited vision of what counts as teaching, knowledge, and learning to children and their families, which often reflects only a Western, white, middle-income conception of these constructs (Brown and Brown 2010). This limited vision is particularly troubling in the United States where students in these publicly supported ECE programs are increasingly culturally and linguistically diverse (US Census Bureau 2010; Maxwell 2014). For instance, researchers project that by 2023 students who are culturally and linguistically talented will become the majority of students in the United States (Frey 2011). Furthermore, more than 80 percent of teachers in the United States are white (US Department of Education 2016). Thus, there is both a political and practical need to ensure our practices address children's sociocultural worlds.

CULTURALLY RELEVANT PEDAGOGY

To address this shortcoming of developmentally appropriate practice, we've turned to culturally relevant pedagogy (CRP) to determine how early educators can interact with children from diverse backgrounds and engage in learning experiences central to them and their community. CRP is a "pedagogy that [empowers] students intellectually, socially, emotionally, and politically by using cultural referents to impart knowledge, skills, and attitudes" (Ladson-Billings 1994, 17–18). It does so by expecting teachers to foster academic success, cultural competence, and sociopolitical consciousness for all of their students. Teachers expect all children to succeed, and they make their instructional decisions incorporating the cultures of the children in their classroom (including the stories they read, the materials made available to the children, and images children see in their learning environment). Teachers also pursue learning topics that reflect and support the realities of their community (such as examining why their community might lack access to such basic needs as fresh food, health care, and so on). These three central components of CRP align directly with RIGOROUS DAP. Fostering academic success parallels *Pushing every child forward*. Cultural competence aligns with *Understanding each learner*, and developing children's sociopolitical consciousness is connected to *Growing as a community*. Moreover, RIGOROUS DAP asks that we *Reach* all children through practices that *See* their entire being.

To engage in CRP requires early educators to develop a complex repertoire of cultural, developmental, and curricular knowledge. They must engage in a humanizing and empowering pedagogy. This pedagogy attends to their students' sociopolitical lives and requires them to view "learning beyond the confines of the classroom using school knowledge and skills to identify, analyze, and solve real-world problems" (Ladson-Billings 2014, 75). Thus, when breaking down the construct into its three core components, teachers foster children's academic success by viewing the process of learning as more than simply conveying the knowledge found within policy makers' content standards. Instead, learning is an interactive and social process in which teachers work with students to construct understandings of their worlds in and out of school.

Tied with academic learning is building children's cultural competence. Building this competence requires teachers to help students "recognize and honor their own cultural beliefs and practices" and provide them with the knowledge and skills needed to access "the wider culture, where they are likely to have a chance of improving their socioeconomic status and making informed decisions about the lives they wish to lead" (Ladson-Billings 2006, 36). Furthermore, as Professor Django Paris (2012) points out, early educators must work to sustain and value the cultural and linguistic pluralities children bring to school. Paris and others worry CRP has been co-opted by many within the education system to justify such goals and reforms that focus solely on improving children's academic achievement, while ignoring the process of fostering children's cultural competence and developing their sociopolitical consciousness. An example of building children's cultural competence would be having community elders visit early education programs to read with the children to help develop their literacy skills and share the history of their communities.

The sociopolitical dimension of CRP, which includes both the politics and policies in which teachers and their students work, require teachers to engage students in ways that have a direct impact on their immediate lives and their communities. To do this, teachers need to see their students as subjects, rather than objects, that live in complex communities and hold a wealth of knowledge about how to live in the various worlds they inhabit in and out of school (Moll and Gonzales 1992). This will assist them in framing children as active participants in the curriculum development process (Ladson-Billings 2014), and by developing children's sociopolitical consciousness, early educators assist children in developing the skills and knowledge needed to work toward illuminating and eliminating the political and structural inequities that have discriminated against nonwhite and low-income individuals for generations (be it policy, access to financial resources, or myriad other factors).

To engage in CRP requires educators to help their students be aware of not only how the process of schooling works, but also how success in that system aligns with, as well as possibly contradicts, their home, cultural, and linguistic experiences. To tie this back to RIGOROUS DAP, CRP reminds early educators to make instructional decisions based on their students' sociocultural experiences (which include their home languages, interests, and political positioning within the classroom and society) rather than off the mandated sets of content standards and assessment measures.

Why ECE Needs RIGOROUS DAP

Young children learn differently from their elementary school counterparts. They have shorter attention spans and are just beginning to develop the skills of an intentional learner (National Research Council 2000). As such, the academic practices and expectations of elementary school cannot simply be shoved down into preschool. To be clear, we recognize that the goal for everyone invested in ECE is to improve the lives of young children in and out of school. These SBA reforms, which include such blunt instruments as readiness tests that deny children access to a particular program or force them to repeat a grade level, can overlook the subtlety needed by early educators to care for their students in ways that attend to their individual, sociocultural, linguistic, and developmental needs. Teachers must also balance meeting the students' needs, while providing them with the skills and knowledge needed for success in and out of school. We designed RIGOROUS DAP to help bridge this gap that has emerged in this era of standardization, academic achievement, and limited resources.

By engaging in the practices of RIGOROUS DAP within their classrooms, early childhood teachers provide learning experiences that help children develop the foundational knowledge and skills they need to succeed in elementary school. Early educators such as Ms. Sanchez do this through engaging in multimodal learning practices like purposeful-play. Activities such as these take into account what is known about how children develop across the cognitive, social, emotional, and physical domains; what they know about children's individual needs; and the sociocultural and linguistic needs of their learning community. They also offer children meaningful choices, opportunities to experiment with new ideas in a safe and comfortable setting, and time to revisit new knowledge and skills.

Not only is RIGOROUS DAP a theory of instruction that early educators can employ to improve their practices in their classrooms, but it is also a framework for early childhood education. Policy makers, public school administrators, classroom teachers, and families can use RIGOROUS DAP to discuss what is and what should be occurring in early learning classrooms so children enter elementary school confident and prepared for the academic and social demands that await them. When teachers explain how the intentionality of their instruction offers children meaningful choices, opportunities to experiment with new ideas in a safe and comfortable setting, and time to revisit new knowledge and skills, colleagues, administrators, and families better understand. They come to realize how RIGOROUS DAP builds on what children know and can do so that they can develop the skills and knowledge needed to be successful in elementary school and beyond.

Reexamining Why RIGOROUS DAP Is Needed

- Discuss with your colleagues how you define the purpose of early childhood education. Think about how your definition does or does not reflect the history of ECE in the United States presented in this chapter.
- Think about whether you agree with our argument as to why RIGOROUS DAP is needed. What do you see being the strengths of our argument? What did we miss but should consider adding?
- Discuss with your colleagues how you define school readiness. Would you define yourself as an empiricist or interactionist? Discuss how your understanding of school readiness affects the ways you interact with your students.

Extending Your Learning

- To learn more about the expansion of publicly funded preschool in the United States, read Elizabeth Rose's *The Promise of Preschool: From Head Start to Universal Preschool.*
- To learn more about DAP, read Carol Copple and Sue Bredekamp's *Developmentally Appropriate Practice in Early Childhood Programs Serving Children from Birth through Age 8.*
- Mary Cowhey is an early educator whose work reflects a culturally relevant perspective. Her website (www.mcowhey.com) outlines her publications and projects.
- Rethinking Schools (www.rethinkingschools.org) is committed to engaging culturally relevant and sustaining practices, while at the same time working toward strengthening public education through social justice teaching and education activism. It offers a range of publications examining these issues.
- Facing History and Ourselves (www.facinghistory.org) is another organization committed to working with children from a range of backgrounds to examine issues of racism, prejudice, and anti-Semitism for the purpose of promoting the development of a more humane and informed citizenry.

Steps You Can Take toward Change

- Of the eleven principles that define RIGOROUS DAP, make a list of those you engage in on a regular basis. Which principles do you struggle with? Over the next few weeks, identify spaces within your teaching where you can engage in these principles.
- Make a short list of activities you engage in on a regular basis that you have difficulty explaining the educational value of to others. Now look at the eleven principles of RIGOROUS DAP and think about how you might use that language to help define your work to others.
- Consider how current and historical education policies affect your life in the classroom and the interactions you have with your students and their families. Talk to other early childhood educators within your community about these policies and how you might work together to become more involved in larger conversations about how best to serve young children.

Examining How Children Develop and Learn across All Developmental Domains

On a warm spring morning, Ms. Anderson, a third-grade teacher, talked with author Beth Feger about success as she watched her students playing on the playground during recess. She pointed to an energetic third-grade boy and said, "I love watching Drew play with his friends during recess. At the beginning of the year, he just couldn't figure out how to play without tackling somebody or having to sit out. It was rough. He didn't know how to be a part of the community. Seeing him learn to be a part of the classroom, to play with the other kids, and to share things—those are the big moments to celebrate. I want my students to learn things they can take with them into the world to whatever they want to do, whether they go to college, choose a trade, or be a parent. They'll know they are capable of achieving great things."

We begin this chapter with this statement from Ms. Anderson because, for her, success in school and life is more than the development of specific academic skills or students attaining a specific test score. Ms. Anderson considers children's growth and development as a "whole person" experience that affects each child and the entire learning community. Growth and development encapsulate who each child is socially, emotionally, physically, socioculturally, and academically. Even as a third-grade teacher in a high-stakes context that uses achievement tests to define success in school, Ms. Anderson understands that Drew's success as a member of the learning community is just as important as a test score. She feels she had an obligation to notice and celebrate such accomplishments with the individual student and the classroom community. By broadening her belief about success beyond standards, testing, and academic achievement, Ms. Anderson fosters opportunities for her and her students to develop as a community across all developmental domains.

Understanding How Children Develop and Learn

From birth, all children are curious, intelligent, and constantly trying to figure out how the world works. When we tie discussions about school readiness or grade-level promotion to children's learning, we overlook their potential and possibilities as learners. Children are often given such labels as *at risk*, and with those labels, questions emerge about their inquisitiveness and ability to function in the classroom. Labels often lead to stigmatizing comparisons, particularly along socioeconomic and cultural lines. Children are negatively compared to peers, previous students, and academic or developmental standards. These comparisons typically lead to conversations rooted in deficits, such as having a limited vocabulary or behavioral issues (Brown 2005).

How teachers see the whole child as a learner affects their interactions with children in numerous ways—be it socially, emotionally, culturally, instructionally, and so on. Take a moment and consider how you look at the children in your classroom setting. Do you start to make comparisons between them? Do you start to seek out differences? Do you worry about how you might manage those differences? We pose these questions because we want you to be aware of such tendencies so that you can move beyond them. We want you to intentionally let go of such comparative and deficit-oriented language.

Instead, we hope you will think about children and their learning through the lens of possibilities. Peter Johnston (2012) calls this a dynamic orientation toward learning—meaning children's ability to learn is not fixed, and instead, they are always learning more. We believe all children will learn whatever we ask of them if given the time, opportunity, knowledge and skills, and academic and emotional support. However, many within early childhood education do not think this way about how children develop and learn. We must move beyond such limiting language and attitudes.

Big Ideas around Children's Development and Learning

Historically, early childhood educators have viewed learning through three major schools of thought: maturationists, behaviorists, and constructivists.

Maturationists (such as Gessell) believe age determines children's ability to learn and that child development is a predictable biological process that automatically occurs. "She is too young to understand that" is a maturationist statement.

Behaviorists (like Skinner) believe that children's environments shape their development and learning. Children achieve learning by breaking down the learning process into a series of sequential steps taught through pleasant experiences (such as teaching children to read through direct instruction of specific skills).

Finally, **constructivists** (think Piaget) propose that child development occurs through children interacting with their environment. Thus, children actively construct or misconstruct their knowledge. A classroom with self-guided learning centers would be considered constructivist.

Thinking back to our discussion of school readiness in chapter 1, an empiricist conception of readiness is closely aligned to behaviorists, and the interactionist is associated with a constructivist understanding of learning.

Recognizing the role of developmental theory as we engage in RIGOROUS DAP is important. First, understanding how children develop and learn provides us with guideposts for our instruction (see table 2.1). Knowing how children typically develop and learn helps us identify what most children can do at different points in their lives. For instance, knowing that block play and playdough help develop motor skills and further creative thinking provides teachers a strong rationale for including these items in their classrooms. Second, an understanding of developmental theory provides professionals who work in early education, such as occupational, speech, or physical therapists, with the knowledge base to identify children who may need early intervention. Moreover, how children develop in one domain influences their development in other domains, and therefore addressing issues that might arise in speech, fine-motor control, or sensory input supports the growth of the whole child.

Child development is dynamic and encapsulates three interrelated aspects. First, there is a sequence of development. Humans change over time based on their physiological development and life experiences. Such knowledge provides educators with insight into what to prepare for next. It is important to remember that each sequence is dependent on the child, including the strengths she brings to the early childhood setting and the sociocultural world she was socialized in.

Second, there is a delayed impact aspect to children's development and learning (Katz and Chard 2000). When children learn something new, such as the alphabet song, or experience a life-changing event, such as losing a parent to cancer or incarceration, it may have an effect on them that will take time to emerge, particularly in relation to those aspects that reflect their affective and personality development.

Finally, there is a cumulative effect of repeated or frequent experiences on children's development; these experiences can be positive or negative. More opportunities for skills practice often leads to mastery, and repeated experiences with negative emotions, such as shame or frustration, can lead to a negative self-image. We highlight this dynamic aspect of development because it ties nicely into our belief that children are always growing and developing as learners.

TABLE 2.1
Typical development characteristics of children ages 3 though 8

Age	Cognitive	Social	Emotional	Physical
3	• Says short sentences • Uses about 1,000 words but can understand up to 4 times more • Experiences great growth in communication • Tells simple stories • Uses words as tools to express thoughts • Wants to understand environment • Answers questions • Is imaginative • May recite a few nursery rhymes or songs • Names colors • Can count to 3	• Engages in parallel play • Enjoys being by others • May begin to take turns in activities and/or games • Knows full name • Enjoys brief group activities • Likes to "help" in small ways • Responds to verbal guidance • Seems sure of self • May be defiant • Can display negative social behaviors • Needs controlled freedom • May begin to follow 2- to 3-step directions • Knows own gender and becomes aware of others' gender	• Finds emotional security from the presence of familiar adults • Begins to develop and express a sense of individuality and personal preferences • Begins to label own feelings and those of others' based on their facial expression or tone of voice • Begins to understand that feelings have causes • Begins to express feelings, needs, and opinions in difficult situations or conflicts, without hurting self, others, or property • Can still fall apart under stress	• Skips on one foot • Copies a circle • Cuts with scissors • Can wash and dry face • Can undress self (unbutton) • Jumps distances • Throws ball overhand • Can ride a tricycle

TABLE 2.1 *(continued)*

Age	Cognitive	Social	Emotional	Physical
4	• Uses complete sentences • Uses plurals and prepositions • Uses about 1,500 words • Asks many questions • Is learning to generalize • Is dramatic and highly imaginative • Can draw simple objects • Repeats four digits • Can identify body parts • Can recognize letters, common words, and possibly write own name • Speaks in decently complex sentences • Can do the same activity for 10–15 minutes • Understands own accomplishments • Knows 6–8 colors • Understands immediate time, but not things far away • Understands daily routines • Asks a lot of "why" and "how" questions	• Plays with others • Enjoys company of other children and highly social • Plays tag, duck-duck-goose, and simple games • Is talkative and self-assured • Is capable of some self-criticism • Imitates adult roles • Enjoys responsibility • Likes to follow the rules • Has imaginary friends • Likes to play with others • Likes dramatic play, role play • Is creative and imaginative • Has intense moods—can feel strong emotions of anger, jealousy, sadness, fear • Is expressive and talkative • Is curious • Is proud • Likes to brag to friends • Seeks adult approval	• Capable of feeling jealous • Enjoys new activities • Is boastful—enjoys showing off and bragging about possessions • Can still struggle to distinguish between real and make-believe • Is fearful of the dark and monsters; has understanding of danger • Likes to shock others by using "forbidden" words • Expresses anger verbally rather than physically (most of the time) • Still throws tantrums over minor frustrations • Can feel intense anger	• Hops and skips • Grooms self • Copies a cross and a rectangle • Has good balance and smoother muscle action • Skates • Rides wagon and scooter • Prints simple letters • Establishes handedness • Ties shoes • Can exercise basic self-care, such as brushing teeth, combing hair, feeding, dressing, washing self • Is developing more advanced motor skills and hand-eye coordination, such as throwing/catching balls, threading beads, forming shapes out of clay • Needs 10–12 hours of sleep each night • Can walk in a straight line, hop on one foot

TABLE 2.1 *(continued)*

Age	Cognitive	Social	Emotional	Physical
5	• Uses 2000+ words • Tells long tales • Carries out directions well • Reads own name • Counts to 10 • Asks meaning of words • Is beginning to know the difference between fact and fiction • Is interested in environment, city and stores • Knows the basic colors like red, yellow, blue, green, and orange • Understands that stories have a beginning, middle, and end • Understands that books are read from left to right, top to bottom • Draws pictures that represent animals, people, and objects • Board games, card games, dominoes, puzzles are ways to stimulate thinking. • Blocks and playdough further develop motor skills as well as help them become creative thinkers. • Child-size tools provide practice with using scissors and pencils	• Engages in cooperative play • Has special friends • Enjoys simple table games requiring taking turns and following basic rules • Feels pride about clothing and accomplishments • Is eager to carry out some responsibility • Feels conformity to peers is important • Takes turns with others and shares and organizes toys in pretend play • Can carry on conversations with other children and adults • Chooses "best friends" to play with and often excludes others • Is sensitive to others feelings, like when others are sad or upset • Prefers the company of only one or two other children, may become bossy or sulky when others come in • Has a sense of humor, enjoys joking and laughing with others	• Sensitive to feelings of others • Tries to please peers and caregivers • Feels more grown up • Seeks adult approval • Enjoys giving and receiving • Is less fearful of the world • Expresses anger and jealousy physically • Not emotionally ready for competition; however, likes to test strength	• Copies a square • Dresses self • Catches ball with two hands • Able to dress self with little assistance • Hand dominance is established • Losing baby teeth • Skips, gallops, runs, and runs on tiptoes • Able to use a fork and knife well • Throws ball overhand • Uses the bathroom independently • May be able to copy simple designs and shapes • Walks down stairs with alternating feet

TABLE 2.1 *(continued)*

Age	Cognitive	Social	Emotional	Physical
6	• Able to put things in order (seriation) • Shifts from egocentric to social speech • Vocabulary increases exponentially • Begins to understand cause-and-effect relationships • Learns best through discovery and active involvement with people and materials • Starts to grasp concept of time—past, present, and future • Has increased problem-solving ability • Attention span is short but long enough for involved stories • Uses language and words to represent things not visible	• Rules of the game are key • Wants to be a part of a team • Shows an awareness of the needs of others and understands their points of view • Learning how to talk to friends, e.g., how to start and finish a conversation as well as negotiation, winning arguments, and listening	• Plays with friends typically of the same gender • Can be bossy and competitive when playing with others • Has common fears that include the unknown, death, family problems, and rejection • Is self-conscious • Inner control is being formed and practiced each time decisions are made. • Feelings get hurt easily, has mood swings, and doesn't know how to deal with failure • Develops sense of humor • Competitive • Fascinated by rules but may make up own rules • Begins to develop a "moral compass" and starts to understand what honesty means	• Copies a triangle • Prints letters • Draws a recognizable man with head, body, and limbs • Skips with alternating feet • Rides a bicycle • Permanent teeth start to come in as baby teeth fall out. • Can tie shoelaces • Can be full of energy, but may tire easily • Has control over fine motor activities (e.g., using scissors or other small instruments) • Tends to be clumsy in the early stages, though as coordinated as adults by the end of middle childhood • Still experiences growth spurts

TABLE 2.1 *(continued)*

Age	Cognitive	Social	Emotional	Physical
7–8	• Is beginning to apply personal knowledge and experience to a particular situation to determine whether it makes sense or not (logical thinking) • Starts to understand the passage of time, day and date • Can copy adult speech patterns	• Has increased ability to interact with peers • Has more same-sex friends • Is developing and testing beliefs that will guide behavior • Has a strong group identity; increasingly defines self through peers • Has a desire to develop a sense of mastery and accomplishment based on physical strength, self-control, and school performance	• Can resolve conflicts without seeking adult intervention • Displays a need for own place, e.g., at the table or in the car • Shows an awareness of the needs of others and understands their points of view • Wants to please important adults • May be easily embarrassed and sensitive to other people's views and beliefs • Has a growing awareness of the outside world, which can lead to/cause fear and/or anxiety.	• Demonstrates increased coordination and strength • Enjoys using new gross- and fine-motor skills • Experiences a steady increase in height and weight

(CDC 2017; Poppe et al. 2011; Healthy Children 2017)

Connecting Development to Learning

Brain-based research provides us with more information about how children learn than ever before. However, it is interesting that brain scans are necessary to convince the public of what early childhood educators have always known—children enter the world as learners seeking to make sense of it. The following are a few key points we must keep in mind to help us make teaching and learning brain compatible.

Alison Gopnik's (2012) research has consistently demonstrated that children are natural-born scientists. She and her colleagues argue that young children are consumed with the desire to experiment with and explore objects, and our job as teachers is to nurture their curiosity. Her work demonstrates that we do not need to provide children with teacher- or parent-directed activities such as flashcards to teach sight words at a young age; rather, we need to provide them with a safe space to explore, experiment, and play. We need to support children emotionally, fill in the gaps when they get stuck or need help in their learning, and provide a safe and caring environment.

Gopnik's work also highlights how we talk about learning. We typically talk about learning in two ways: the process of discovery and the process of mastering what we discover. For instance, there is the process of discovering how to tie our shoes, and then there is the process of mastering that skill. These two ways to talk about learning are connected directly to how we learn. We absorb new information through guided discovery, which for Gopnik is how we increase our capacity for learning. There is also routinized learning, which is about perfecting procedures so our minds are free to make new discoveries (such as learning math facts so that we can focus on algebraic principles). Both are necessary, but unfortunately, guided discovery is often pushed out of early childhood learning spaces in favor of routinized learning.

Early childhood author Marilou Hyson (2008) argues that our goal as educators is to create environments that simultaneously facilitate the acquisition of knowledge and skills and the desirable dispositions for learning. To do this, we focus on what she terms the two elements that shape how we approach learning: our feelings (enthusiasm) and our actions (engagement). Hyson notes that since emotions serve as the primary motivator of all behavior, children must be motivated by their emotions to engage in positive learning behaviors. To do this, we want to develop children's capacity for interest. Hyson defines interest as the capacity to lose oneself in an outside activity or concern. Although children will not develop the traits of an intentional learner for some time, we should nevertheless help our students work at integrating and managing these emotions, which they will need to harness for their future learning. It's not just being happy or excited about a topic. We want our students to be interested, motivated, engaged, flexible, and able to self-regulate. By paying attention to children's emotions and actions, we create environments that facilitate and sustain their interest in learning. By helping children develop their interest in learning, their teachers, families, and peers will see them as learners. Our goal is to facilitate the simultaneous acquisition of knowledge, skills, and desirable dispositions. To do this, we must balance our intention in our instruction between these goals of skill acquisition and fostering children's dispositions toward such acquisition.

Gopnik, Hyson, and many others unpack the complexity of the learning process. While humans are naturally curious, we are not very good thinkers. Thinking involves using our short-term and long-term memory, specifically through our working memory, which is essentially our consciousness (what we are thinking about right now). When we enter a new learning experience, we take in the information in front of us through our working memory, and depending on what we're asked, we pull from our long-term memory to help us make sense of the learning situation (Willingham 2009). Consider, for example, your response to being asked how many toes you have. You would likely be able to recall the answer quite quickly but would not be thinking about that information until you were asked to retrieve it.

This process of taking in new information and making sense of it during a learning experience is a slow and difficult task that requires much mental effort. Because of this, researchers have found that our brains try to avoid such work (NRC 2000; Willingham 2009). We typically try to apply what we already know to a new situation, which is why having a range of learning experiences is critical.

Think about the process of learning to drive a car. It's a somewhat difficult task at first, but it becomes easier with more experience. However, if you've ever driven in Great Britain or in a nation they colonized, you've had to drive on the opposite side of the road. Driving on the opposite side of the road causes you to devote more of your attentional resources to making sense of the demands of this new task. This novel, unfamiliar situation requires you to abandon your otherwise habituated responses. You must rethink a habitual process that is part of your long-term memory, which can be quite exhausting and confusing. You might yearn to drive like you've always known how to, which is less taxing on your brain but not safe for you or your passengers.

You must remember that children have limited experiences and fewer resources and memories in their long-term memory to apply to new situations. Consequently, they need more support to help them focus, engage, and persevere as they work through the challenges presented in the learning event. To provide this level of support, you must be patient and recognize the complexity in what you are asking children to do, as well as offering them multiple opportunities to comprehend and internalize skills and knowledge. Second, children are looking for patterns in their world to make sense of it. Offering predictable routines and learning experiences that build off what they already know in a nurturing and stable environment is essential for them to pick up new knowledge and skills. If the classroom is in a constant state of flux without offering children predictable routines, they will struggle to move beyond making sense of their environment. They won't be able to let their brains slow down and focus on learning new skills and information.

Not only is learning something new a difficult process, but it requires children to do more than simply internalize information. It requires children to possess a range of mental skills associated with executive-level functioning; these functions form the neurological infrastructure for such noncognitive abilities as perseverance, resilience, and creativity. These skills develop in our brain's prefrontal cortex, the part that controls our most complex intellectual functions, including our ability to self-regulate both emotionally and cognitively (Miyake et al. 2000). Some of these functions include maintaining information in our working memory, which allows us to keep facts in mind while working with them as well as follow multistep instructions; cognitive flexibility, such as reasoning, problem solving, and identifying/correcting errors; planning and prioritizing; and organization. Developing these skills along with the ability to self-regulate is essential for development and learning, and it takes time.

To be clear, you cannot simply teach children these skills in a lesson or expect them to become intentional learners because you ask them to be. Rather, children's executive functions develop through many of the actions that define RIGOROUS DAP, such as establishing consistent and appropriate routines, modeling appropriate behavior, and maintaining supportive and caring relationships.

Often, children who grow up in stressful environments or have insecure relationships with adults do not possess these skills, or their development is delayed (Raver, Blair, and Willoughby 2013). Lacking these skills does not mean that children cannot develop them. Rather, it will take more time and explicit instruction for these children to acquire such skills than it might for their peers who grew up in more nurturing environments. Early childhood stress and trauma (homelessness, food insecurity, abuse, neglect, or medical trauma) cause a child's brain to focus on survival rather than exploration and appropriates the development of the child's executive function. Rather than develop the prefrontal cortex, the brains of children experiencing trauma are instead developing the limbic brain, which scans the environment for danger. Children with these early childhood experiences will need additional support within a safe early childhood classroom to develop skills that other children the same age may already demonstrate.

TRAUMA-INFORMED RIGOROUS DAP

There has been a great deal of research into the differing needs of children who have experienced developmental trauma; notably the work of Purvis and her colleagues (2013) and the Texas Christian University (TCU) collaborative for children. As you consider creating classrooms where students are engaged in meaningful and challenging work, remember that these children may have different or additional needs. You must intentionally engage students affected by trauma in the following components of RIGOROUS DAP: *Offering choices, Seeing the whole child,* and *Pushing every child forward.*

By offering choices and listening to a child's emerging capacity to ask for what she needs, you facilitate a child's sense of worth. By seeing the whole child, you will become aware of what specifically each child needs, and this will allow you to focus on connecting with the child and meeting the need. Such experiences begin to build the connections in the child's prefrontal cortex that allows that child to fully engage his executive functions and move forward in her learning. For instance, when teaching children affected by trauma, offering choices and compromises is one way to give that child a voice. Children, particularly those who may have been ignored or neglected, need to have control over what they are doing. Finally, as you push each child forward, ensure you offer challenges that are appropriate for the individual student. You may need to ask a child to wait for her turn or use a mindfulness strategy to deal with a stressful situation.

ADDITIONAL PROSOCIAL AND EMOTIONAL TEACHING STRATEGIES

The strategies outlined above are designed to assist you in creating a peaceful classroom environment where everyone is working toward *Growing as a community*. Proactive strategies you can use to support all children (including children affected by trauma) include intentionally designing a supportive physical learning environment, ensuring that noisy places (like the block center, pretend and learn/drama center) are near each other while also providing quiet places for children where they can get regulated and feel safe. Also, embedding home materials such as class pets and plants helps children feel secure. Having pictures of children's families posted within the classroom lets them know you care about their entire family.

Children benefit from routines and a predictable schedule. If your schedule needs to change, inform children at the beginning of the day to help them with that transition. Additionally, consider providing children with classroom jobs or responsibilities, such as watering the plants, feeding the class pet, serving as a line leader, and so on.

Teachers should model prosocial behaviors with children and with other adults in and outside the classroom. Authors Marilou Hyson and Jackie Taylor noted, "To highlight this modeling, teachers can comment on what they are doing and why ('Oh, Carla, I see that you are having trouble with that. How about if I help you? It makes me happy to help children when they need it.')" (2011, 78).

When teachers verbalize or label emotions within the classroom, children can begin to recognize the terms associated with particular feelings and use them in their interactions with others (Johnston 2012). For instance, a teacher stating, "Class, I want you to look at my face. This is what I look like when I am confused. If you see me give you this reaction, I may not know how to respond and need a moment to think through what you are asking me." Think about those times across the day when you might have conversations that involve other's feelings, for example, having a morning meeting or sharing one's writing in an author circle. Those are easy moments for you and the children to discuss emotions associated with particular behaviors—"Louise, show us how you feel now that you've completed that story you've been working on so hard for the past two weeks."

In determining how to foster prosocial behaviors in the classroom with your students to promote their social/emotional and cognitive growth, consider your expectations for how your students present themselves to you as learners in the learning process. Unfortunately, some teachers believe children must be silent or quietly sitting before they can learn. Such expectations not only tend to mischaracterize the skills, knowledge, and capabilities of children, but they also impede your ability to connect with your children on a personal level. By forcing children to sit a particular way and be quiet before conversations or learning can take place, you ignore the fact that learning is an interactive process. You may also set up your students for failure and interrupt learning when you redirect those children who cannot sit still for long periods. We know there are times when you must require self-control or silence in your early childhood classroom, but such expectations are often not needed as much as you think they are. As you engage with your students across your day, think about why and when you ask them to behave in a particular way and what message your actions and expectations convey. Engaging in RIGOROUS DAP with your students requires a strong personal connection, and when you silence and control children, you may be hindering the development of such relationships.

SOCIOCULTURAL INFLUENCES ON LEARNING

The learning process is often framed from a cognitive perspective. Learning is not simply about developing an understanding of how the world works. It is a process that entwines all of children's developmental domains, which means you must develop the whole child. For instance, the work by Kagan, Moore, and Bredekamp (1995) for the National Education Goals Panel framed children's learning and development as it relates to school readiness through five dimensions: (1) physical well-being and development, (2) social and emotional development, (3) approaches to learning, (4) language development, and (5) cognition and general development.

While the constructs developed by the National Education Goals Panel in 1995 define school readiness expand the process of learning and development to the whole child, they still leave out the importance of the sociocultural contexts in which children develop and learn (Kagan, Moore, Bredekamp 1995). This omission is significant for multiple reasons. First, various cultures view the role of the child and the learning process differently, which can affect how the child views the world, approaches new problems, and has a significant impact on his long-term memory, which shapes how he thinks about and interacts with learning opportunities in the here and now. Second, what occurs in the home environment affects children's development and learning in significant ways. For instance, children who come from high-stress home environments or from homes where caregivers are emotionally unavailable to them often show delays in their cognitive functioning. Third, the sociohistorical positioning of the learning experience in the here and now plays a significant role in children's learning as well—such issues as gender, class, sexual-orientation, or the physical location of the learning environment. Finally, while developmental theory and psychology makes it appear as if there is a natural course of development, there is not. The factors we just listed demonstrate that we need to incorporate these developmental theories and ideas into our teaching, but our decisions must first be through coming to know the individual children in our programs and their sociocultural worlds.

Three theorists who help us think about and highlight the significance of the role children's sociocultural worlds have on their learning and development are Urie Bronfenbrenner, Barbara Rogoff, and William Corsaro. All three view children's development and learning through a sociocultural perspective, meaning that development is an interaction between the child and her immediate environment. This notion of sociocultural development emerged from the work of Vygotsky (1978), whom we'll discuss in more detail later on.

Urie Bronfenbrenner

Bronfenbrenner takes on what he terms an ecological systems perspective, which focuses on the impact of the larger world on children's development and learning (see figure 2.1). He defined children's development and learning occurring across microsystems, which include the family and local community, as being the most immediate in their lives, and macro systems, which include such larger systems as schools and politics/policies (Bronfenbrenner 1979; Bronfenbrenner and Morris 2006). While Bronfenbrenner located the construct of culture as a component of the larger macrosystem, we've repositioned it in our interpretation of children's learning and development as a component of the children's familial system. Children are not blank slates, and as such, they interact with these systems. Their interaction with these systems is dialogic, meaning they interact with as well as influence each other. Each child is unique and possesses her unique temperament, learning styles, and intelligence, which all affect the way she approaches learning. Remember that you are helping children develop skills across these systems so they can succeed in school and the larger systems they inhabit.

When assisting children using Bronfenbrenner's systems, it is important to recognize where children are in their development and learning. Use those places as a starting point, rather than focusing on what is missing and why (and possibly blaming the child or parent). As you move into the family system, recognize that children's bonds with their family members significantly influence not only their development but also what takes place in the classroom. These familial relationships affect children's willingness to engage in class, take risks as learners, and form strong relationships with their classmates and their teachers. Your job is to support these relationships—not add stress to them.

As noted above, we've positioned children's culture/cultural practices within the family system. We've done so because children's cultures influence how

FIGURE 2.1
Our interpretation of Bronfenbrenner's ecological framework

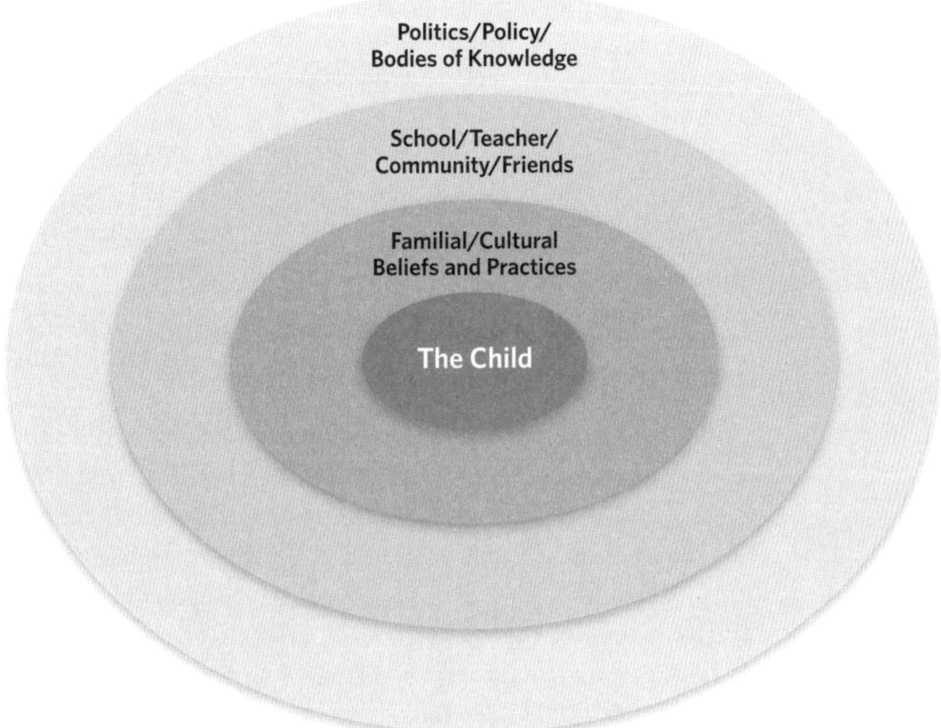

they approach everything they do, including schooling and learning. For children, their culture is "something to be enacted or expressed, something that is dynamic and agentic" (Goodwin, Cheruvu, and Genishi 2008, 6). Children's cultures influence their persistence, attentiveness, and self-regulation. When moving into the school/teacher/community/friends circle, understanding your culture is important. The US culture, which is an individualistic society, conflicts with most of the world's cultures, which are more collaborative/interdependent (Rogoff 2003). Teachers who are successful with children from a range of cultural backgrounds respond to these differences and strive for warm and personal relationships that have high expectations for all their students.

Regarding the school system, you and your colleagues play a key role in helping your students become lifelong learners. You can be a positive influence in how you display yourself as a learner (mastery orientation: learning to become more competent rather than simply learning to pass a test/get a reward, and discussing mistakes as a normal part of learning a skill). Engaging with your students (communicating clear expectations, encouraging children's active involvement and collaboration, and giving helpful advice without controlling them) can also have a positive influence.

Finally, politics, policy, and bodies of knowledge are woven throughout all these circles. Policy and politics affect such things as access to food, shelter, health care, and even income for the individual. Policies affect what schools teach and assess, and how nonwhite/nondominant cultures and languages are valued. Policies affect such cultural issues as immigration, which affects families in multiple ways, and access to governmental resources (like schools) and capital (such as securing loans). Remember, teaching is an inherently political act (be aware of how policy affects you, be involved in the policy process, and seek out alliances for support). Finally, bodies of knowledge reflect the systems of thought that are most valued by the larger society. Meaning what you teach in your early education program or classroom reflects the bodies of knowledge the larger society values, which continue to reflect a Western, white, middle-income conception of teaching, learning, and knowledge.

Barbara Rogoff

While Bronfenbrenner's systems approach is extremely beneficial in thinking about the complexity of children's sociocultural worlds and how they influence children, his view of culture is of a system that encapsulates the school, family, and child circles we detailed earlier. As we stated earlier, we disagree with this framing of culture. Instead, we view culture as a verb (Goodwin et al., 2008), meaning that while we recognize that culture encompasses a broad set of ideologies and practices shared by groups of people, it is also the meaning-making process through which children make sense of the world (Rogoff 2003). We cannot separate culture from the child. For instance, in some communities, it is appropriate and expected for children to talk back to their elders, while in others it is not, and that is why we embedded it in the family and their cultural beliefs and practices circle.

Child development is not a set of skills that children acquire in lockstep order at particular times in their lives. Rather, it is something that is constantly occurring, and for each child, is dependent on his immediate experiences. Teachers must recognize that developmental milestones or guideposts provide limited insight into the development of our students and often do not consider the priorities, expectations, and practices of nondominant cultures and languages. As such, it is essential that we get to know children and their families personally. Interactions with families should not only focus on how they can contribute to the education of their child, but also include efforts to honor the knowledge and cultural assets they can bring to the school community.

William Corsaro

The work of Corsaro adds to Bronfenbrenner's systems approach and Rogoff's notion that development is constant and occurs through children's participation in their local communities. Corsaro focuses on the sociology of children rather than their development and learning. Doing so makes us aware that childhood is both a period in which children live their lives and a structural form, like social class (Corsaro 2015). Thus, by being social agents within society, children are constrained by existing social structures and by societal reproduction; meaning, the world in which they live affects how they respond to it. Still, children evolve as members of their cultures by striving to interpret and to participate in them. In doing so, children create their peer worlds and cultures, and they contribute to cultural change in the larger society through their interaction with it.

Corsaro also contends that children live in a dynamic system constituted in routine practices collectively produced at various levels of organization. As Corsaro and his colleagues pointed out,

> We must consider the nature of children's *membership* in these local cultures and *the changes in their degree or intensity* of membership and participation over time. We also must consider how different structural and institutional features constrain and enable the collective processes of interest. From this view . . . *the development of humans* is always collective, and transitions are always collectively produced and shared with significant others. (Corsaro, Molinary, and Rosier 2002, 325)

For Corsaro, children enter their culture through their families and then interact with institutions (like schooling, medical) and other children and adults who are not part of their family. These interactions shape their development and participation in the larger society. Such participation in these various groups and institutions affects them and the groups themselves, and thus their development within the world is a process that is collective in nature, always in flux, never static, and does not progress in a lockstep or linear manner.

Lev Vygotsky

As Bronfenbrenner, Rogoff, and Corsaro point out, children do not develop and learn in isolation. They are doing so in relation to the complex worlds in which they operate, and as teachers, we must be aware of these varied worlds and support children's participation in them.

Vygotsky's contribution to child development helps us to make sense of how culturally produced tools and sign systems change the nature of children's cognition (their way of knowing) through the simultaneous acquisition of language. Unlike his contemporary Piaget, Vygotsky did not attribute children's cognitive development to maturational and internal processes alone. Rather, Vygotsky believed that culture played a role in the advancement of mental functions and operations, which include thinking and communicating.

According to Vygotsky (1978), up until age three children's capacity for abstract thinking is limited/subordinate to their reliance on and use of sensorimotor and perceptual skills as they explore and manipulate objects in their environment. This exploratory activity consequently contributes to children's understanding of cause and effect relationships, which in effect enhances their problem-solving capabilities. For instance, a toddler will begin to anticipate the sound of a jingle each time he or she shakes a rattle.

Vygotsky also contends that from infancy to toddlerhood, children's language acquisition progresses concurrently alongside their cognitive growth, but still with neither developmental domain (language and cognition) intersecting or influencing the development of the other. Capacity for speech production occurs as infants visually cue and auditorily adjust their vocalizations to match their caregiver's speech sounds and patterns. From eighteen months of age into toddlerhood, a child's vocabulary will undergo a significant increase of up to two hundred words (Berger 2009). This rapid uptake in the child's language acquisition along with his increased cognitive activity and acuity will converge by age three. Each domain motivates and enhances the development of the other and leads to increased capacity for symbolic thinking; that is, the ability to convey and comprehend information through the production and exchange of sign systems and symbols, which are products of the child's culture. The use of signs makes learning more efficient by allowing the child to store information in memory for longer periods of time. This storage conversely influences his ability to attend to more difficult and complex tasks that require the coordination of higher-level mental processes related to executive-level functioning (for example, memory, attention shifting, and self-regulation).

The transmission of culture occurs as children interact with both human and nonhuman objects, which include texts, symbols, and artifacts, such as toys. When a young child plays with a Barbie doll, she is making meaning of a culturally produced construct related to gender (girls wear makeup), race (straight hair is beautiful), and class (it is desirable to wear fashionable clothing and drive a sports car). The child's identity, however, is not completely determined by these cultural artifacts and sign systems. The child will also exert her influence on the signs and objects with which she interacts. Two children in the same classroom might play with the doll in different ways. For example, a young Latina girl, who is aware that Barbie looks different from her, might imagine the doll as a white character on her favorite television program. A white middle-income girl, on the other hand, might pretend she is the Barbie doll, going on dates and shopping for clothes—enacting what she perceives as a version of herself as a teenager. Although both children are playing with the Barbie within the culturally defined parameters of what it means to be a white, middle-income girl, the play scenarios they act out are quite different due to each child's individual experience in her sociocultural world. Hence, signs and artifacts both influence and are influenced by the individuals who interact with them.

Literacy learning, texts and sign symbols, such as letters and print, have a similar culturally mediated and symbiotic effect on the child's identity and perception of how to think, talk, and interact with others. For example, children who speak English as a second language experience a positive impact of becoming a bi- or multilingual learner on their development. Neuroimaging research demonstrates the extensive capacity of the human brain to learn multiple languages during the early childhood years (Conboy and Kuhl 2011). Moreover, bilingualism influences the organization of the language processing systems in young children's brains in a positive manner (Conboy 2013). Early bilingualism has been shown to have a positive impact on children's cognitive skills, such as executive function abilities (Ramírez et al. 2016). Such advantages in cognitive development are larger in children with advanced skills in their two languages. Still, early educators must recognize that they should attempt to use children's first language in instruction because empirical research consistently demonstrates that such instruction often leads to higher social, cognitive, and academic achievement levels for bilingual learners (García, Kleifgen, and Falchi 2008).

Thus, the sociocultural worlds in which children grow and develop, including their linguistic worlds, have a significant impact on their development and learning across all developmental domains. Children influence and affect the worlds in which they operate.

The Importance of Physical Development and Learning

Because we frame the learning process through a whole child approach within RIGOROUS DAP, we want to highlight the significance of physical development and its connection to learning. Research shows that schools place less emphasis on physical education and have reduced the amount of physical activities children engage in across the day (Anderson, Butcher, and Schanzenbach 2011; Dee and Jacob 2011). Many early educators misconstrue silence and being still as a necessary precursor for children to learn. This is disconcerting for two reasons. First, children can and do learn while moving, fidgeting, and talking with you or their classmates. Second, there is ample research linking increased physical activity in school with improved academic achievement and enhanced executive functioning (Mavilidi et al. 2015; Chang et al. 2012). Moreover, researchers have found that spending as little as six to ten minutes engaged in physical activity can improve children's performance (Barcelona 2017).

Many within early childhood education are becoming aware of the importance of children being allowed to move, fidget, and take physical breaks across the day to keep them engaged in learning. Furthermore, early educators in a range of school contexts are using such web-based programs as Go Noodle (www.gonoodle.com) and texts to facilitate physical activity in their classrooms. Physical activity must be an essential component of your instructional strategies in and out of the classroom to support the whole child in your teaching.

A Dynamic Framing of Learning

Professor Peter Johnston wrote *Opening Minds* in 2012. In this book, he reminds us of the importance of the words we employ in our work with young children. He contends that our language choices have serious consequences for children's learning and for who they become as individuals and as a community, which is connected to fostering a strong democracy. In his work, he advocates for a dynamic framing of learning, which hinges on the idea that one can cultivate intelligence. This mind-set contrasts with what Johnson identifies as a fixed framing, whereby ability and achievement are seen as immutable and inherently determined regardless of instruction. When you talk with children, you must be aware of how your words position them as learners, as well as influence how they imagine the process of learning itself. Your words have the potential to frame how children see themselves as learners, which when you think about it, means that teachers have an awesome amount of power over their students.

Johnston gives the example of how one word can shape the way a child views the world or even herself as a learner. Simply introducing a spelling test by stating, "Let's see how many words you know," versus, "Let's see how many words you know already" creates two different learning environments (Johnston 2012, 2). By adding the word *already*, the teacher tells the child that "any words the child knows are ahead of expectations, and, most important, that there is nothing permanent about what is known and not known" (12). Thus, Johnston's work demonstrates how we have three major points of influence in assisting children to take up a dynamic-learning frame.

CHOSE YOUR WORDS WISELY

The first point of influence lies in the words teachers choose to say to children when they are successful or unsuccessful at something. For instance, how you give feedback and praise (smart versus worked hard), or when children behave poorly or break classroom rules (bad student versus bad choice). As the child's teacher, you also need to legitimize and consider your students' comments as they talk about themselves as learners and not judge them.

CONSIDER HOW YOU FRAME LEARNING

The second point of influence is the way you frame learning. Do you think there is only one way to see the world or to learn? Do you ask children for the "right" answer or see who is the quickest to complete their work? Instead, early educators should ask children how they solved the problem at hand or ask them to identify the problem they found to be the most interesting and why. You, as well as the children in your classroom, also need to recognize that mistakes are just that, and as such, can be fixed and learned from before moving on.

Three Issues to Consider

Author Carol Dweck (2006) raises three important issues about how teachers frame learning. First, while having a dynamic framework for learning is an important aspect of teaching, we have to recognize that children's effort in learning is not enough. We must help children see where they make mistakes and offer specific skills instruction when appropriate so that they can become more efficient in their learning and progress toward more complicated skills and tasks. When praising children, we need to focus on what Dweck calls "process praise." We should praise the effort that allowed the child to complete the task or progress in his learning. We also need to teach children to ask questions about why they are failing or not making progress. Learning to determine how to move forward or who to turn to when they are stuck is an important skill. Finally, Dweck makes it clear that no one has a growth mind-set in everything all the time. There are triggers that can push us back into a fixed mind-set. For example, if you've always seen yourself as performing poorly in math, being asked to take a math test can push you back into a fixed framework. She contends we are mixtures of fixed and growth mind-sets, and thus we need to help children (and ourselves) recognize when and what led us back into a fixed mind-set.

TEACH CHILDREN HOW THEIR BRAINS WORK

Early educators need to explicitly teach children how people's brains and minds work. For instance, Johnston suggests letting children know the brain grows new cells each time they learn something new, or simply saying, "I think I see your mind growing" when they are engaged in a learning activity. This allows children to imagine how their brains are becoming more efficient through the process of effort and perseverance.

SUMMING UP THE POWER OF YOUR WORDS

Johnston's three points and Dweck's three issues reiterate how your words can push your students forward as learners. Moreover, they tie directly into what motivates children intrinsically to learn. For children to be motivated to learn, they have three psychological needs. The first is having a sense of autonomy, which means children feel they have a sense of choice in the learning activity. They must also feel competent that they can complete the task at hand, which means the learning situation should be attainable but not too easy. Finally, they should feel a sense of relatedness to those within the learning situation, which means feeling that their teachers and classmates value and respect them.

If children feel unsupported in any of these three needs, it negatively affects their motivation and engagement with the learning experience (Deci and Ryan 2002). Thus, teachers who create classroom environments rooted in a dynamic orientation toward learning that offers children autonomy, builds and supports their confidence, and creates a sense of relatedness are more likely to develop learning environments where children are highly motivated to learn.

Putting This All Together into Four Steps for Instruction

Considering how to address everything we've covered up to this point in teaching young children can be quite overwhelming. When we talk about these ideas with practicing teachers or teachers in training, we draw from the work of the National Research Council (2000) and their text *How People Learn*. The council argues that four strategies must be incorporated for one to learn with understanding.

USING STUDENTS' PREVIOUS EXPERIENCES

First, early educators need to draw on and work with their students' preexisting understandings (*long-term memory*). By making a personal connection, early educators help children make an emotional connection (for example, interest). If teachers do not tap into children's preexisting conceptions of the world, students will either fail to grasp what is taught or after learning for the test revert to their previous conceptions of that learning objective (think back to some of your classes where you simply studied lists of facts).

Children possess both behavioral and representational knowledge. Behavioral knowledge encompasses those scripts we employ to accomplish various roles, tasks, or procedures. For instance, many children have a bedtime script they follow at home. Representational knowledge consists of the mental framings of ideas, propositions, facts, and schema that children develop through direct and indirect experiences. For instance, a three-year-old understanding how to put the result of her eating one of three cookies into the mathematical formula of 3–1=2.

In early childhood classrooms, teachers provide children with both types of knowledge. Behaviorally, early educators teach children the scripts they need to employ to operate in school (for example, how to ask a question and how to line up for lunch, recess, and so on). When trying to walk a group of restless and talkative first graders returning from a field trip back to the classroom, the teacher could regain some order by giving the children a clear directive linked to a meaningful purpose, such as, "Remember to be considerate and quiet so that other students in their classrooms can concentrate on learning." Early educators also teach such representational knowledge and skills as reading. As children come to school, they take in new experiences and use these events to rewrite their behavioral scripts of how to operate in the larger world. They develop their representational understandings of how the world works around them and how they can use those skills and knowledge to affect their worlds. Remember that young children are better at learning scripts than representational knowledge. Moreover, some children will know more scripts than others, and in some instances, the cultural scripts children bring may not align with the practice you use in your classroom.

To tap into children's previous learning experiences, we need to observe and document what they know (we discuss this more in chapter 6). We need to foster multiple conversations in our learning environments (not interrogations) about what we're learning, studying, and discovering. Remember that young children are not always reliable sources. We also need to interact with families—such as asking families to send in a couple of sentences about their child's experience with sinking and floating objects.

PROVIDING IN-DEPTH LEARNING EXPERIENCES

The second strategy is to provide in-depth learning experiences, as well as numerous learning opportunities for any new investigation or unit of study. Recognize that you cannot simply teach your children facts or lists. You must help your students recognize how facts are structured within an area of thought, an instructional strategy that can assist the student to transfer knowledge into new learning environments. You should provide students with learning activities that reflect their experiences. Providing in-depth learning experiences, such as project-based learning, allows students to develop comfort with a topic and center their attention on learning this new information. To provide in-depth learning experiences, you need to spend more time on a topic than a fifteen-minute activity. A lot of pressure is placed on early educators to cover standards, be they local, district, state, or Common Core, and because of this pressure, they feel they must cover content quickly. However, that's not how children learn. Educators should think about how they can integrate a topic across subject areas. Thematic units (a series of lessons based on a theme, such as winter, pumpkins, or magnets) can do this as well as project-based work (an in-depth investigation focused on finding answers to students' questions about a topic, experience, or event).

One way to help students recognize the complexity embedded in a topic is to create a learning web, a KWL(H) chart (what do we Know, Want to learn, what have we Learned, and How can we learn more), or Venn diagram.

Recently, Beth observed a teacher using a Venn diagram to help students brainstorm writing ideas and make connections in their everyday lives. The teacher began by comparing two comic book heroes using a Venn diagram. Students were asked to write or draw in their writer's notebooks using the Venn diagram to organize their thinking. Students then generated their own Venn diagrams that compared such topics as having different pets, teachers, and their favorite cartoon characters, and used these diagrams to create new stories.

Teachers help facilitate in-depth learning experiences through rich conversations with children. Remember that children are more likely to open up to you in small groups, and making comments prolongs conversations more than asking questions. Avoid a "formal interrogation" of your students. If you want to ask children questions, think to yourself, "What's the purpose behind my question?" Author Brian Mowry shared an example of the ineffective and inappropriate practice of unnecessary interrogation of children's thinking. Brian's principal wanted all the teachers to implement a highly metacognitive element to learning, what Resnick (1995) termed "accountable talk." This practice involved asking students how they knew their work was of quality. In compliance with this mandate, Brian questioned the quality of a journal entry one of his students had just completed. Specifically, Brian wanted to know why she had decided to write words along with the picture she drew, and how she knew this was her best effort. The child responded, "Because a clown told me so." As this incident shows, teachers should solicit comments from children's opinions and ideas about the world. Early educators should offer comments that generate agentive actions in students. Instead of asking whether the child put forth her best effort, Brian could have first affirmed her effort by noticing the complexity of her work, and then he may have asked if there was anything she might consider editing to improve or extend her work.

TEACHING STUDENTS TO THINK ABOUT LEARNING

The third strategy asks for teachers to integrate metacognitive skills into their instruction (teach students to think about their learning). This strategy helps students stay motivated and learn to self-regulate when problems arise. Early educators can show children how to tap into their background knowledge (like using the KWL[H] charts mentioned on page 43). Educators also need to show the importance of predictions, which can be easy to practice during story time. Teachers need to show students how to plan ahead, which can be difficult with children since they typically have difficulty understanding the concept of time. You must ask children to explain their solutions to learning problems/challenges so you are not simply checking for the right answer. You also need to teach them that failure is a natural part of learning so they don't feel defeated (for example, using your failures as an example). Making mistakes in front of your students (such as, "The clock says it's fourteen o'clock, so it must be time to go home") not only shows children that you make mistakes all the time, but it also keeps children engaged in your classroom conversation. You also need to show children how to use their new knowledge to make future inquiries (for example, ending a project by asking children what new questions they want to investigate).

CREATING A POSITIVE LEARNING ENVIRONMENT

The fourth strategy for learning with understanding is to create a positive environment where the classroom community works together to foster learning for all. This strategy includes creating a safe space for the child to take risks, ask questions, and share personal stories with the classroom community. Consider the words you use about children and their learning. For instance, are you using such fixed words as *best, smartest,* or *nicest*? Or are you engaging dynamic conversations with children that emphasize effort, taking risks, using new strategies, and working as a community? Employing dynamic words helps children grow cognitively and grounds them emotionally. You want them to come to see you and their classmates as support mechanisms that they engage with as they tackle new learning experiences. Research has shown that children spend less than one-third of their time in school interacting with teachers (Jerome, Hamre, and Pianta 2009), and when they do, many of those interactions are negative (such as having their behavior redirected). Focus on relationships and interact with your students throughout the day—not just during instructional time. Doing so has repeatedly shown to have a positive impact on students' academic performance. Your goal should be to create learning environments where children feel they belong. Create a learning space that tells children they can tackle what you are asking them to do. Their confidence as learners will grow as they complete these learning activities, and the learning activities themselves will have value for them (Farrington et al. 2012).

Thus, according to the NRC (2001), to foster learning with understanding, teachers need to develop their students' enthusiasm and engagement. You can accomplish this by doing the following:

- Tapping into children's previous knowledge, including their cultural construction of learning by observing and documenting their learning
- Having in-class discussion
- Talking with children's families
- Providing in-depth learning opportunities that are integrated across the day
- Verbally connecting the dots for children regarding what is to be learned and why
- Creating a positive learning environment where the classroom community works together to foster learning for all.

These interconnected points provide an outline to ensure you are allowing children to bring what they already know and understand to the learning experience and are providing students with an opportunity to engage with the new material and skills in deep and meaningful ways. All of this should be done in a positive and nurturing learning environment.

Why Knowing How Children Develop and Learn Is Important

If, as Amos Hatch (2002) pointed out, our goal is to ensure children learn something new every day, we must know the curriculum we are expected to teach, the children in our classroom, and how children develop and learn. Understanding how each learner develops and learns will help us ensure we are *Seeing the whole child, Reaching all children with our instruction, Growing as a community,* and *Pushing every child forward.*

AVOIDING INAPPROPRIATE PRACTICES

Still, in this current era of accountability, where high stakes are used to motivate children and teachers, teachers face an inordinate amount of pressure to demonstrate that their students are learning. Unfortunately, this has led to teachers implementing a range of inappropriate practices and having unreasonable expectations for children. For instance, one of our favorite statements about teaching and learning is from Katz and Chard (2000). They note that just because children *can* do something does not mean they should *have* to do it. They provide the example of what they term the "calendar ritual" (23), which we see in almost every pre-K and K classroom we visit. The ritual typically entails the teacher and/or a student helper identifying the day, month, and the year, and counting the numbers of days children have been in school. Developmentally, most four- and five-year-old children do not possess conceptual knowledge about time for this activity to make sense, and yet, as Katz and Chard pointed out, they act as if they do to please the teacher. Another example comes from a conversation Beth had with a first-grade teacher whose students were reading *Harry Potter*. While they may have all the required skills to tackle this text, it doesn't mean the topic, which entails verbal and emotional abuse by adults toward children, darkness, fear, and parental death, is appropriate for young children. When thinking about the dynamic aspects of development, repeated exposure to a learning event that does not match children's conceptual level can have both immediate and long-term negative effects on them as learners. Immediately, it can make them feel incapable or not smart. Over the long term, such feelings and experience can "undermine their confidence" as learners (Katz and Chard 2000, 24). Thus, you need to see the whole child, and in doing so, ensure that when you try to push them forward in their learning that you are not pushing them in a way that shakes their confidence as learners.

Furthermore, with the prevailing myopic focus on student achievement, researchers have found that external pressures lead to teachers using controlling and didactic teaching strategies with children, which negatively affect children's motivation to learn. Such practices do not offer children autonomy or support their confidence as learners. They also decrease the likelihood of relating with the teacher and negatively affect teachers' interactions with children.

Policies that emphasize standardization and increased academic achievement while providing limited resources have led to many teachers, schools, and communities using rewards and even punishments, such as suspending children from school to motivate children to learn. Unfortunately, such strategies do not align with how children develop and learn. For instance, researchers found that rewards for children "have a substantially negative effect on intrinsic motivation. . . . Even when tangible rewards are offered as indicators of good performance, they typically decrease intrinsic motivation for interesting activities" (Deci, Koestner, and Ryan 1999, 658). It is essential to consider how what you ask children to do supports their autonomy, builds their confidence as learners, and creates a connection with you, their classmates, and their communities. The use of extrinsic rewards also negatively affects teachers. It undermines their autonomy, decreases their enthusiasm for teaching, and affects their creativity within their instruction. Thus, what motivates children to learn also motivates teachers to want to teach.

Reexamining Why It's Important to Understand How Children Develop and Learn across All Developmental Domains

- Discuss with your colleagues how you have traditionally thought about the ways children develop and learn. Then, discuss what ideas from this chapter you see yourself incorporating into your teaching.
- Using Deci and Ryan's (2002) idea that successful and motivating learning experiences offer the learner autonomy, builds and supports the learner's confidence, and creates a sense of relatedness with others, discuss an instance when you were successful as a learner. Were these three ideas present in that experience, and if so, how? Then think about an unsuccessful learning experience, and think about whether these three ideas were present in that experience, and if so, how?

Extending Your Learning

- To learn more about the intellectual development of young children, read *The Scientist in the Crib: What Early Learning Tells Us about the Mind* by Dr. Alison Gopnik and her colleagues Dr. Andrew Meltzoff and Dr. Patricia Kuhl (New York: HarperPerennial, 2001).
- To learn more about the significance of attending to children's social/emotional development in their learning, which includes their executive function skills, read *Helping Children Succeed: What Works and Why* by Paul Tough (New York: Houghton Mifflin Harcourt, 2016).
- To learn more about working with children who have experienced early childhood trauma, visit The National Child Traumatic Stress Network (www.nctsn.org/) and their child trauma toolkit for educators (https://schoolleaders.thekeysupport.com/pupils-and-parents/pupil-health-and-wellbeing/pupil-wellbeing/supporting-pupils-who-have-experienced-traumatic-events).
- The website for the Center on the Developing Child (http://developingchild.harvard.edu) at Harvard University provides a range of resources on child and human development for early educators.
- Child Trends (www.childtrends.org), a nonprofit organization, conducts and shares research around issues affecting the lives of children and their families.
- The Office of Head Start's website (https://eclkc.ohs.acf.hhs.gov/hslc/hs/sr/approach/elof/se_dev.html) provides teaching and research resources dedicated to children's social and emotional development.
- Dr. Ross Greene works with addressing challenging behavior in young children's lives. He has two websites that offer insight into his collaborative and proactive solution to working with children: www.livesinthebalance.org/educators-schools and www.cpsconnection.com.
- To learn more about how you might support children who are struggling with learning or attention in your educational setting, Understood (www.understood.org/en) is an umbrella organization for fifteen nonprofits seeking to assist families in the education process.

Steps You Can Take toward Change

- Consider how you approach learning with your students—are you tapping into their previous knowledge? Are you allowing them to experience new content/knowledge/skill in depth? Are you teaching them how to think about their thinking, and are you doing this in a safe learning environment? If you answered no to any of the above questions, think about what aspects you can address in your teaching.

- Think about how you talk about learning with your students, colleagues, administrators, and the families you serve. How are you using a dynamic learning framework? In what ways are you using a fixed framework? What is one way you could change your statements and intent so that you project a more dynamic understanding of growth and development?

3

Knowing Your Students' Worlds

Ms. Anderson, a third-grade teacher, begins every day with a class meeting where she and her students check in about what is going to happen in school that day and what is going on in their lives. In a meeting shortly after winter break, Susan, a third grader, stated, "I think we have changed over the last few months." Ms. Anderson responded, "Yes, we have all changed over the last few months. Each of you, as well as myself, have learned so many new things, and each of you has become a better problem solver. You've become better friends, and we've come to know each other as a learning community. These changes are good for us. That's how we grow and develop into better people, a better class, and a better community."

Ms. Anderson's response to Susan's insight about how she and her classmates were changing was an attempt to build on the idea of growing together, be it academically or becoming a more cohesive learning community. However, Ms. Anderson soon realized that Susan had another idea about the changes taking place in their classroom. Susan continued, "Yes, but I was talking about how some of us have different hairdos." Ms. Anderson laughed. Realizing that new hairstyles were just as important to her class as all the changes she listed, Ms. Anderson responded by saying, "New hairdos. Some of us do have different hairdos. You are right. Some of us have had the same hairdo all year. Mine is a little longer than it was when we started school, and it looks like your hair is shorter." Susan nodded her head.

Ms. Anderson's response demonstrates how building caring relationships within the classroom community required her to relate to her students and discuss what was important to them. She continued, "Who else had longer hair at the beginning of the school year?" Carla responded, "I did, remember? It was down to here," and pointed to her midback. Stephen added, "I know my hair is going to get long if I don't cut it, right?" Ms. Anderson agreed. Ms. Anderson continued with the class meeting and made sure each student had the opportunity to share whatever news he or she deemed important for the class community.

In Ms. Anderson's morning meeting, we see how growing as community is not simply a matter of attaining specific academic or social goals over the course of the school year. It requires teachers to see the whole child and understand that each child has her own goals and desires within the classroom—including their own interpretation of what is and should be important to their learning. In this case, Ms. Anderson realized that her students saw change differently than she did, and in doing so, she immediately began to relate to and expand on her students' interests in hairdos. This could not have happened without Ms. Anderson creating the space for such dialogue to occur within the daily morning meeting. Such activities allow early educators to come to know their students on a personal level, which is a necessary component of a classroom that encourages the growth and development of all children.

To be an effective teacher who engages in RIGOROUS DAP, you must get to know your students and their families. However, there are two primary challenges many early educators face that hinder their ability to get to know children and their families. The first is policy makers' standards-based accountability (SBA) reforms. The second is the construct of developmentally appropriate practice itself.

The Challenge of Standards-Based Accountability Reforms

Policy makers' high-stakes SBA reforms, such as NCLB and Common Core, have affected educators working in publicly supported early education programs in numerous ways. The policies strive to create aligned systems of education in which all children demonstrate their mastery of a particular set of content by attaining a certain level of proficiency on standardized exams.

While high-stakes exams typically do not begin until third grade, these policies redefine the purpose of pre-K and kindergarten programs (Brown 2013; Sherfinski 2013). These policies also deemphasize such practices as developing a positive interaction between early educators and the children and families they serve, which in turn affects children's readiness for school. For instance, recent Head Start reforms requiring the increased use of student and teacher assessments created conflicts between following the new policies and meeting the needs of students (Bullough Jr. et al. 2014). Many early childhood educators are ignoring traditional early childhood teaching practices and instead are making instructional decisions based on policy makers' demands for standardization and improved academic achievement (Brown, Weber, and Yoon 2015).

Such a conception of ECE (or public education in general) shifts the measure of student performance from individual children and their personal, developmental, linguistic, and cultural needs to a test score all children must attain.

Doing so fails to capture the field's research-based understandings of children's learning and development and the assessment process.

Shortcomings with Developmentally Appropriate Practices

Many within the field of ECE have advocated for teachers to respond to these changes through practice rooted in NAEYC's construction of developmentally appropriate practice (DAP). By following DAP, teachers make instructional decisions that focus on the growth and development of individual children across all developmental domains in a manner that addresses the sociocultural contexts in which they live (Copple and Bredekamp 2009). While some teachers can actively balance the expectations found in their state policy makers' SBA reforms with DAP, DAP can still fall short in addressing the needs of culturally and linguistically diverse children (Edwards, Blaise, and Hammer 2009).

Because DAP is primarily rooted in developmental psychology, which places children at the center of the learning process, children can be seen as isolated figures who are either acted upon by others (such as their teachers or families) or they themselves act on others. This understanding of development does not capture the role and influence of the sociocultural community and context in which children develop. Children's development should be framed through the social worlds in which they exist, which include their family, teacher, school, the larger community, and so on. Such a vision of appropriate practices frames early education as a social and coconstructed process influenced by the networks in which children live. As such, "children, peers, teachers and families are actively, authentically, and meaningfully engaged in the social and coconstruction of knowledge and skills" needed to thrive in school and the larger society (Langford 2010, 121).

If the focus of DAP is on the development of children at an individual level, the gendered, racialized, and sociopolitical contexts in which children are being educated aren't recognized. The constructs that define children and their families are influenced by the policies and politics of that community. When taking into consideration these and other sociocultural/political factors, framing children as middle-income for example, or identifying them as Latinx, may not only differ across nations but also across local communities.

Having a limited understanding of how children develop and learn creates an opportunity for a standardized or ideal image of a "normal child" to emerge. This standardized image excludes those who do not match the culturally and income-biased norms found in DAP (Brown 2013). Children who do not match certain developmental markers (which are a key aspect of DAP) or sociolinguistic expectations of the teacher are then labeled as at risk by preschool or elementary school personnel. This, in turn, will lead to these children being given remedial instruction, being excluded from the classroom, or being made to repeat the program.

The idea of incorporating culture to the spectrum of appropriate practices with young children, or framing development through a collectivist rather than individualist lens, is not new to ECE. Collectivism, as a cultural perspective, emphasizes the needs of the family or the community before the individual and leads to a stronger sense of community and less competition. An individualistic culture, which is the dominant perspective in the United States, often results in a strong sense of competition. The revisions of DAP have expanded the role of culture in the development of young children. However, adding high-stakes SBA reform policies to the early education context, in which educators must teach children with a range of cultural assets and linguistic abilities, specific skills and knowledge, complicates matters further.

Children's Culture and Their Learning

Children's culture influences their learning and how they approach schooling. Children live their lives through their culture. As such, their cultures influence such social/emotional traits as their persistence, attentiveness to work, conversations within their learning community, and self-regulation. Teachers cannot expect all children to approach or demonstrate their learning the same way.

Successful teachers respond to these cultural differences in a positive, humanizing manner and strive to establish warm and personal relationships with their students, while still having high expectations. By humanizing, we mean building reciprocal relationships with children and their families that are rooted in dignity and care. Early childhood educators, children, and their families must share their interests, goals, thoughts about schooling, and other issues to foster humane interactions that seek to value and incorporate understanding and voice within the early childhood classroom.

To move beyond the issues surrounding DAP and the impact of policy makers' high-stakes SBA reforms on teaching in ECE settings, we turn to the work of Gloria Ladson-Billings (1994, 2006) and her conception of culturally relevant pedagogy (CRP). It is a theory of instruction that puts forward a more complex understanding of the impact of culture on children's development and learning, as well as of the impact of teachers' own cultural history. CRP attends to the sociopolitical context, which includes both the politics and policies in which you and your students work. We must pay attention to sociocultural worlds children and their families bring to the classroom and how such worlds may be privileged or discriminated against in the larger sociopolitical context. At the same time, we critically examine our ideological beliefs and pedagogical practices toward our students and their families. Being intentionally critical and reflective of one's practice and teaching context helps us become aware of the issues central to children and their families, which leads us to develop curricular and instructional opportunities that attend to the children's sociopolitical contexts.

WHY CRP?

Ladson-Billings (1994, 17–18) defines CRP as a "pedagogy that [empowers] students intellectually, socially, emotionally, and politically by using cultural referents to impart knowledge, skills, and attitudes." As such, CRP is framed through three criteria you can implement with your students: fostering academic achievement among all students, cultivating their cultural competence, and developing their sociopolitical consciousness.

The suggestions put forward in DAP are difficult for early educators to implement in a high-stakes teaching context. While DAP recognizes the impact of policy on teaching, NAEYC's current guidelines advocate for an increased use of and political support for DAP (Copple and Bredekamp 2009). This framing limits the role of the children, their families, and the educational context in shaping the early education process. By adding CRP to our conceptual understanding of RIGOROUS DAP, we attend to the role of the sociopolitical. This not only affects the actions and lives of children who participate in public ECE programs, but also aids teachers in addressing the societal (for example, a high incidence of poverty among culturally and linguistically diverse [CLD] children) and political issues (for example, being told what to teach and when) in their teaching.

We see these challenges creating a different space for instruction, and therefore, they do not align easily with other examples of teachers in non-high-stakes contexts who have been able to engage in DAP or CRP on a regular basis (for example, Cowley, 2006). We believe that advocating for more developmentally appropriate practice in the classroom or in policy makers' reforms does not necessarily attend to the current instructional demands many teachers' face. Still, while CRP offers a political response to policy makers' high-stakes reforms, at its core, this framework advocates for structural changes not only to the education system but also to the larger society.

THREE CONSTRUCTS THAT FRAME CRP

Engaging in CRP, which is an essential component of RIGOROUS DAP, requires educators to foster academic success, cultural competence, and sociopolitical consciousness for all their students. To foster academic success, you must transition from a view of teaching and learning as an act of transmitting knowledge to one in which you work "with students so that they can reflect, theorize, and create knowledge" (Nieto, 2002, 7). Entwined with academic learning is your responsibility to build children's cultural competence. You must help students "recognize and honor their own cultural beliefs and practices" and provide them with the knowledge and skills needed to "access the wider culture, where they are likely to have a chance of improving their socioeconomic status and making informed decisions about the lives they wish to lead" (Ladson-Billings 2006, 36). By doing this, you help students use cultural knowledge and experiences outside of their formal schooling to succeed academically.

Research has shown that while early educators may be trained in or have received professional development about CRP, they still struggle with implementing these practices in their classrooms on a consistent basis (Gichuru et al. 2015). Specifically, teachers have difficulty taking up the sociopolitical dimensions of CRP, which requires them to engage with children in ways that go beyond the mandated curriculum and have a direct impact on their lives and communities. To build children's sociopolitical consciousness necessitates interacting with students as subjects, rather than objects, and including them as active participants in the curriculum development process.

Researchers have demonstrated that early educators need continued and sustained support either via professional development or working with collaborative communities of educators to assist them in the process of fostering and maintaining culturally relevant instruction with their students (Brown and Weber 2016). Such continued support from colleagues and administrators can help early educators make sense of the process of engaging in CRP within the standardized teaching context. If these opportunities are not available, you could do something as simple as starting a children's literature group, where you and your colleagues would seek out, review, and plan to incorporate stories that reflect either the children and communities in your classroom or issues that are important to your students.

WHAT IT MEANS TO ENGAGE IN CRP

Teachers often struggle to address their students' needs, whether cultural or developmental, and they are increasingly asked to defend their teaching practices to school or district personnel when they deviate from what is typically expected (Brown and Weber 2016). For instance, we work and do much of our research in Texas, and we've witnessed firsthand how many teachers must provide weekly documentation to show how many minutes they spend on specific instructional activities that address such curricular domains as literacy, mathematics, science, and social studies.

Engaging CRP requires you to question your own cultural identity as well as your conceptions of teaching children from a range of cultural, linguistic, and socioeconomic backgrounds. Ask yourself, "How do I identify culturally?" For some, it's an easy question. For others, those who are typically white, middle income, and raised as a part of the dominant culture in the United States that benefits from structural inequities, it's a more difficult question. It may be difficult to acknowledge being raised in a family dynamic where culture, discrimination (both personal and systemic), and so on were rarely discussed. We recognize that asking yourself these questions might not be easy, but it is nevertheless important to determine whether you are engaging in CRP. In understanding your cultural, linguistic, and socioeconomic identities, you'll find that your multiple identities intersect in different ways, depending on the context (for example, being an African American female student in a classroom is very different from being an African American female parishioner in a church). This intersectionality of identities represents the complexity of who you are as an individual and helps you see how the power you possess varies depending on the context in which you are operating.

Once you recognize who you are, what your position is within the larger society, and how you maintain or resist the dominant structures, you then need to reflect on your own beliefs about teaching culturally and linguistically talented children, which can be a major influence on your classroom decision making. For example, researchers have found that teachers often favor students who sound or look like them. Teachers can develop biases and even discriminate against those who do not (Kumar, Karabenick, and Burgoon 2015). Ask yourself how you react to or address others who are different from you—be it the color of their skin, their gender, their language or dialect, their sexual orientation, or their mannerisms. Are you framing the "dynamic cultural and linguistic dexterity" of your students "as a necessary good, and see the outcome of learning as additive, rather than subtractive, as remaining whole rather than framed as broken, as critically enriching strengths rather than replacing deficits" (Paris 2016, 6)? Asking yourself these questions is critical for you in engaging not only in CRP but also in RIGOROUS DAP. Research has consistently shown how teachers react to children's varied cultural and linguistic actions or statements can create a sense of cultural or linguistic insecurity for children (such as responding to a child's statement with, "That doesn't sound like English to me"), which negatively affects their academic learning (Charity, Scarborough, and Griffin 2004).

You should also question the type of learning environment you've created for children and their families. Ask yourself, when children and families come into my classroom, what does my classroom say? One thing we tell our preservice teachers is to go outside their classroom and walk back in on their knees, and as they do that, think about what they see. Some questions to consider are: Do the images posted on the walls or materials available in the classroom reflect who students are physically and linguistically? Would a child or family member understand the purpose of your classroom? Would they feel valued and secure in this learning space? If students do not feel welcomed, valued, or secure in your classroom, how can you expect them to grow and develop as learners and members of your classroom community?

It is just as important to study and understand how both local and larger sociopolitical issues affect your children's lives, as well as what you are expected to do with the students in your classroom. Understanding how the sociopolitical context (both local and national) creates inequities among different populations of students is an important first step and makes engaging in CRP more plausible. To come to know a child, you must come to know the child's community. If you do not live in your students' communities, shopping for groceries, walking the neighborhoods, or spending time at the park, movie theater, or local restaurants will help you gain insight into your students' worlds. Students are always excited to see you outside of school, and engaging with them and their families in a nonschool context can lighten the mood for everyone. The ability to make familiar conversations about their lives as well as your own in and out of school allows your learning community to develop naturally.

The secret behind culturally relevant pedagogy is "the ability to link principles of learning with deep understanding of (and appreciation for) culture" (Ladson-Billings 2014, 77). Learning in this sense is more than what is tested in third grade or what is found in any mandated curricula. Rather, it is a process of children understanding how to exist, thrive, develop, and learn through their sociocultural worlds. The learning experiences you provide children in your program/classroom are tied directly to the skills, knowledge, and dispositions they need to thrive in their communities.

Bringing Your Students' Sociocultural Worlds into Your Learning Community

We believe that engaging in CRP is an essential aspect of RIGOROUS DAP and will assist you in getting to know the children and their families on a personal level. When we bring up CRP with teachers, they often think there is some secret set of practices they need to use to be able to say they are teaching in a culturally relevant manner. There isn't. It's a matter of your awareness and actions as a teacher with each student in your classroom. It's linking effective instruction with the cultural backgrounds of your students and ensuring your practices are sustaining children's cultural and linguistic practices. As we said earlier, that means you need to know yourself as a cultural being as well as your students. We warn, however, that the term *cultural* is not a one size fits all category. Rather, culture is child/family specific. Therefore, you first must show your students that you are interested in getting to know them and that you want them to be a part of the classroom community.

To do that, you must show children that you care about them from day one. Simple acts, like sending home a postcard or email to children and their families welcoming them to your classroom and having the children's name prominently posted around your classroom lets them know you want them there. Other welcoming activities we've seen include having a scavenger hunt during the first day of school to get to know the school's layout and important people (principal, school nurse, and so on) within the school; creating class books that mimic stories the students have read; and remaking songs that include or incorporate students' names.

MORNING MEETINGS TO GIVE STUDENTS VOICE

Another activity to consider including in your classroom is a morning meeting like Ms. Anderson's, where children get to check in with you and the class. For instance, in Chris's kindergarten classroom, each day began with the class meeting in a circle where each child had time to share their news with the class. They would pass around a Koosh ball, and whoever had the Koosh had the floor. This activity took only about ten minutes a day, but it was a way for everyone to check in with one another and know that they had a voice in the classroom community. At the beginning of the year, the children may not have anything to share or know how to share, so this will take a lot of modeling on your part. You can also have class meetings across the day to find out specific information about children to help you know them in a more personal manner. For instance, you might ask if they have any brothers or sisters. If so, how many? Do they have pets? What's their favorite (or least favorite) thing to do? What's their favorite song, story, movie, and so on?

Morning meetings can also be used to address important issues. For example, in Ms. Jackson's third-grade class one day, police asked school personnel to keep all students in their classrooms while they attempted to subdue a man with a gun resisting arrest across the street. The next day, Ms. Jackson brought students to the carpet for their morning meeting to discuss this issue. She knew that the school lockdown had caused a great amount of fear, anger, and frustration, and she hoped the class meeting would allow students space and security to talk about their feelings. Some students complained about missing lunch and being hungry, while others were mad about the media attention surrounding the lockdown. Ms. Jackson probed, "Why were you mad about the cameras?" The students were concerned that people might perceive their neighborhood as ghetto. While Ms. Jackson rejected the term *ghetto*, she acknowledged the reality of their lives in a high-crime area. "You can say, 'I might live in an area with crime, but if I go to school, get an education, do what I am supposed to do, and focus on doing better, I can be anything.' But you must focus on wanting to do better. You hear what I am saying to you?" By allowing this space, Ms. Jackson furthered her goals of knowing and understanding her children's lives both in and outside the classroom.

The goal of the morning meeting or any activity where the class works together is to develop a learning community that is growing together. Engaging in such acts as a morning meeting provides children with the opportunity to interact as well as begin to develop an understanding of other peoples' perspectives. This allows children to learn how others think about the same issue. When sharing personal stories in morning meetings, you and the children provide one another with insight into issues surrounding your lives.

BEING OBSERVANT OF POSSIBLE SOCIOCULTURAL ISSUES

As you engage in these practices that allow you to *See the whole child* as well as *Grow as a class community*, pay attention to children's daily activities, conversations, and play scenarios that might indicate an issue or dilemma is occurring in the children's homes, communities, and broader sociocultural worlds. For example, when teaching preschool, coauthor Brian missed an opportunity to probe deeper into a sociopolitical situation that his students (all of whom were from immigrant families from Mexico) had confronted and were subsequently reenacting through their dramatic play. At the dramatic play center, which was set up as a home, a group of girls removed household items (such as pots, pans, and clothing) from the counters and storage bins and placed them inside a make-believe truck that a group of boys had constructed at the block center. The two groups of children pretended to be on a road trip, with one child playing the driver while the other children sat among the items carefully packed inside the truck. At one point during this complex, hour-long dramatization, the children pretended to cross a river. Upon crossing, some of the girls screamed, "La migra!" (the Spanish term for *immigration*) and immediately hid underneath a blanket. After waiting a few minutes under the blanket, which muffled a few giggles, the children removed the blanket and continued their pretend journey. Then center time came to an end, and the children cleaned up—returning the housekeeping props back to the dramatic play center.

Unfortunately, Brian failed to revisit this dramatization during circle time and did not inquire deeper into what was happening and if the children wanted to discuss the event in greater detail. Doing so might have allowed Brian to explore a potentially (although risky) sociopolitical topic with the class that is relevant to many immigrants who fear the risk of deportation. Although the children were only four and five years old, they nevertheless had experienced this traumatic event at some point in their young lives. Their experience could provide a bridge to discussing the issue of immigration at their developmental level.

GETTING TO KNOW YOUR STUDENTS' FAMILIES

An essential component in getting to know your students' worlds is getting to know their families. Making connections with families has a long history in early childhood education. However, family involvement in early education programs, particularly in public education systems, has become less common.

It is important to examine how you view the families you work with—are they your allies, or do you see them as an inconvenience? Your thoughts will affect your actions. To engage in RIGOROUS DAP, you must know the whole child and grow with them and their families as a community, and to do this you must know each child's family.

How to Foster Positive Relationships with Families

There are several ways that you can gain access to and foster positive relationships with families, starting from the first day of school. For instance, you can send home questionnaires to families: How does your child learn best? What are your child's interests? What are your child's strengths? With what may your child need help? What do you hope your child accomplishes this year? What type of relationship would you like to have with me and our classroom/program? Would you be willing to volunteer in our classroom, and if so, when are you available? What additional information should I know that you think is important? Finally, ask them to send in some family pictures so their child will be able to see them in your classroom each day.

Some early education programs emphasize home visits, and while we see value in this activity, we know that not all families, school districts, or early childhood programs support this. Some families might not feel comfortable having teachers or school personnel visit their homes. If your program requires home visits or you find value in doing so, offer to meet family members in a public place, like a library, coffee shop, or fast-food restaurant, rather than the family's home. Doing so lets them know that you're interested in them and not where they live.

Other ways to build relationships with families before the start of a new school year include having a potluck dinner before the school year where each family and teacher brings a food item that is important to them to the meal. You can also have an informal open house welcoming families and their children to meet you and see your classroom. Many public school programs have a formal back-to-school night, which is a wonderful way to welcome families to your classroom/program, but also offering an informal meeting can be another beneficial way of getting to know them.

You may also want to call all your families before or during the first week of school to welcome them and their children to the classroom. Families appreciate these types of affirmations, and spending a few minutes at the beginning of the year letting them know you care and appreciate the work they have done with their children helps put your relationship with them on a positive trajectory. Moreover, if you must make a call later in the school year about a negative issue, having already built a trusting relationship will make that conversation much easier.

You can also send a handwritten postcard to them and the child. Email works as well, but in our experiences as teachers and as parents of school-age children, it seems less personalized and can be easily overlooked.

Once the year is under way, there are several ways to interact with families: phone calls, newsletters, emails, class blogs, web-based portfolio programs such as Seesaw (http://web.seesaw.me) or ClassDojo (www.classdojo.com), teacher-family conferences, back-to-school nights, and so on. In each of these situations, consciously choosing your words is essential. Remember, your goal is to help families understand and appreciate what's going on in your classroom, and you want them to know that you understand and appreciate what's going on in their families. Moreover, you should affirm their children as well, and tell them you appreciate their hard work. Finally, be sure you're contacting each child's family on a consistent basis—set aside a specific time each week or every other week to call families and inform them of the wonderful things happening in the classroom.

Words Matter

As you set out to establish successful relationships with students' families, remember that this partnership requires you to use positive and appropriate communication skills—be intentional in what you say, and be an active listener.

When communicating with families, think about your message. For example, which note would you like to receive from a teacher?

> Dear Families,
>
> That chill in the air has returned, which means it's that time of year again when we ask that you please send a coat with your child. We try to spend time every day outside to give children a chance to be active and get fresh air, and when children do not have coats, they usually do not last long outside. So please be sure to check that your child has a coat when you send him or her to school in the morning!
>
> Thanks,
> The Teacher

• • •

> Dear Families,
>
> I noticed that some families again forgot to send coats to school with their children. If you fail to send a coat to school, I cannot allow your child to go outside. Be sure to send your child to school wearing a coat, or your child will not have recess.
>
> The Teacher

Both notes convey the same message to families, but one does so in a way that is both helpful and positive. Ask yourself if the message you are trying to convey and what you are asking them to do fosters a positive relationship.

Another way to encourage positive relationships is to invite parent volunteers in the classroom. If you do this, let parents know your expectations and how you would like them to interact with the children in your class. Try to plan an interesting and fun activity they can do with your class, ask them to share a story about their family or childhood, or to read a favorite children's book with the class. Personally, when we had parents in our classrooms, we usually asked for their help during small-group time so we could work with children one-on-one or in targeted groupings.

You may want to consider conducting class-based in-person family interviews that ask different students' families to visit each week to share with the class about who they are, their family practices/traditions, their community involvement, and their hopes and dreams for one another. Such interviews provide you and your students with deep, personal insight into each family and, when planned ahead of time, give children the chance to learn how to prepare for and conduct interviews. After the interviews, have the children create two family books (one book for the class and one for the family) that share what they learned about each classmate's family through the interview process.

Teacher/Family Conferences

One of the most important interactions early educators have with families is the teacher/family conference. Essentially, there are four goals to accomplish during a teacher/family conference. First, establish or strengthen the relationship between home and school, and develop shared purposes between you and the child's family. For many families, arranging work schedules, child care, and transportation to and from school can be quite difficult, so be sure to thank them for making time in their busy schedule to discuss their child. Second, gather information from the family about the child; for instance, what they see as their child's strengths and growth areas, what goals they have for the child, and so on. Third, share information about the child with them; for example, you outline what you see as the child's strengths, their growth areas and how you plan to address them in the classroom, and your plans for the remainder of the year. Make sure everything you say within the conference reflects your respect for the child's capabilities and potential for success. Support your statements with facts, details, evidence, and documentation, and be clear to the family that it's your responsibility to support the child in the classroom and that you are committed to ensuring that the child grows and develops across the school year. Finally, answer questions family members might have, as well as make a plan of action for how to continue to build a positive relationship with them and their child. If there is a question you can't answer, it's okay to say, "I don't know, but let me look into it. I promise to get in touch with you by (give day and time)." Moreover, it's important to say "I'm sorry" if you made a mistake. Either way, the goal is to keep moving the relationship forward, which requires you to listen to what families say, follow up when you say you will, and apologize when you make a mistake.

To know children's worlds requires you to establish a strong and positive relationship with their families. Doing so allows you to engage in instructional opportunities with children that reflect not only their sociocultural worlds but also content, issues, and ideas that their families value and think are an essential component of their education.

TABLE 3.1
Conducting Effective Teacher/Family Conferences

Goals	Actions
Establish/strengthen the relationship between home and school and develop shared purposes	• Begin by sharing your knowledge of and affection for their child (e.g., be sure to pronounce their child's name correctly; share an anecdote about their child in the classroom). • Express your gratitude for the hard work they do at home to help their child develop and learn. • Explain your vision of the partnership and shared purposes.
Gather information from the family about the child	• Remember, families know much more than you do about their child, so invite them to share their knowledge. • Provide them with opportunities to gather their thoughts *before* the conference by sending home a letter/email that asks family to think about such things as the topics that spark their child's interest; the activities that engage their child's focused attention; what they would like to see their child accomplish this year at school and at home; any cultural practices they would like you to be aware of; and how you might work together to help their child reach their goals.
Share information about the child with the family	• Begin by sharing their academic and developmental strengths through documentation/evidence. • Share their child's growth areas using the same types of documentation. • Share your instructional plans to address these growth areas specifically and build on their strengths. • Always talk about children's development and achievement in relation to grade-level expectations and in a tone that emphasizes continued progress.

TABLE 3.1 *(continued)*

Goals	Actions
Answer questions from family members and make a plan of action for continuing to build a positive relationship together	• Give families a chance to ask any questions they might have. In answering them, remember that it's okay to say, "I don't know" or "Let me find out more about that. What's the best way for me to reach you to tell you what I learned?" or "That's interesting. What have you been noticing at home?" • Remember, if you made a mistake or misinterpreted a situation, it's okay to say you're sorry. • End the conference by thanking the family member for coming, remind them that they can contact you anytime, and provide them with directions on how to do that (such as I am available to talk on the phone at this number most days between 2 and 3 p.m.). • Finally, give them a message (verbal or written) to share with their child. "Please tell Lucille how much I enjoy the stories she writes. I always look forward to reading her journal because she's such an expert with developmental spelling."

Putting What You Know about Your Students into Action

Knowing your students' worlds is essential for you to engage in RIGOROUS DAP and to ensure children can develop and learn to their fullest potential. We end this chapter with an example of what this means in practice; specifically, an example of teacher Ms. Santos engaging in a series of activities around the issue of incarcerated parents (Brown and Mowry 2016). This example provides a bridge between this chapter and our next, which examines instructional strategies you can use to instruct your students through RIGOROUS DAP.

This investigation into parental incarceration emerged from Ms. Santos's observations on the playground. She commented, "I've noticed the children were playing jail on the playground, and I know some of the children have family members who are or have been in jail. I wanted to understand how they perceived jail. I wanted to know: Why do they think people are in jail? Why do they think their parents go to jail?"

While Ms. Santos was nervous to pursue this topic with her students, she knew it was an issue present in many of her students' lives. We think it is important to include it in this book because most early childhood educators in the United States will have children in their classrooms who have had an incarcerated family member. Up to 15 percent of all school-age children have a parent who has been incarcerated sometime during their childhood (Lee, Fang, and

Luo 2013). Currently, about 3.6 percent of all children in the United States have an incarcerated parent (Uggen and McElrath 2014). Furthermore, researchers have found that children with incarcerated parents typically do not have anyone in their lives to talk to about this issue (Clopton and East 2008). Thus, teachers can create a space within the classroom that allows children to discuss and explore issues related to their sociocultural worlds.

Because Ms. Santos was nervous about going off script in her high-stakes teaching context, she decided she would follow a lesson plan format that mirrored what she typically did. She began by reading stories like *Jack and the Beanstalk* (Ottolenghi 2002), and then she read the opposite version in which the giant is the good guy (Braun 2011). She did this because she wanted students to see that there are different perspectives to every story. She hoped her students would be in a frame of mind to think differently about why someone might see something as good and somebody else might see it as bad. She added, "I wanted to scaffold their thinking about the complex issues surrounding why someone may go to jail." This lesson plan demonstrates how Ms. Santos scaffolded children's understandings of the world beyond what they typically see in their everyday lives (Metz 2004; Vygotsky 1978), and it also reflects how she engaged in culturally relevant practices with her students. Specifically, she assisted her students in reconsidering the power dynamics that exist within the larger society. In this case, she helped her students begin to understand how certain taken-for-granted assumptions about why people go to jail are much more complex than a simple matter of right and wrong.

Next, Ms. Santos read a story that specifically examined what it means to have an incarcerated family member: Wittbold's (1997) *Let's Talk about When Your Parent Is in Jail*. Before the story, she asked the students what they knew about jail, and afterward she planned to have students work with her in small groups during center time to write their thoughts about the story.

Ms. Santos had the children sit on the reading carpet. She showed them the cover of *Let's Talk about When Your Parent Is in Jail*, which has a drawing of two hands holding the bars of a jail cell. She asked the children, "What do you know about jail?" Ms. Santos noted, "It was kind of shocking to them. They seemed to act as if no one had ever talked to them about jail before."

After a moment, a few children raised their hands, and she called on them to share their thoughts. Alejandra, in a distraught voice, stated, "My dad was in jail, and if he did not pay [a court fine], he would have to go back to jail." Ms. Santos tried to calm Alejandra down by stating, "Everything will be okay, and remember, your daddy loves you." Ms. Santos noted after the lesson, "I am very close to Alejandra's family. Her grandma talks to me, and so I knew everything that was going on. I think that's the reason why she decided to be open in the classroom."

After students had made a few more comments, including Francisco, whose father had been in jail, and Verónica, whose father was currently in jail, Ms. Santos began to read the book. She asked, "What is jail? Jail is a place where people go as a form of punishment. If you have had a dad that has been in jail, you're not alone; there are many children whose fathers have been in jail." Lucia added, "And mothers too." Ms. Santos repeated her statement, "And moms too." As she continued reading, she paraphrased the text for the children. She stated that when a person doesn't obey the law, he hurts someone he loves." She continued, "But listen to what it says here. When someone breaks the law, it doesn't mean that person is bad. Because someone goes to jail, it doesn't mean he is bad. Do you understand me?" Ms. Santos then said, "I have an uncle who broke the law, and they took him to jail. But he's my uncle, and he is good to me. If your mom or dad breaks the law, can she or he still be a good person?" The children responded, "Yes." Ms. Santos added, "Sometimes people break the law, and if they do, there are consequences. But they can still be a good person."

Ms. Santos continued with the story and stopped to ask or answer questions when they came up from the children. Toward the end, she stated, "The book says many children feel sad because their relative is in jail and you may feel sad sometimes." She then added, "I understand if you feel sad, but remember, it wasn't you who made the decision to break the law. You should remember that no matter what, your parents love you."

As she finished the book, she asked the students if they had anything they wanted to share or add. Francisco told the class about how his father had been in jail many times before he was deported back to Mexico. Ms. Santos asked Francisco how he felt about that, and he said, "Sad." She then reminded Francisco that his father loves him very much, which seemed to comfort him.

Ms. Santos told the students that during center time she would call a few of them over at a time to draw, write, and/or dictate their thoughts about the story. As the children rotated through the center with her, many of their drawings involved having a fictional person in a jail cell with the police standing outside it. For instance, Javier drew this type of picture and explained, "The man was in jail because he took something. The police threw him into jail." Four of her twenty-two students drew pictures of their fathers being in jail. For example, Verónica drew a picture of her dad in jail with a sad face and her standing outside it with a happy face. When Ms. Santos asked about the picture, Verónica told a story of her dad going to jail for "drinking too many beers." She explained that her father is still in jail, and when they go to visit him, "My mom cries, my sisters cry, but I don't." Ms. Santos said, "I am sure it is very hard for you, your mom, and your sisters to visit your dad. It's okay to cry about it, and remember, your daddy loves you." Verónica responded, "I know," and proceeded back to the centers. When reflecting on this experience with Verónica, Ms. Santos noted, "I was worried about the students going home and telling their families, 'Ms.

Santos talked about jail today,' and that's what Verónica did. However, her mom said she was glad that Verónica could talk with me about it, which was a relief. It was nice for her to feel comfortable enough with me to tell me that it helped Verónica." This statement demonstrates how Ms. Santos intentionally created a learning environment where she listened to and accepted Verónica for who she was and built off her strengths so she could move forward in the classroom. While Verónica's and her classmates' parents may still be in jail, Ms. Santos supports her students by addressing this issue head on and seems to assist them in making decisions about the lives they want to lead.

Moreover, Ms. Santos noted that by engaging in this lesson she felt empowered and planned to pursue more topics that reflected her students' lived experiences. Doing so will help her students flourish in school and in life. By taking this curricular risk to expand her instructional practices, Ms. Santos incorporated her students' sociocultural worlds into her teaching activities.

Instructionally, she did this by first observing her children across the school day. Next, she provided them with space for their voices to emerge so that they and their interests could be the focus of their learning. Then she implemented an activity that allowed the children to reflect on what they learned/shared in their discussions about jail.

For teachers working in a high-stakes context, like Ms. Santos, this lesson touched on such academic domains as literacy development where she asked her students to use, demonstrate, and extend information learned from informational texts in their work. Socially, this lesson expanded her students understanding of others' diverse experiences in the world and touched on what it means to live in a community. Finally, on a personal level, this lesson assisted children in developing their sense of agency, specifically, in coming to understand the link between actions and consequences in one's own life.

Still, it is important to recognize that the combination of high-stakes for teachers and students and the complexity involved with examining such issues as parental incarceration can make culturally relevant investigations a risky teaching endeavor both personally and professionally. Looking at such personal issues with young children will take time, and often it will not go as expected. As you take risks, plan for time to personally reflect and review what occurs with the children, and seek support from others who are committed to making school meaningful for young children. If pursuing such a topic does not go well the first time, please do not give up on these practices. Change cannot occur without action, and if you give up because the first time you try to move beyond standardized instruction with your students does not go well, change will never occur.

Reexamining Why You Should Know Your Students' Worlds

- Discuss with your colleagues your thoughts about what it means to engage in culturally relevant pedagogy and how it falls under the principles that define RIGOROUS DAP. If possible, provide an example of where you taught or experienced a lesson that incorporated the principles of CRP, and share your thoughts about how it affected you as either a teacher or a learner.
- Discuss the ways you've tried to get to know your children's sociocultural worlds. What were some of your successes? What were some of your struggles? Provide an example of how getting to know a child in your classroom on a more personal level affected your instruction of and interactions with that child.
- Discuss the ways you've tried to get to know your students' families. What were some of your successes? What were some of your struggles? What are your growth areas in reaching families, and how might you address these growth areas?
- Discuss your thoughts about Ms. Santos's examination of parental incarceration with her students. Do you think her plan of action for addressing this issue was effective? Could you implement such a lesson with your students? Why or why not?

Extending Your Learning

- Teaching Tolerance (www.tolerance.org), a project of the Southern Poverty Law Center, states its purpose is to reduce prejudice, improve intergroup relations, and support equitable school experiences for children. It offers teachers a range of resources that seek to support them in accomplishing these goals.
- Dr. Paul Gorski founded EdChange (www.edchange.org), and he and his colleagues have developed resources, workshops, and projects that offer insight into engaging in culturally relevant pedagogy across a range of education sites and with various learning communities. Moreover, the site offers a range of articles, handouts, and other resources for teachers to engage in CRP.
- The Harvard Family Research Project (www.hfrp.org/family-involvement) and the newly formed Global Family Research Project (https://globalfrp.org) are nonprofit organizations seeking to improve home-school relations so that all children can be successful in school.
- Teaching for Change (www.teachingforchange.org) offers a range of resources for teachers and parents designed to create schools where students learn to read, write, and change the world.

- The state of Virginia has a website dedicated to language variation in the classroom (www.doetest.virginia.gov/instruction/english/literacy/language_culture.shtml). It provides videos that examine how teachers can address linguistic and cultural diversity in their classroom.

Steps You Can Take toward Change

- Draw two columns on a piece of paper. On one side, list your shortcomings in getting to know the worlds of your students and their families. On the other side, list actions you can take to address your shortcomings and what it would require to implement these actions.
- Seek out professional development learning opportunities or create your own professional learning community that allows you to foster and maintain culturally relevant and sustaining leaning activities with your students. If you are creating your own group, you can curate a collection of children's stories that reflect your communities.
- Take a moment and reflect on how you react to others (be it children or adults) who are different from you. Do you act/react differently toward others with a different skin color, from a different sociocultural or socioeconomic background, of the opposite gender, who speak another language, or have a different sexual orientation than you? Think about why you react that way and what you might be projecting to those individuals who are different from you. Then make a list of steps you can take in the immediate and long term to break those habits/reactions. Consider ways to foster and display respect and appreciation for those who are different from you. Remember, part of being an early educator is being an active learner, and thus your goal should be to learn from those who are different to engage in culturally relevant practices with them and your students.
- Think about the range of communities your students and their families live in. Generate a list of potential ideas, topics, or issues you think the children might find worthwhile to investigate. Then pick one topic, research how you might explore it in a way that connects directly to the community (for example, think about bringing community experts, visiting local sites, or asking families for help in planning your lessons/activities), develop your lesson plan/activity, implement it, assess it, and evaluate the outcomes. Plan for the next investigation either based on this experience or on an idea, topic, or issue from your original list.

Teaching to All Developmental Domains

Over the course of the school year, Ms. Salinas provides her first graders with a series of maker challenges. In these challenges, she asks the children to figure out how to make certain objects, such as a kazoo using a cardboard tube, wax paper, and a rubber band, or provides them with a collection of recyclable materials to make a container that can protect an egg dropped from the top of a step ladder. With each exercise, she provides space for her students to problem solve, work with their classmates, and try and fail with their thinking within a safe learning environment. She also introduces the students to a range of scientific concepts and strategies for investigating the world around them. For instance, with the egg drop, she introduced such scientific concepts as gravity, energy, force, and absorption. Today she is asking her students to create a recipe for oobleck.

She began this challenge by introducing oobleck through Dr. Seuss's book Bartholomew and the Oobleck, *a story about how the King of Didd wanted his royal magicians to create something new to fall from the sky. They give him a gooey green substance called oobleck, which falls from the sky and wreaks havoc in the kingdom.*

Following the story, Ms. Salinas asks the class the following question, "I wonder if we could make oobleck?" Camille says, "Ooo, I think I know how to make oobleck. We made it in my pre-K. I think its glue and water, something else, plus food coloring." Ms. Salinas knew that some of the students might have had experience with oobleck before and did not let this distract her. Instead, she tried to build off Camille's background knowledge and experience. She asked if anyone else had made oobleck. She heard some nos, but most children were not sure if they had made it or not. Looking at Camille, she asked, "Camille, do you remember how oobleck felt or maybe how it smelled?" Camille responded, "I have no idea how it smelled, but I think it was sticky. Like, you'd squeeze it and it kind of stuck to your hands." Ms. Salinas said,

"That sounds like what I want you to make, but let me give you a little more background knowledge about how we are going to make oobleck in class today."

She continued, "I would like you to work in groups of four. In your group, I want you to try to create a recipe for a substance that when you squeeze it together it feels like a solid, but when you let it go, it falls out of your fingers and hands like a liquid."

Stevie immediately shot up her hand, and Ms. Salinas saw her excitement and called on her. Stevie said, "It sounds like we're making wet sand." Ms. Salinas replied, "What do you mean?" Stevie continued, "When I went to the beach last summer, we made drip castles by getting the sand wet, and when we squeezed it, it felt like a solid. But then I'd let it go, and it would drip like a liquid. That's why we called them drip castles, and they were so fun to make." Ms. Salinas said, "Yes, that sounds very similar to what we are going to make today, Stevie."

Making sure she had the attention of the entire class, Ms. Salinas continued, "The oobleck we are going to make in our small groups is called a non-Newtonian fluid. *I know that's a big word, but what it means is that we are making a liquid that's viscosity—or what you might call thickness—changes based on how much force you place on it. Remember, we talked about what force is with our egg drop challenge. I want you to make a substance that moves like a liquid when it's left alone, but when we squeeze it, apply some force to it, it feels like a solid. Like Stevie's drip sand, when the substance you're making is wet, it moves, but when you squeeze the substance together, it feels like a solid. Any questions?"*

Alfredo raised his hand, and Ms. Salinas called on him. "I am kinda confused Ms. S. You keep saying we're going to make a recipe for a substance, but with what?" Ms. Salinas responded to Alfredo by saying, "Oh, Alfredo, that's a really good point. I forgot to tell you what we are going to use to make our oobleck. Thinking back to what Camille said, we will make oobleck using cornstarch, water, and green food coloring. Essentially, you are creating a cornstarch substance that when you squeeze it, you squeeze the water out from between the particles. This makes the substance resist the flow, and the particles grind against each other to feel like a solid. By letting go, or what a scientist might say, 'releasing the pressure,' you allow the water to seep between the particles again, and the substance flows more easily. I want you to use measuring cups to figure out how much cornstarch and water you will need to make oobleck. Does anyone know what cornstarch is?"

Althea raised her hand, "I've seen my mom cook with it, but I don't remember what for." Several children nodded their heads in agreement. Ms. Salinas said, "Yes, Althea, cornstarch is a thickener that chefs, like your mom, use to make things like gravy thicker." Althea quickly replied, "My mom's not a chef. She's my mom." Ms. Salinas smiled and continued, "Yes, she's your mom, but she also cooks. If you celebrate Thanksgiving, you may have seen your mom, like Althea, or whoever cooks in your house, use cornstarch to make gravy. But to be clear, even though we are using cornstarch in our oobleck, we are not going to eat what we make today. We are just going to play with it because it doesn't taste good."

This example provides an introduction into meaningful activities that teach the whole child. In this case, Ms. Salinas's challenge is a lesson that offers children the opportunity to employ all their developmental domains while exploring this non-Newtonian fluid. Beyond the academic language, skills, and knowledge they learned and employed in this activity, the children had to generate new knowledge. Ms. Salinas did not provide the children with a model; instead, she expected children to interpret the challenge, create a solution, and analyze whether it fit the definition of a non-Newtonian fluid. The challenge also required them to engage in prosocial behaviors to work together. Emotionally, the activity required such interpersonal skills as self-regulation, persistence, and creativity. Physically, they used both gross- and fine-motor skills to make the oobleck, as well as their senses to ensure the substance felt both like a solid and a liquid. Combined, this challenge was both rigorous and appropriate for the students in Ms. Salinas's classroom.

Teachers need to honor and address the complexity of children as learners and recognize that learning is a cultural and developmental process. It is okay to teach children content beyond where you might believe they are in their knowledge and development. Teachers do children a disservice by expecting them to know every nuance of a lesson before moving on to new information.

Early educators also need to recognize that if children fail to grasp a concept, it may not be the content itself but rather some feature of the task. For example, during a whole group read-aloud, you may ask children to make a prediction using the title of the story, such as *Clifford and the Big Storm*. However, some of the predictions children give you may have nothing to do with the story title. For instance, Vivienne might say, "I like stories about Clifford." The issue may not be that Vivienne or other children in the class do not know how to make a prediction, which they actually do on a regular basis throughout their days. Rather, Vivienne and some of her classmates do not understand the term *prediction*. Early educators must think about the immediate children in their classrooms rather than some conception of how children are supposed to develop or demonstrate their learning.

Furthermore, when teachers focus their teaching soley on the content children are to acquire, this often reflects what Freire (1970) defined as a banking model of teaching in which children are empty vessels that must be filled with specific sets of knowledge and skills. Not only does such a conception of teaching and learning frame early educators as mere technicians who deliver a prescribed set of information to children, but it also positions the children themselves as passive and compliant consumers of knowledge while failing to consider their interests and desires to learn.

Recognizing the Difference between DAP and SBA Reform

The theory of action underlying SBA reform, which focuses on all children attaining a specific set of knowledge and skills at particular points in their schooling, is fundamentally different from the theory of DAP. In DAP, children, rather than the content to be taught, are the central focus or pivot on which all decisions are made, and the knowledge children are to acquire and what is of most value depend on each child's cognitive, social, emotional, and physical skills. While teachers can implement prescribed curricula within this theory of practice, decisions about what to teach and how are still based on the skills, knowledge, interests, and sociocultural understandings of the world children bring to their early education classroom. Furthermore, this construct of academic achievement is framed through a normative conception of children's growth and development and focuses on the performance of each child rather than the performance of the entire education system.

As we think about implementing RIGOROUS DAP, it is important to consider both theories of action and how they align with our ideas about teaching and learning. To *Push every child forward* in your teaching through a range of instructional strategies and curricula requires you to think about DAP as a tentative rather than absolute form of practice. You must also recognize the limitations SBA reform places on teachers and students. To implement RIGOROUS DAP in your classroom, you must engage in a variety of instructional practices that go beyond developmental conceptions of children and the standards or mandated curriculum you might be expected to teach. Instead, employ such instructional strategies as inviting "students to engage in research to answer a question that truly matters to them" (Souto-Manning 2013, 59). Think about the effectiveness of the teaching/learning tasks you implement, and document the effectiveness of your strategies through a teaching journal.

Framing Teaching as a Mediated Social Act

In chapter 2, we discussed the work of Lev Vygotsky and his influence in recognizing the sociocultural nature of learning and development, as well as the process by which children internalize such mental tools as language and the processes that guide their learning. These ideas highlight the importance of the early educator in mediating these processes between the world and the child. The most well-known idea of Vygotsky's is the zone of proximal development (ZPD), which is the distance between the point where a child can problem solve on his own and the point where he can problem solve with the assistance of a teacher or more capable peers. Vygotsky saw this as the ideal target of instruction. However, he did not address the practical side of this construct, which has made it difficult for many to conceptualize what this means in terms of teaching. The term *scaffolding* provides insight into the role of the teacher in the process of teaching the child within her ZPD, although it is not a term Vygotsky used. Another phrase we often hear associated with this process is *gradual release,* meaning the teacher offers a high level of support when she first works with the child on the new skill and gradually diminishes that amount of support as the child learns the skill.

As Patsy Cooper (2018) pointed out, the work of Wood, Bruner, and Ross (1976) provides teachers with six tools they can use to help scaffold children's learning.

- Secure child's interest in the task at hand.
- Simplify the task.
- If necessary, supply motivation to the child.
- Show the child the discrepancies between what she can do and might be able to do.
- Ensure the task does not to frustrate, overwhelm, or cause stress for the child.
- Demonstrate to the child how to solve the task.

A teacher does not have to implement all six tools in a lesson but should consider what she can do to help a child learn the idea at hand, even if that means demonstrating how to solve the task. Remember, for Vygotsky, being able to solve a problem independently or demonstrate a new skill is a process, and thus showing a child how to do a task assists that child in moving from mimicry to mastery.

MEDIATORS

One way to facilitate eventual progress toward mastery of a concept is to provide children with mediators, which are tools (both material and human) that offer support in accomplishing a learning endeavor. One example of a mediator is a number line. In the case of a child who can count but is unable to identify numerals, she could start on a happy face affixed on top of the numeral one on a number line and then continue arranging each object being counted in a left to right, one-to-one progression directly underneath the other numerals in the sequence. The numeral right above the last object signifies to the child which symbol she should use to label the set. Once children no longer need a mediator, however, the teacher should remove or substitute another anchor of support that leads to the next step in the progression of skills necessary for the acquisition of the desired concept.

FRAMING TEACHING AND LEARNING IN YOUR ECE SETTING

One of the joys of teaching young children is that they are eager to learn new information about the world around them. Moreover, they are usually confident in their abilities to take on new challenges. Yet as children progress through school, they tend to lose this desire to learn academic skills and knowledge and become less confident in their abilities to learn. Why this happens has been tied to numerous factors, such as irrelevant curriculum, rushed schedules, high-stakes learning environments, and the use of external rewards (Dutro and Selland 2012).

However, as we noted in chapter 2, there are several things you can do psychologically and pedagogically to counter children's decline in confidence and motivation. Children need to know that you care about them and want them to succeed. If you are not providing an environment that is nurturing, supportive, and full of meaningful relationships, no instructional strategy we discuss in this chapter will help them move forward as learners.

The way you communicate with children daily also has an impact. Research has shown that early educators do not interact with their students often, and when they do, it is to redirect behavior or to tell children what to do (Fowler et al. 2008). This should not be your only interaction with children.

We must also think about how we frame development and learning for children. For instance, early educators need to maintain a dynamic rather than fixed framework focused on growing as a community. You should concentrate on children's effort rather than ability and point out specific strategies they used that aided or impeded their success. It is also important that students understand failure is a part of the process of learning, and rather than get stuck in it, they can learn from it. Learning is a group endeavor, not a competition.

Finally, it's crucial to engage in practices that reflect a growth mind-set, such as offering challenging tasks and providing children support when they need it. For instance, if you are going to implement academic challenges like the oobleck challenge, you must prepare your students to demonstrate and wrestle with strong emotions, such as anger and frustration. As part of the preparation for engaging in such activities, you need to talk with children about their emotions and how to deal with them; for example, taking a break or using breathing exercises to calm down. Providing them with the language to express these feelings is essential so you and their classmates can move from operating in a mode of frustration or anger, where they are more likely to be reactive to the learning situation, to a place where they can use reason and interact with you and others in a more intentional manner.

BE INTENTIONAL IN YOUR TEACHING

Teachers who successfully engage in RIGOROUS DAP are intentional in their practices. You must commit to instructional practices that *Push every child forward* in their learning and development. You must also strive to clearly define learning objectives for all children, employ a range of instructional strategies that help children achieve these objectives, continually assess students' development, and adjust your teaching strategies based on those outcomes. This includes knowing when to use a given instructional strategy to differentiate instruction for individual children in your classroom. Implementing a range of engaging learning activities in which children are asked thoughtful questions to push them forward, while at the same time providing them emotional and instructional feedback, is also necessary.

LETTING CHILDREN KNOW OUR EXPECTATIONS FOR THEM

Part of being an intentional teacher who frames teaching as a socially mediated act is informing your students how you view the learning process and what your expectations are for them as learners. We must let children know that we see their growth and development as an ongoing process. We expect to see their ideas, thoughts, and beliefs about their worlds, as well as their abilities to share, represent, and explain them, to be always evolving. To help them achieve this, you must acknowledge their ability to change and grow within the learning process. With young children, one of the easiest ways to do this is to discuss their ability to write their names—from one letter to all letters, or from all capitals to a capital and lowercase. You also must let children know that in learning everyone will make mistakes. Highlight your own mistakes as you interact with children and discuss what you learn from them—be it calling a child the wrong name, telling students the wrong answer to a question, or forgetting that you promised your class you'd read a certain book after snacktime.

Early educators also need to help children be aware of their thinking during the learning process, helping them see the causal connection between engaging in particular activities and their growth in understanding the world around them. For example, when Ms. Salinas interacts with her first graders as they attempt to formulate a recipe for oobleck, she could say to one group, "What are you noticing about yourselves as you try to create a recipe for oobleck?" or "I noticed you started by pouring a half cup of water in your bowl and then a half cup of cornstarch. Tell me how you came up with this strategy and what you found out?" Once the students come up with their recipe, have each group share with the entire class how they solved this challenge. They can compare how each group's thinking solved the problem. Children should recognize that everyone's goal is to produce a learning community. This community is a place that emphasizes togetherness over competition, that offers each child tasks that push him forward.

Play Is an Essential Instructional Strategy in the ECE Classroom

Play is not a break from learning so students can better focus; it is an essential component of instruction within every early childhood setting. When many parents, educators, and administrators hear the term *play*, they automatically tend to shift their thinking away from education and toward ideas about fun or not working. It is as if the term itself cancels out any notions of formal learning, growth, or development. For some reason, most adults struggle with the idea that play leads to learning. Adding to this complexity is the fact that it is quite difficult to define play formally. *Play* is one of those words like *happy*: you know when you see or feel it, but a clear definition everyone understands is difficult to create.

We think of play as a state of mind in which children are purposefully engaging in spontaneous, enjoyable, voluntary activities. Play is voluntary and not stressful, and the means are more valued than the ends. Play typically involves structure that children create. Thus, an act like kicking a ball against the wall can be play for one child and not another. Moreover, as children get older, their play changes. Toddlers typically play with the objects in their immediate world, while preschoolers begin to engage in a range of dramatic play scenarios. As children enter formal schooling, their play becomes more structured and often game oriented. This is not to say that they do not engage in dramatic or imaginative play, but rather the structuring of their lives by school and families, as well as access to a wider range of materials, makes it more difficult for them to do so.

Play is important because it assists children in developing their cognitive, physical, social, emotional, and moral skills and knowledge. Play accomplishes this by helping children expand their knowledge and insight into the acts they are either reenacting or making anew. Play also assists children in developing their knowledge of themselves, their imagination, their reasoning abilities, and their language and communication skills. For example, Beth's daughter Michelle, who is four, uses a small playhouse to re-create and reauthor events from her life, changing the details to fit her imagination. She will engage her brothers using the dolls to give voice to new ideas, requests, and resolutions. She will also invite others to join her in her make-believe world.

Physically, play allows children to develop their gross- and fine-motor skills, their physical stamina, and body control. Emotionally, play helps children work through their feelings/responses to the world, develop their self-awareness/self-esteem, and begin to develop such emotional skills as persistence and self-direction. Socially, play offers an opportunity to interact with others, which helps children develop skills such as sharing, taking turns, cooperation, competition, perspective taking, self-control, and communication with others. Play also creates situations where children begin to make sense of right and wrong, and it offers adults the chance to work through some of these ideas using play scenarios.

There are many different types of play: physical (running, jumping, playing chase), expressive (sharing feelings through drawing), manipulative (puzzles, taking things apart), symbolic (putting dolls in a time-out), dramatic (playing school), and games (playing a memory game). Children play in multiple ways: solitary, parallel (playing side by side but not with each other), associative (with others but without rules/structure), and cooperative (goal-based with others and clear delineation of who is and is not part of the group).

While play of all types is an important part of children's learning and development across all their developmental domains, be aware that play differs for children and their families across cultures. For instance, the work of Liz Brooker (2002) used a sample of Bangladeshi children in a preschool program in Great Britain to demonstrate how children may not know how to play in ways that white, Western cultures typically think of play, and their families may expect them to do something other than play at school. Brooker argues that we need to develop dialogues with families about our beliefs and goals for our students, and we must focus on relationships as the foundation for children's learning and development, and not solitary exploration through isolated play.

Consider your own beliefs about play. Play should not be thought of as a linear process that moves from one stage to the next. What do you consider to be appropriate or inappropriate play and why? Do you hold biases against particular types of play (quiet versus loud) or do you tolerate different types of play by boys and girls (such as allowing boys but not girls to engage in rough and tumble play) or between younger and older children? Furthermore, if you say you give children free choice within their play, what does that mean? Do children really get to choose what they want to do? Or are they selecting between two to three choices you've given them? Ask yourself these types of questions. Doing so will help make you aware of how your practices are or are not *Seeing the whole child, Reaching all children*, and *Pushing every child forward.*

CREATING A PLAYFUL CLASSROOM

To facilitate play you must make time and space for play within your classroom and outdoors. You'll need space for children to play in large and small groups. They will need places where they can store materials or come back to play activities. Consider your role in play and discuss what the rules for play are. For instance, in Vivian Gussin Paley's (1992) kindergarten classroom, you could never say, "You can't play." You must discuss with your students what is allowed and what is off limits, how to use equipment appropriately, what it means to share and negotiate needs, how to clean up, and so on. These conversations should be revisited regularly and adjusted to meet the changing needs of the classroom community.

Think about what materials you make available to children, such as blocks, games, repurposeable art materials, dress-up materials, real-life materials, and props for dramatic play, and how those materials can help facilitate children's development and learning. For example, wooden blocks help develop children's problem-solving and prediction skills, both of which are essential in mathematics and science. Dramatic play allows children to develop such social-emotional and cognitive skills as self-regulation, rule following, conflict resolution, literacy, and creativity. Some materials may always be available, such as blocks, but you can rotate others in and out of the classroom based on what you're exploring at that time of the school year (for example, creating a grocery store in the pretend and learn area). Evaluate children's use of the materials and rotate those that no longer generate interest or remain unused by the children out on a regular basis.

One often overlooked benefit of play is the way it naturally allows for differentiated learning to occur. If a teacher selects play materials that allow for a range of different uses, meaning children with a range of skills and knowledge can use these materials and it offers children the chance to engage with each other in meaningful ways, differentiated learning using these materials will occur.

YOUR ROLE DURING PLAY

Play offers time to assess children's knowledge and skills as well as to get to know them on a more personal basis. In any classroom setting, some children might need help initiating play.

Remember, play offers children time to make decisions about their lives, so it is important that you do not immediately step into play scenarios when things are not going as you believe they ought to be. Children need the chance to work through issues and explore outcomes. Moreover, they need time and space to figure out what's going on not only in your program but also in their lives.

By being present during children's play, you can assist them in finding materials and ask them questions to move play scenarios forward and facilitate them in teaching each other. Your presence allows an important opportunity to learn about the children in your classroom outside of formal learning experiences. Finally, your presence allows you to help children develop their metacognitive skills and self-regulation skills.

The Continuum of Instructional Practices That Reach the Whole Child

Sue Bredekamp and Teresa Rosegrant's (1995) conception of a transformational curriculum is a useful tool as you consider which instructional strategies will help children succeed in your classroom. Bredekamp and Rosegrant place the child and not the curriculum or the instructional strategies at the center of the schooling process. By doing so, you prioritize the child's needs in your pedagogical decision-making. Your instructional decision-making also depends on your normative and dynamic understanding of child development, which includes your understanding of the cultural, social, and physical variations that exist among children in your classroom. Such a framing of your decision-making process helps deprioritize the curriculum you are expected to teach. Bredekamp and Rosegrant's work provides a continuum of teaching practices that range from the nondirective behavior of acknowledging (giving children your attention or positively acknowledging their engagement in an activity) to mediating (strategies such as facilitating, supporting, scaffolding, and coconstructing) to more directive behaviors (demonstrating, directing, and providing specific instruction or feedback to students about their work).

We want to summarize briefly some of these instructional strategies, as well as include a few more to illustrate the different ways you can support young children in their growth and development. Also, we want to point out that Vygotsky's notions of ZPD and scaffolding play a significant role in how we conceptualize these practices.

POSITIONING

The first idea we consider is how we are positioning ourselves in relation to our students. We must be conscious about where we position ourselves throughout the day. Our physical presence in the classroom affects how children not only see us but also how they interact with each other. Their position in relation to each other will affect learning as well. There are times when we need to be physically near children for them to stay regulated or move forward in their learning. At other times, we need to step back and let children take risks or try out new things without feeling as though they are being watched. Other learning experiences require children to be close to one another; sometimes they need space. Think about where you position yourself and your students throughout the day. Finally, we encourage you to experiment with your position to see how it affects children during different learning activities. For instance, during choice time, position yourself near the blocks one day and near the pretend and learn area the next. During both days, document what you notice. Continue alternating positions over several days and compare notes.

ACKNOWLEDGING

When acknowledging children in our instruction, we pay attention to their learning and determine which children need to develop their ideas socially and internalize them. Think about the language and vocabulary you use to respond to them. A more complex response assists children in recognizing the complexity in their work and develops a keen sense of awareness as to what is happening around them. However, sometimes children might struggle with a complex description or new vocabulary, so be prepared to rephrase your statement if this occurs. Still, acknowledgment offers you the chance to encourage the children to move forward and confirm that their work is meaningful. For example, you might say, "I noticed that your new building has some interesting details. You've made it symmetrical; it's the same on both sides." Finally, we can transform these acknowledgments (or any of the instructional strategies we outline below) into anecdotal records that document children's learning to monitor our own instruction and inform others about children's learning and development.

LISTENING

To be effective at acknowledging children's learning, we need to be good listeners. We must pay attention and concentrate on what children tell us. Doing so will help us understand who they are as learners and what their interests are, and help us plan for future instruction. When we listen, children know we value what they have to say. This is important for fostering a positive learning community, and at the same time, we model for them how to interact with others. Listening to and acknowledging children's learning requires us to make time to do so.

MODELING

When we model a skill (such as writing our name) or an action (how to put a dress on a doll) for children, we demonstrate how we want them to perform a task (sharing materials), or we assist them with a task they are struggling with (buttoning up their coat). Essentially, teaching by example gives children insight into an important skill or task, helps develop their relationship with us, and builds their vocabulary and understanding about how the world works.

FACILITATING

To facilitate children's learning means to step into the learning sequence/experience and offer children assistance. When thinking about Vygotsky's notion of scaffolding, we act as mediators working toward releasing ourselves from the learning situation. Within early childhood settings, facilitation also encompasses all the work we do to make learning possible for children. Facilitation includes the way we schedule our day, the materials and equipment we select and offer children, and the way we organize our learning environments, including the space itself and the children and teachers within in it. Each of these decisions facilitates the way our students go about their days.

OFFERING SUPPORT, SCAFFOLDING, AND COCONSTRUCTING

Building off the idea of facilitation, Bredekamp and Rosegrant (1995) introduce three other acts that mediate children's learning. The least amount of teacher involvement occurs by offering support, while the greatest amount of teacher intervention occurs as the teacher and child are coconstructing the learning event, with scaffolding falling somewhere in between this continuum. While the three strategies are similar, there are clear distinctions in how to use them. To offer support, you give a fixed form of assistance to help children learn the skill or knowledge. For instance, you might suggest a child use a ruler to draw a straight line when creating a triangle, provide an example of her name so that she can begin to write it out herself, or give her a grip for her pencil so that she can write more legibly.

Scaffolding means that you work within a child's ZPD and offer tasks or challenges that push the child just beyond her current level of competence. For instance, young children often have difficulty with the teens when learning to count to twenty. As you work with the child on her counting, step in as she says things like "three-teen" or "five-teen." Or, if a child is having difficulty using scissors to cut out pretend cookies, you might ask about her grip or suggest another strategy.

Finally, when we coconstruct with children, we work collaboratively or side by side as they engage in a task or learning situation. For instance, we might work with a child to complete a puzzle or create a simple circuit in science using batteries, foil, electrical tape, and a small lightbulb.

Across these instructional strategies, our role in assisting children in their activity increases—moving from providing a tool to working with the child within the learning situation. Moreover, as we move from nondirective to directive learning experiences, our feedback to children also increases. To be clear, feedback is information or ideas, given verbally and nonverbally, in reaction to what children are doing within the learning experience. Remember, our goal is to facilitate dynamic learning environments, so when we give feedback, we focus on the learning scenario, not on the child's abilities or talents. Our goal is to push children forward in their learning, and thus it cannot be evaluative. For instance, "It looks as though you're stuck (or are struggling) with X; why don't you try Y?" Or nonverbally, you might simply point to or act out the next step in the learning sequence, the key being that your comments, both verbal and nonverbal, are focused on completing the process and not critiquing the person.

DEMONSTRATING

When we demonstrate a learning activity, we show children how it is done. For instance, when demonstrating to children how to draw a triangle or write their name, we show them how to use a writing instrument to accomplish a specific task. Sometimes all we need to do is step in and quickly show them how to do the activity, and that will be enough. In other instances, we might have to provide verbal directions or comments about what we are doing so the children understand our thinking about the activity. Either way, we ensure our demonstration is clear and easy to follow, is brief, and follows a logical sequence that children can repeat. Again, thinking about Vygotsky and learning, provide children with enough guidance so that as they develop these skills and knowledge, they will eventually be able to do the task without your assistance.

DIRECTING

The most directive form of instruction is directing children's learning, meaning that we tell children how to complete a task in a specific manner. For instance, a reading curriculum that uses direct instruction tells the teacher to say, "Children, point to this letter. This is the *B*. Say, 'B.' Now say, 'Buh.' That's the *B* sound. It's a bouncing sound, so we should say it quickly." While this method of instruction places the control in your hands, there are certain skills or knowledge that you will want to teach children directly.

When discussing directing as a form of instruction with early childhood educators, conversation often revolves around whether an activity is teacher directed versus child directed. Essentially, the difference between the two is who is leading the learning activity—the teacher or the children. If it's teacher directed, the teacher makes instruction decisions in relation to what she needs to teach, meaning the content is the pivot on which she decides on the lesson. If it's child directed, the child makes decisions about what he learns, meaning the pivot is not the content, but rather the child and his interest.

Elizabeth Green (2015) helps us think about directing children in our instruction more deeply by offering two scripts for instruction: the "I-You-We" script and the "You-Y'all-We" script. With the "I-You-We" script, the teacher (I) introduces the skills, the student (You) demonstrates the skill, and the class (We) checks in and addresses any issues. The focus of this script is on mastering a particular set of knowledge or skills. So with a lesson around the five senses, the teacher might begin by introducing the five senses to the children. Then the children employ or demonstrate that knowledge in some fashion (for example, completing a worksheet identifying things they like to see, touch, feel, taste, and smell). Finally, the class comes back together to check in and make sure everyone has understood what needs to be learned.

With the "You-Y'all-We" script (see table 4.1 for how we've combined Green's scripts with other instructional strategies), the teacher provides the children with a task or problem they must complete (such as providing a mathematical word problem). Then "You," the student, is asked to solve that problem. After some time, "You" and other classmates become "Y'all" and share what they've done and help each other solve the problem. Finally, all, "We," come back together and share how they addressed the problem and the answers their strategies generated. The focus of this script is not simply on the content or skill to be covered, but rather the processes by which children understand/are thinking about that content/skill. While both scripts have their strengths and growth areas, the "You-Y'all-We" script frames learning as an intellectual activity, which is something we emphasize in this book by advocating for RIGOROUS DAP.

TABLE 4.1
A continuum of instructional practices

I Do/You Watch	I Do/You Participate	We (All) Do Together	I Watch/You Do
• Directing children (e.g., a read-aloud)	• Demonstrating • Scaffolding (e.g., creating a class graph)	• Modeling • Coconstructing • Scaffolding (e.g., a community walk)	• Offering support • Acknowledging • Giving feedback (e.g., play or self-selected learning centers)

We want to be clear that across the day you will engage in all these instructional strategies we've outlined in table 4.1, including child-directed learning activities. Your instructional decisions will depend on the children in your classroom, the knowledge and skills you want them to learn, and the specific activity you want them to accomplish. If you find yourself stuck on one strategy, take a step back and think about how you can assist your students in such a way that you are gradually releasing yourself from the learning process to allow the children to eventually accomplish the task independently. Remember that we do not need to wait to move forward until a child or the class has mastered a specific set of knowledge, skills, or tasks. They can move forward even if they are still developing their independence in relation to that knowledge, skill, or task.

SMALL- AND WHOLE-GROUP INSTRUCTION

Across the day, you instruct children through one-on-one experiences, as well as construct groups of children to teach specific knowledge and tasks. Depending on what you hope to accomplish within that learning situation, you will either create whole or small groups. Whole group instruction focuses on a skill the entire class is learning. Small-group instruction allows you to teach the task at hand to a smaller number of children. You may choose small-group instruction due to the amount of support each child will need, or select a group of students at a similar point in their knowledge/skill acquisition who need to learn the same information to progress in their development. Teachers often form small groups based on such constructs as age, ability, and interest. Small-group instruction offers you more opportunities to provide direct feedback to children about their learning, mediate social interactions among peers, and get to know them on a more personal level.

With both whole- and small-group instruction, you decide how best to bring children together to assist them in their learning and development. Such groupings can occur formally, meaning the group is constructed to achieve a particular learning goal or task, or informally, meaning it arose spontaneously. Again, no matter what type of groupings you create, focus on ensuring the students learn, and across the day provide children with opportunities to engage in both whole- and small-group instruction. Finally, if you use small groups often in your instruction, make sure you are mixing up how you construct those groups. Teachers often tend to strictly create groups around ability and maintain these groups for extended time periods, which may send the message to children that their ability to learn is fixed rather than dynamic.

USING QUESTIONING TO PUSH CHILDREN'S THINKING FORWARD

Early educators use questioning within their instruction to support, reinforce, and stretch children's learning. Questions give insight into children's thinking. There are two types of questions: closed and open. Each makes a different cognitive demand on children. Closed questions seek a particular response or piece of information from children; for example, "How many children are in our classroom?" Open questions do not seek a particular answer. Rather, they are designed to provide children with the opening to provide multiple answers; for example, "How did that story make you feel?" Such a question asks children to share their feelings, thoughts, theories, and understandings about the world.

Asking effective questions takes time and practice. Moreover, it requires you to establish a strong, positive bond with children. If that bond is not there, children may feel you are interrogating them rather than trying to learn about their thinking. Beyond ensuring you have a positive relationship with children, be sure to ask them a range of different types of questions (how, when, where, what, or why). With young children, be sure your questions are easy to understand and reflect their experiences and knowledge. Respond to children's answers with warmth and sincerity, which again develops a positive learning community. Be prepared to support children in their responses to your questions. You may need to provide a prompt to get them started. Finally, make sure you offer both closed and open-ended questions. If you use only closed-end questions, you create a fixed rather than dynamic learning environment, and children will believe that there is one right answer to any question you ask.

Asking effective open-ended questions can be difficult, but we should use them as much as possible with young children. Such questions tap into children's curiosity and wonder about the world, and they demonstrate that teachers trust children to have good ideas, think for themselves, and contribute in valuable ways. To ask open-ended questions, we need to be genuinely open to children's thinking; when we are not, children know. We also need to provide clear boundaries in our questions. Denton (2007, 3) explains that "How can we use the markers to show what we know about butterflies?" might result in children making a butterfly using markers; a clearer question might be "How can we use the markers to draw what we know about butterflies?" Denton also says that we should use words that encourage cooperation and not competition, and avoid such terms as *best, most,* and so on.

The Importance of Questioning

Educator Deborah Meier (2007) reminds us that questions allow us to gain insight into children's thinking and can also help us teach children how to think about the world in a more complex manner. Questions prompt children to consider how things work and how to see the world from many different angles. For Meier, we can use argumentative questions to help children develop the habits of mind that will expand their intellectual understandings about the topic of study or the world around them. Good teaching and good learning are in constant dialogue. To facilitate that dialogue, early educators need to engage children in rich conversations about their learning. Below are some questions Meier (2007, 140) believes help foster good teaching and good learning:

- So how do you know it? What's your evidence?
- What does the other guy think? Is there another viewpoint?
- Is there a connection, a pattern here?
- If you did x instead of y, would it make a difference? Supposing that . . .
- Who cares anyway? Why does it matter?

Meier points out that these questions also teach the importance of good listening in the learning process. Such listening also allows for the dialogue to evolve and move forward.

Using Children's Questions to Examine Contentious Issues

Facilitating dialogue with children can lead them to ask uncomfortable questions. For instance, when discussing jobs in the community, a common social studies theme in pre-K and kindergarten, we've heard several children in classrooms across Texas, who are often white, ask, "Why do we only see people with brown skin working in people's yards?" We should not ignore or acknowledge but move on from such questioning. Professor Jean Anyon (2010) contends that to encourage children to participate in the larger society, which includes teaching them how to contest acts that negatively affect particular children or communities, we must recognize and embrace such questioning. We must help children interpret and understand the current economic and political situations of their communities. From there, we can help them see how to work toward change through existing institutional and organization forums and take advantage of social and community networks and movements. Finally, we need to provide children with the physical and emotional support necessary to ask such questions and engage in acts for change. Anyon asserts that by doing all this we will help children develop an identity as an active agent who can work toward change in their own lives and in their communities.

With Anyon's steps in mind, a teacher might respond to a child's question about people with brown skin and landscaping by first asking, in a caring and responsive voice, why she thinks that is the case. From there, using the child's answer, the teacher might begin to explore what type of training is required to do certain jobs and how accessing that training requires such things as an education, time, and money, which might open another discussion about discrimination and how certain peoples and cultures have not had access to those institutions. Or, depending on the child's answer, the teacher might explore issues of worker's rights or look at such historical figures as César Chávez and the fight for worker's rights and connect those issues to labor discussions within the local community. Finally, the child's answer may lead the teacher, particularly in Texas, to examine the histories of Native peoples, the various forms of colonization that occurred throughout the Southwest, or the issue of immigration. No matter how the discussion within the classroom evolves, the teacher must acknowledge children's recognition of societal or structural inequalities on their terms (for example, even if they are white, they know what it means to be discriminated against for their size, age, or maturity level) and work with them to understand why things are the way they are and how they might work to change things.

STRATEGIES TO SUPPORT MULTILINGUAL CHILDREN

Throughout this text, we have made a case for engaging in practices that are culturally sustaining and responsive, including supporting the linguistic development of multilingual children. To help us provide suggestions as to how you might accomplish this, we turn to the work of Dina Castro and her colleagues. They have identified the following strategies to promote language and literacy development of young bilingual children.

Provide Explicit Vocabulary Instruction

While most monolingual children can learn vocabulary incidentally through conversations and by listening to words in their everyday routines, second language learners are often not able to take advantage of such learning until they become proficient in that language. There is also the issue of exposure. Multilingual children learn vocabularies in more than one language, so their exposure will be limited to the frequency that word is used in that language. You should strive to create conditions in which students learn words in an effective and efficient manner. To do so requires you to plan for purposeful and repeated exposure to and opportunities to use specific words multiple times in a variety of settings (Gillanders, Castro, and Franco 2014). Research has demonstrated that explicit and strategic instruction accelerates vocabulary learning (Carlo et al. 2004). Such instruction can occur through read-alouds as well as the direct teaching of core vocabulary. Early educators can use pictures of vocabulary to demonstrate meaning and use hand puppets and gamelike activities to illustrate concepts and actions while engaging children physically with the vocabulary.

Use Academic Language

You should strive to develop children's academic language in specialized content areas, such as science, language arts, math, and social studies. Such language is dense with information and syntactically complex and includes many nouns, adjectives, and prepositions to describe abstract and complex ideas in content areas, creating a semantically challenging task for young learners. To help multilingual children develop this language, which is different from conversational skill, provide explicit instruction of the academic language related to concepts and skills discussed/covered in varying content areas. Teach children not only the specific academic vocabulary you want them to learn (*introduction, addition,* or *prediction*) but also the vocabulary that signals to the reader/listener the meaning of the term and the associated academic domain. For example, the word *table* means something very different when it is used in science versus everyday speech. When engaging in activities such as read-alouds, think about the academic language you want children to learn, as well as the phrasing associated with it, so children can make connections between the academic language and the domains of study associated with that term.

Provide Small-Group Activities

Another suggestion is to provide focused small-group activities—four to five children maximum. Children who are learning in more than one language need opportunities for additional exposure to and use of new concepts and words in all languages. Small-group and peer-assisted support allow children multiple opportunities to receive explicit instruction on vocabulary and phonological awareness, to practice reading skills, and to respond to questions.

Conduct Ongoing Assessments

Early educators need to conduct ongoing assessments to monitor development in children's first and second languages. Doing so will allow you to plan practices for children that are aligned with their levels of proficiency and target specific areas where they may need additional support. As you do this, recognize that there are few valid and reliable assessments of young multilingual children's development and learning, and your selection of assessment tools needs to be well informed. When you use a particular assessment, read the handbook or guidelines provided to verify that it was designed for multilingual children. Employ a combination of standardized measures and systematic observational methods to obtain the most accurate information about their development and learning.

Promote Social-Emotional Development

Early educators need to promote social-emotional development to support multilingual language development. This occurs by fostering positive teacher-child relationships and facilitating children's participation in the sociocultural group of the classroom (Castro et al. 2011). If multilingual children receive instruction in English only, they will have difficulty communicating with others. They will also have difficulty following directions and responding to questions consistently. Receiving instruction in English only can lead children to feel withdrawn, insecure, and even stressed (Santos and Ostrosky 2002).

Engage Families

Finally, early educator programs should allow teachers to use children's primary language in their instruction and engage families to support their children in both their primary language and English (Castro, Espinosa, and Páez 2011). Employing a multicultural curriculum, offering and supporting professional development, and constantly striving to incorporate practices that support the development and learning of multilingual children is essential.

Curricular Approaches to Teaching

Alongside the various instructional strategies we've outlined above, there is a range of curricular approaches to teaching young children. Like instructional strategies, many put these approaches on a continuum that spans from teacher directed to child directed. For this text, we want to focus on the following approaches: units of study, learning centers, integrated curricula, thematic teaching, emergent curricula, and projects.

UNITS OF STUDY

Units are an area of study around a topic within a specific content area. For instance, in science you might do a unit about magnets. Using this approach, the teacher selects the unit and plans the daily, weekly, and possibly monthly (depending on the topic) lessons examining that unit of study. The teacher considers the academic goals, the process by which children will attain those goals, and how she will assess children in relation to those goals. As you can see, the teacher directs these learning experiences.

Teachers can implement multiple units at one time. For example, a teacher can have children study magnets in science, the *-at* word family in reading, and addition facts in math. This content is not integrated or related to the other parts.

LEARNING CENTERS

Learning centers are areas within the classroom, typically around a table or play area, where children engage in a specific activity or series of activities to develop their knowledge and skills around some content or area of inquiry. By providing children with options within these centers, you increase the likelihood for differentiated learning experiences that support children in relation to where they are as learners.

Learning centers are very common in early childhood settings, and increasingly we've noticed that they tend to center around academic content areas (math center) or skills/knowledge (writing center). Nevertheless, when creating a learning center, think about what you want children to learn, how you might facilitate that learning through materials that children can engage with independently, and how you might check in on or document that learning. It is important to remember that young children do not separate learning into categories or content areas as adults do. Thus, learning centers offer an easy way to integrate content across different sets of skills or academic domains, which will help them make sense of their world and connect their learning to what they already know.

If you set up learning centers within your early education setting, remember that children will need specific strategies and skills, such as making decisions, carrying out plans, cooperating and sharing with others, and problem solving, to be able to play and learn independently within the center. One of the key benefits of learning centers is that they offer children the opportunity to learn through social interaction; think about how you can create tasks that require children to work with each other and share materials to complete the task at hand.

You will need to be there to support the children as they engage with the centers, particularly if a center is new or if this is the first time children have ever worked independently at a learning center. Such support may include asking questions, participating in the activity, sharing your expertise and knowledge, or engaging in discussions that help students make discoveries and connections.

INTEGRATED CURRICULUM/THEMATIC TEACHING

An integrated curriculum or thematic teaching is a theme that the teacher preselects for the class and all the classroom activities, lessons, and learning experiences focus on that theme. For example, in the fall many early childhood programs do thematic units around pumpkins, and in the spring many do themes around seeds as they begin to grow. The benefit of this type of instruction is that children begin to see how learning is interconnected and not a piecemeal process broken up around particular content domains.

The terms *integrated curriculum* and *thematic teaching* are often used interchangeably. However, educational consultant Judy Harris Helm (2015) distinguishes the two by stating that with an integrated curriculum the teacher selects the topic of study, determines which content to cover, and does most, if not all, of the instruction. Helm views thematic teaching as being less teacher directed in that children can initiate the theme to investigate or they may select some of the learning experiences on their own.

Nevertheless, both approaches center the teacher's instruction on a theme. For teachers working in more standardized contexts where they are expected to teach children a particular set of knowledge and skills, integrated/thematic teaching offers an easy opportunity to plan a range of learning activities on one topic aligned with a range of content standards. If a teacher is doing a pumpkin unit, she can have children engage math standards by weighing, counting, and measuring pumpkins; literacy standards by reading, writing, and discussing pumpkins; science standards by dissecting a pumpkin, discussing the life cycle, and so on. Essentially, teachers in high-stakes contexts incorporate as many content standards as they can into the theme.

Still, a teacher does not have to select a theme such as pumpkins to integrate her curriculum. In fact, she can turn to the content standards for her context to think about how to weave a curriculum around a particular strand of content. For instance, authors Marjorie Kostelnik and Marilyn Grady (2009) provide a useful example of how a second-grade teacher wove the concept of patterns across the curriculum: in science, children build and record patterns using different types of rock; in art, children create an abstract piece using multiple patterns; in language arts, children write one to two paragraphs describing their artwork; in math, children build patterns using such manipulatives as Unifix cubes; and in social studies, children seek to identify patterns in how their families approach bedtime routines at home.

EMERGENT CURRICULUM

An emergent curriculum is a framework for play-based and child-centered learning that encompasses a range of activities and learning experiences, routines, transitions, and schedules (Stacey 2009). This flexible and adaptive curriculum emerges from the daily life of children within the early childhood classroom—not from a mandated set of learning experiences. Teachers facilitate learning experiences across the day that are rooted in the children's interests at that time. For example, a child arrives on Monday with a bug in a jar and students become interested in the bug, so the teacher plans a series of lessons or learning experiences that center on investigating bugs. Still, the focus for the teacher and the children within this curricular approach is learning, and the teacher can incorporate such documents as well as early learning standards into the curricula.

An emergent curriculum begins with observing children's play themes, learning interests, and developmental skills. Based on those observations, you develop a planned learning environment that offers children a range of opportunities to delve more deeply into their interests about the world around them. You not only structure their play environment so they explore what interests them more deeply, but you also plan activities that provide children the opportunity to learn about what interests them. This plan can include learning centers, teacher-directed activities, field trips, and bringing in family members and community experts to your classroom. Across the day, the children need the opportunity to represent what they learn. Such representations not only offer the teacher documentation about children's learning, but documentation offers children the opportunity to clarify what they are learning, and they can also analyze and re-represent their initial thoughts.

THE PROJECT APPROACH

The project approach is a curricular approach that centers on investigating a topic and question for an extended period, most often based on the children's interests. It is different than an emergent curriculum in that it centers on the investigation of one topic or question. An emergent curriculum is an organizational strategy for an entire program, and the project approach is only one component of your instructional program.

The project approach is divided into three phases: the planning phase, where you establish common ground among participants and the basis for your investigation; the progress phase, where you enable children to acquire new information; and the reflections/conclusions phase, where you bring the project to completion and summarize your work. Lilian Katz and Sylvia Chard (2000) contend that project work can and should foster habits such as making sense of experience, predicting and checking predictions, grasping the consequences of actions, and persisting in seeking solutions to problems. Helm (2015) adds that projects offer children a chance to discuss what they are interested in studying with other children and adults; investigate the topic alone or together by researching, collecting data, and possibly visiting sites; represent what they've learned; and share those representations either through displays or presentations.

Children should reflect on what they have accomplished individually and as a group. Projects typically end with a culminating activity. Think of the presentation as a communicative rather than performance-based activity—children share what they have learned. Helm (2015) notes that representing one's learning is what differentiates project work from thematic teaching or teacher-directed learning activities. The teacher, with the help of the children, needs to evaluate the project—both collectively and individually, and allow time to consider the next project.

Documenting student learning through various forms of representation not only demonstrates how the project progressed and what was learned, but it also provides the children with an opportunity to interact with and reflect on their learning. This form of documentation is different from the type typically used within public schools as a source of information for teachers, parents, and other stakeholders—demonstrating that children have learned particular skills or sets of knowledge. Documenting children's learning through representations gives you a chance to provide your colleagues, families, and the larger school community with insight into your work. As you collect and share information, think about the narrative of learning you generate—you want to tell a story of whole-child learning across the three phases of the project.

Lesson Planning

Many of you will work in contexts where you are required to write out formal lesson plans for your administrators, following a specific format.

Common lesson plan formats typically include a title, objectives, content standards addressed in the lesson, the materials needed, preparation required, procedures for executing the lesson, and the evaluation used to ensure students' learning. More and more lesson plan formats also include the plan for differentiated instruction and extensions or how the lesson taps into children's sociocultural knowledge. To meet the needs of students who are emerging English language learners, some lesson plan formats also include English language proficiency standards (ELPS).

Another model that we've seen used in several school districts is the 5 E model (Barufaldi 2002). Rather than the teacher leading the students through a series of planned events, he creates a learning situation that aligns with what we've learned about how children develop and learn. The following list specifies what the five Es represent:

- Engage. The teacher engages children around a topic of interest. Prior knowledge is accessed, and the teacher asks questions about the concept being learned.
- Explore. The teacher allows children to engage with the concept through a hands-on activity.
- Explain. The teacher leads a conversation, prompting students to explain the concept being studied. This requires the teacher to provide students with such things as vocabulary and to address issues that emerged during the students' exploration of the topic.
- Elaborate. The teacher encourages the students to apply (for example, new vocabulary), revise, extend, or enhance their understanding of the concept being studied through their interaction with the teacher and the class.
- Evaluate. The teacher allows students to demonstrate understanding of the concept, hopefully through some form of authentic assessment.

Across all lesson plan formats, you need to have a firm grasp of what the children in your classroom know about the topic/concept being studied. You must also be aware of their strengths and growth areas, the content/skills you hope they learn from this activity, ways to differentiate that learning experience, and strategies for documenting children's learning.

THE "WHAT" OF THE LESSON

Think about the big idea behind your lesson, the linchpin that holds it all together. For instance, in pre-K many teachers focus on developing children's phonological awareness. They do so to assist children in becoming readers.

Essentially, the big idea of reading is broken down into a set of discrete skills, knowledge, and concepts, and phonological awareness falls under that larger idea. By recognizing the big idea behind a lesson, you will have a better sense of your direction as well as how you might differentiate for children who already know how to read, or children who struggle with rhyming. Before you teach any lesson, you need to know the big idea, and then you can successfully lay out your lesson—be it listing the objectives, procedures and so on, or using the 5 E model.

DIFFERENTIATING INSTRUCTION

To differentiate, teachers need to know their students and their content, including the big idea. Teachers should also consider how they manage the learning environment, including grouping, instructional methods, and so on. Many teachers differentiate their teaching using small groups. You can arrange these groups around the children's interest in the topic, their understanding of the topic, or a mixture of these constructs.

Still, teachers can easily differentiate instruction by adjusting the following (Smutny and von Fremd 2010):

- the product (students produce/reproduce different products)
- the degree of participation
- the instructional input method (video, books on tape, computer, visual aids)
- the length/amount of work required (more or fewer problems, pages, sentences)
- the level of support provided (work alone, with a buddy/tutor, or with you; or, for instance, allow some children to write, others to dictate to an adult)
- the time allowed for completion (more or less time)
- the difficulty/depth/breadth (more or less complexity, allow for ambiguity)

When we talk about differentiated instruction with early educators, questions often arise around whether changing the lesson to meet the needs of individual children is fair. The focus in any classroom should be on ensuring that all children learn what they need to succeed in school and life. To do that, we view teaching through an equitable rather than equality lens. As we've said throughout this book, we hold high expectations for all students. Asking a student to simply write one word today does not mean that's our expectation for the entire school year. Rather, this one word is the first step to writing an entire sentence. Moreover, for the child that can write an entire sentence, our expectations will change as well, and as the year progresses, we will need to seriously consider whether both children need to participate in the same activities at the same time. We must continually ask ourselves if we are supporting and challenging students without creating frustration. For example, asking every second grader to read the same text at the same time might frustrate some students while being effortless for others, and thus not everyone is learning within that instructional activity.

Equitable Teaching

First, it is important to highlight the need for your instructional decisions to reflect your students' sociocultural worlds. You should question whether you are making decisions about your teaching that ensure all children are offered the opportunity to achieve and succeed to their fullest capabilities in your classroom. You should spend time reflecting on your teaching and making sure that you're not advantaging certain children over others. To prevent bias, ask the following questions:

- To whom are you always giving your time?
- Are you focusing on only those who have the most challenges?
- Are your ignoring the quiet, easygoing child?
- Are you expecting more or less from a child based on their gender? Their sociocultural background? Their socioeconomic status?

Engaging in equitable practices means giving each child what he or she needs to succeed in the classroom. To achieve this, we need to engage in transformational teaching, which encompasses student-centered ways of teaching and a multicultural curriculum. We must offer a curriculum that gives children the chance to pursue their questions and interests. Furthermore, the curricular experiences should facilitate developing the skills required for both students and teachers to question whether what we investigate advocates for an equitable learning environment. For instance, when investigating social or historical issues in your class (such as Thanksgiving), ask questions such as who is telling the story, whether there is another way to tell it, whose perspective is represented, and whose perspective is left out. Finally ask yourself, when children and their families walk into the classroom, what do the materials and media offered say about the world? Are multiple voices and cultures represented?

For Souto-Manning (2013), who frames curricula through a multicultural lens, the goal is to provide all children with the knowledge/skills and attitudes to work toward transforming society in a positive way so that all children can live in an equitable and socially just world. This last statement may seem overwhelming or unattainable, but change requires time and effort. As we've said many times before, change is often evolutionary rather than revolutionary. But consider the example of Ms. Valenzuela, who brought her students' sociocultural worlds into her classroom by engaging in the act of *testimonio* to examine the issue of fighting in a personal and powerful way (Brown and Mowry 2017).

Testimonios are oral language forms of art from Latin America in which the narrator shares a personal account of an event in his or her life to give it immediate and emotional attention. Ms. Valenzuela wanted to investigate the issue of fighting with her students because it was happening in her classroom and she heard from her students that it was happening at home. To do this, she shared a personal story of how her husband, before she left him, was physically abusive to her. She did this because she had already had many conversations with her students about hitting and many mentioned their parents hit them at home. After sharing her personal story, she asked if any of her students wanted to share their stories, and many did. For instance, Luis discussed how his mother and father fought and how it made him sad.

While the primary goal of this activity was for Ms. Valenzuela to create a space for her and her students to bear witness to the impact of fighting on their lives, she also wanted to give them a strategy for addressing these issues in the classroom. Instead of hitting someone, she wanted students to stop and think before they act. Throughout her discussion and the children's testimonies, she continually asked if they, their parents, or her ex-husband were stopping and thinking before acting. The students repeatedly said no, and she would then ask, "Do you think doing so might have made a difference?" Most said yes.

Ultimately, what Ms. Valenzuela did was give her students a voice about an issue that all of them had experienced in and outside the classroom. By doing so, she challenged violence as a strategy for resolving conflicts and provided insight into how to solve interpersonal conflicts appropriately. By broadcasting her and her students' experiences to the whole class, she created a caring environment that reduces the potential for further physical and psychological harm. These *testimonios* by Ms. Valenzuela and the children not only addressed children's sociopolitical consciousness, but they also required and attended to the academic skills of oral language development, narrative construction, and understanding one's community, which falls under the content area of social studies.

We share this example from Ms. Valenzuela to help you see that addressing topics that work toward equity and social justice is possible. We cannot demand *testimonios*, but we can plan for moments across our day, either via planned lessons or conversational moments, in which we draw children's attention to issues of equity and social justice. We must be open to such opportunities and willing to begin such conversations with children. The first time you do this might be difficult for you, but it gets easier with time.

We recognize the pressure you face in your high-stakes contexts, and throughout this chapter we've provided you with a range of strategies to begin to expand your teaching beyond these expectations. To change your teaching is a difficult task. We hope you can begin to see change as an evolutionary process in which you intentionally plan to improve and expand your instructional repertoire a little more each day. As you do this, you'll find some strategies that work and others that don't. Some you will enjoy implementing and others you will not, and of course, your students will have preferences as well. Nevertheless, changing your teaching is a process, and we believe the strategies we've outlined in this chapter will help you become a better teacher.

Reexamining Why We Should Teach to All Developmental Domains

- Discuss with your colleagues how you strive to teach to all developmental domains across your day. What are your strengths in accomplishing this goal? What are your growth areas, and how might you address them?
- Go back to the example of Ms. Salinas teaching about oobleck and identify the different strategies she employs to teach to all her students' developmental domains. Next, discuss how you might teach this lesson and what you would do differently to ensure all your students were learning from this activity. Would you teach a similar lesson? How can you employ some of these strategies to teach to all your students' developmental domains?
- Discuss the different approaches to teaching early childhood education (emergent curriculum, the project approach) and whether you've implemented any of these approaches. What were some of your struggles? Provide an example of how getting to know a child in your classroom on a more personal level affected your instruction and interactions.
- Discuss your thoughts about Ms. Valenzuela's examination into fighting in her classroom through her sharing her experience with domestic violence. Do you think she was effective in covering this topic? Do you think you could implement such a lesson with your students? Why or why not?

Extending Your Learning

- If you're interested in learning more about the emergent curriculum, review Jones and Nimmo's 1998 text, *The Emergent Curriculum.*
- To learn more about the project approach, review Katz, Chard, and Kogan's 2014 book, *Engaging Children's Minds: The Project Approach*, third edition.
- Also, if you're interested in seeing some projects teachers have conducted in their classrooms, view the following website: http://projectapproach.org/project-examples.

- To learn more about how blocks facilitate children's learning, read Kinzer, Gerhardt, and Coca's 2016 article, "Building a Case for Blocks as Kindergarten Mathematics Learning Tools," or look at Rosanne Hansel's 2016 book, *Creative Block Play: A Comprehensive Guide to Learning through Building*.
- The Utah Education Network provides a very useful resource for developing a range of learning centers in your classroom at www.uen.org/k-2educator/learning_centers.shtml.
- For more strategies to support English language learners in the classroom, visit Everything ESL at www.everythingesl.net.
- The Cult of Pedagogy is designed for anyone who teaches, and examines such issues as teaching about issues of social justice (www.cultofpedagogy.com/social-justice-resources), being a new teacher (www.cultofpedagogy.com/marigolds), and supporting English language learners (www.cultofpedagogy.com/supporting-esl-students-mainstream-classroom).

Steps You Can Take toward Change

- Draw two columns on a piece of paper. On one side, create a list of all the instructional strategies in this chapter that you engage in with your students on a regular basis. Then on the other side, develop a list of instructional strategies you would like to implement in your classroom and what it would require to do so.
- Pretend a child's guardian asked why you allow children to play in the classroom. How would you respond to this question? What would you want the guardian to learn from that conversation so he would see the value in your teaching?
- Consider a topic or unit of study that you typically teach. Ask yourself where the children have challenges and choices and whether you are addressing all developmental domains. How can you recreate this unit to better reflect your emerging understanding of RIGOROUS DAP?

5

Knowing Your Teaching Context

SBA reforms have encouraged many school districts to implement scripted and highly didactic curricula that potentially encroach upon teacher autonomy (Brown and Weber 2016). This has led to early educators teaching and enacting curricula emphasizing student performance on a set of standards under intrusive administrative surveillance at both the local (such as diagnostic classroom walk-throughs conducted by principals and district officials) and state level (such as standardized academic achievement tests). This emphasis on performance has led to what researchers describe as an intensification of the teaching profession (De Lissovoy 2013). Standardization of the curriculum affects and trickles down into preschool, pre-K, and kindergarten (Brown 2007), which signifies the importance of knowing your teaching context, including understanding how content, performance, and proficiency standards affect your teaching; knowing the curricular expectations of your district and school; and understanding the culture of your school community.

Historically, early childhood classrooms have been shielded from high-stakes testing because research has shown that young children develop and learn differently than their elementary peers. However, preschool, pre-K, and kindergarten are becoming increasingly normative and academic focused. Although there is empirical evidence that some early childhood teachers do rigidly adhere to scripted curriculum at the expense of culturally relevant, individualized instruction, other studies reveal that this is not necessarily the norm (Parks and Rhoades 2012). Some teachers who are intentional and proactive find creative ways to sidestep components of prescribed curriculum that do not resonate with their beliefs, expertise, and individual student needs (Brown and Lee 2012). This evidence is important to note because it gives early childhood teachers and those who train them reason to believe they can employ the practices related to RIGOROUS DAP.

Aligned Curriculum

In this chapter, we share interviews with early educators who wrestled with these challenges in one school district, as well as provide examples of how educational reforms affect their teaching. Although each teacher has a unique instructional delivery and student makeup varies, they all are held accountable for what they teach through a district-created and mandated aligned curriculum (AC). This AC specifies how teachers must sequence and coordinate their state-adopted resources (such as basal books and supplemental units) to assure coherent and sufficient coverage of the state standards to prepare all children for the third-grade achievement test.

This expectation for teachers to implement the AC in their classrooms is not unique. Early educators in public school systems and charter school programs across the United States are provided with curricula such as *Success for All* (www.successforall.org/Home), SRA's DISTAR (www.sradirectinstruction.com), or other localized reforms that require them to follow scripts or series of lessons every day in their classrooms. These scripts assume all children learn the same way, have a basic understanding of how to act within a school situation, and are passive and compliant consumers of knowledge whose interests and desires to learn do not matter. Such a conception of schooling supposes the purpose of school is to produce children who are successful learners and who will become earners participating as consumers in the larger society.

ADMINISTRATIVE SURVEILLANCE

Some of the more experienced teachers we introduce in this chapter began their career when standardization via high-stakes accountability and testing was not so extreme and severe. Ms. Worth, a kindergarten teacher with more than thirty years of experience, recalls a time as a new teacher when there were no standards that specified what and how to teach kindergarten:

> Everybody did their own thing. We had this little box of cards that was the curriculum, and you were supposed to pull out what you wanted to do. That's where I learned to teach off the cuff. If a child walked in and said, "Look at that bear!" we did bears all day.

In addition to providing considerable autonomy to teachers to decide how and what to teach, the school officials within the district where Ms. Worth worked during her early years as a kindergarten teacher placed very little emphasis on academic skill acquisition, such as letters and numbers. According to Ms. Worth, "[The administrators] came in, and if they saw stuff in your room that emphasized reading and writing, they got really upset. Or true arithmetic, one plus one, you couldn't have any of that."

Now in her thirty-third year of teaching kindergarten, Ms. Worth finds herself in a very different context. Not only is she required to adhere to the scope and sequence of standards outlined in her district's AC, but she and her kindergarten teammates also experience administrative walk-throughs. During these walk-throughs, both her campus administrators and district specialists appear in her classroom unannounced carrying clipboards and check off a list of indicators to provide evidence of each classroom's instructional alignment with the district's expectations. Ms. Worth recounts this dramatic experience, which created a significant degree of anxiety and shame for her and her kindergarten colleagues:

> A district specialist walked through our rooms and wrote the most horrific stuff: "These children are not going to learn anything—these teachers are not following the AC." In my very politically correct way, I went to the principal and said, "These people are not allowed in my room anymore." To think they can say this kind of stuff. They don't know our children or anything about us. They looked to see what content standards were posted on our walls, and they said our children were never going to learn anything and were bound for failure.

Understandably, Ms. Worth was deeply affected by this negative feedback. As she recalls, "I went home and cried every day for six weeks."

The contrast between what teaching was like for Ms. Worth in her initial years as a kindergarten teacher, which offered her a considerable amount of autonomy, to the level of surveillance by administrators she experiences in her current school shows just how different kindergarten has become. As Ms. Worth described, many of the teachers we have observed are required to follow a scope and sequence of instructional units based on state standards and then post those standards along with evidence of this learning as shown in student work on classroom walls. This practice of overt display and monitored performance is evidence of the breadth and depth of accountability that can adversely undermine a teacher's agency or willingness to attend to the individual and sociocultural needs of children as recommended in DAP.

GRADE-LEVEL EXPECTATION SHOVEDOWN

As these teachers carry out their day-to-day professional decision making and instruction under the scrutiny of their campus and district administrators, they must also contend with the critique by their first-grade colleagues. These colleagues question the kindergarten teachers' ability and effort to prepare children for the academic rigors and expectations of the next grade level. In other words, the press to meet the state's accountability markers creates a trickle-down effect or academic shovedown. Each subsequent grade level seeks to increase the academic expectations of the grade level below so that students enter prepared and ready to meet the content standards established by the state.

Ms. Melching, Ms. Worth's kindergarten teaching partner, describes the disappointment she experiences at the start of each school year when the first-grade teachers contest the leveled reading scores she and her colleagues assigned at the end of their kindergarten year:

> It's this panic. Part of it, I think, arises every year at the beginning of the school year, because you are sending learners up and saying, "I tested with your instruments, and this baby can read easily, independently, at a level 6." Then, they go to the next grade level, and they're tested, and "Oh my word, you sent up all these 6s, and they're scoring a 2 in first grade." You start getting this nasty feeling from the other grade-level teachers that you're inflating your scores. It has nothing to do with it, and we wouldn't do that.

At Ms. Melching and Ms. Worth's school, kindergarteners are expected to enter first grade reading at a level 6 on the state-adopted, Developmental Reading Assessment (DRA). The district expectation, however, is that the children will leave kindergarten reading at a level 3, which reflects the child's ability to decode simple, repetitive, and patterned text. To read at a level 6, the child needs to be able to answer questions that show adequate comprehension of the story. Apparently, the discrepancy in the scores Ms. Melching and her team gave on the end-of-year DRA was attributed to the way they administered the test. The kindergarten teachers could read passages to the children and then ask the comprehension questions, whereas, in first grade, the children had to both read the passages on their own *and* answer the questions.

However, the real issue with this discrepancy is that the kindergarten teachers on Ms. Melching's team sense that their first-grade colleagues see them as unsuccessful teachers. This sense of failure affects how Ms. Melching plans her instruction and schedules her day, most notably her decision not to make room for play:

> You used to have observations of children to figure out where they are in their play development; we don't let them do that anymore. I don't let them do that, probably because I know I'm supposed to have these kids reading at a 10 when they walk out the school door, to be quite honest with you.

Ms. Melching confesses that her sense of urgency to prepare her kindergarteners to be successful and competent readers at the beginning of first grade has caused her to disregard her prior, primarily play-based instructional and assessment practices. RIGOROUS DAP removes the unnecessary dichotomy of the play-versus-academics dilemma. Play is not antithetical to learning. Before rethinking ways to reconcile this dilemma, we look at one additional obstacle: content.

CONTENT SEGMENTATION: PLANNING AND TEACHING IN SILOS

The district-developed AC the kindergarten teachers in this chapter used is a compilation of documents, each of which is categorized under a specific content domain: language arts, mathematics, science, social studies, and health; some of these documents are organized by units of instruction, whereas others are divided into nine-week reporting periods. Each document contains a list of big ideas and essential understandings, which are features based on the instructional principles of Understanding by Design, a pedagogical framework developed by Jay McTighe and Grant Wiggins. They define a big idea as "a concept, theme, or issue that gives meaning and connection to discrete facts and skills" (Wiggins and McTighe 1998, 5). The big idea is included in the AC document to foreground the state standards that are covered within that unit of instruction. There are also specifications explaining what level of mastery the students are expected to demonstrate on each standard. Finally, at the end of each document, there are suggestions for both formative and performance-based summative assessments that clarify how the students will demonstrate a deep understanding of the content taught during the unit.

Although many of the organizational and structural features inserted in the AC documents can be useful and helpful for planning units of instruction, the extensive volume of information pre-K and kindergarten teachers must review is problematic. For example, the kindergarten language arts document alone for each nine-week reporting period is twenty-six pages long.

Some teachers manage the time dilemma that comes with having to plan instruction aligned to these documents by assigning content areas to each team member. Each teacher reviews the AC planning guide for their assigned content domain before meeting as a team to plan. These planning sessions occur weekly after school and last approximately sixty to ninety minutes.

The kindergarten team at one of the campuses Brian visited makes this planning time more efficient and streamlined for all members by developing a standard electronic template divided into four columns by content areas. During the meeting, every team member verbally summarizes the content she reviewed from the domain she was assigned (found in a separate document that is part of the district's AC). As they talk, each teacher also simultaneously types on her laptop, filling the respective column on the template. At the completion of the planning session, each teacher will have access to the final weekly lesson plan template, which will be available to download from a campus share drive folder.

This documentation not only provides an assurance of standardization across each classroom but also cuts down on the amount of time each teacher must devote to the individualized planning necessary to effectively and thoroughly address the standards and big ideas from all four content area domains. Ms. Alvarez, one of the four kindergarten teachers from this team, explained the team's rationale for adopting this streamlined planning strategy: "If we were to come to our weekly planning meeting and try to plan all four content areas right then and there, we'd be there forever. We're already there for an hour to an hour and a half as it is."

The decision to assign each teacher as an expert in one content area does help conserve time, a considerable amount of which is already taken up by gathering resources and preparing the necessary materials for the teachers' individual classrooms. However, despite its efficiency, this organizational plan can limit each teacher's capacity to sufficiently understand all four content areas to an equal level of depth necessary to integrate subject matter strategically and meaningfully in a way that is supportive of RIGOROUS DAP. While teachers do become experts in the domain they are assigned, they may not have adequate understanding, preparation, or background knowledge to see how the big ideas can be cohesively linked to the areas they have left to their peers. They are essentially relying on their team members' level of expertise.

Additionally, when teachers plan their content areas as silos, the instruction they deliver and the experiences they offer children suffer accordingly. This fragmentation is evident in Ms. Melching's schedule, highlighted in figure 5.1. The day is organized into blocks of instructional time that rigidly adhere to a specific content area focus. Rather than label each time segment with terms traditionally used in ECE classrooms that describe the mode and format of instruction—whole group, small group, circle time, centers—Ms. Melching explicitly indicates what content she will teach. Calendar and announcements are followed by a mandated two-hour language arts block, which includes phonemic awareness, shared/guided/independent reading, vocabulary instruction, and literacy workstations. Within this block of time, instruction is further interrupted by a forty-five-minute teacher planning time where the children leave the classroom to attend a rotation of art, physical education, or music. Center time, which the district calls Language Super Centers, is scheduled at the end of the day for twenty-five minutes when all the required content areas are completed.

Ms. Melching explains that she often does not get to other content areas, particularly science and social studies, due to the vast amount of content she must cover in language arts and mathematics:

> I can't teach science. How am I going to get through everything in the state-adopted reading program to follow this directive? Then, I have to teach science, I have to teach math, but there is no time for any social studies. Most of my day is gone by the time I get to the end of what I have to cover. It became this paring down. What can I not afford to sacrifice?

The sacrifices that Ms. Melching feels compelled to make to accommodate the required curriculum within her daily schedule mirrors a trend across the

FIGURE 5.1
Ms. Melching's Daily Kindergarten Schedule

7:40–8:15	Announcement; Pledges; Calendar; Attendance; Songs; Morning Message; SEL (Social Emotional Learning)
8:15–8:30	Phonemic Awareness/Heggerty Phonics
8:30–8:45	Social Studies/Health/Poetry
8:45–9:30	Specials (Music, Art, or PE)
9:30–10:45	Language Arts Block (shared reading; independent reading; phonological awareness activities; literacy workstations; buddy reading; guided reading; ESL; vocabulary instruction; Response to Intervention [RTI])
10:45–11:15	Lunch (leave at 10:44)
11:15–11:40	Writing Workshop
11:40–12:30	Science (core; experiment, read aloud, journal)
12:30–12:50	Words Our Way
12:50–2:10	Math Block (numerical fluency; problem solving; core instruction; guided math groups, counting, and construction; RTI; math centers)
2:10–2:35	Language Super Centers
2:35–2:44	Review and Closure
2:45	Dismissal

nation, where science, social studies, and play-based centers are being cut down (or removed all together) for the sake of teaching reading and math (Bassok, Latham, and Rorem 2016).

HOW SURVEILLANCE, SHOVEDOWN, AND SILOS AFFECT TEACHING

The impact that regimented schedules and exclusive academic focus in kindergarten classrooms have on children's engagement in learning deserves more consideration. In this case study, Ms. Alvarez's class gathered around a dry-erase board as she introduced a word problem that is part of her campus's required daily numerical fluency practice. Ms. Alvarez's kindergarten team chose to conduct this routine right before their block of forty-five-minute core math instruction.

It is 1:10 p.m. The class is discussing how to solve the following problem posted on the board: "There are two chairs and three people. Are there enough chairs for everyone?" Ms. Alvarez asks, "How do we want to solve this? Do we draw it or act it out?" The children choose to draw it, which Ms. Alvarez does as the children talk. The children are adamant that there are not enough chairs because someone would be left standing. Ms. Alvarez draws two chairs with dotted lines drawn to two stick figures. One stick figure has a line with no corresponding object so the children can see that one more chair is needed. Ms. Alvarez allows the children to respond to the suggested solution by making a thumbs-up sign if they agree and thumbs-down if they do not agree.

The class then discusses how to represent the situation with symbolic notation. Ms. Alvarez says, "We are not taking away; we are putting one more." This statement causes some confusion when she states that she will need to put the bigger number on top to subtract. She writes 3–2=1 in vertical notation underneath the problem and illustration.

The conversation shifts to an investigation the children have been doing throughout the week to determine whose name has the most letters. The children have made connecting cube trains to represent the number of letters in their names. Individual letters are written on white dot stickers, which are affixed to each cube in the child's name train. Ms. Alvarez selects two cube trains that have the names Maya and Rodolfo. She asks the children how many letters are in Maya's name and then in Rodolfo's name. Once she has helped to clarify that Maya's name has four letters and Rodolfo's name has seven, Ms. Alvarez challenges the children to determine which name has more letters: "What do we need to do?" She orients both trains extending horizontally on top of each other, with Rodolfo's on top. She purposefully holds Maya's name train so that it does not align directly underneath where Rodolfo's name begins. Maya's train juts out a little farther to the right of where Rodolfo's name ends, apparently in Ms. Alvarez's attempt to deceive the children's perception so that they must consider the number of letters rather than focus on the length of the name. Most children agree that Rodolfo has more letters, even though Maya's extends farther out to the right.

The children notice that Ms. Alvarez is trying to trick them, and she challenges them to explain what is wrong. One child responds, "Because there is not so much at the bottom." Ms. Alvarez helps to clarify this observation by stating, "It's like cheating; you have to start at the same place." Ms. Alvarez continues to allow other children to share observations. One girl points out that to have the same number of letters as Rodolfo's name, Maya's name would need three more letters. Ms. Alvarez affirms this response, saying, "Good observation."

After approximately twenty minutes, Ms. Alvarez distributes the name trains to each child so they can compare their names with classmates' names. The children scatter around the room, some conferencing at tables, while others remain on the carpet. They are all on task, counting and comparing their trains as Ms. Alvarez moves about prompting them to talk about their findings. One child points to another classmate's train and says, "My name is the same as that one."

After about ten to fifteen minutes, the children return to the carpet, where Ms. Alvarez asks the group to focus for the debriefing session. She affirms children who are ready to move on: "I see José is ready." Once everyone has joined the group, she asks the children to determine which child has the longest and which has the shortest name in the class. The children agree that Fernando, which has eight letters, is the longest name, and that the name with only three letters (Ely) is the shortest. Fernando, notably content to have the longest name in the class, comments that the name of a friend of his would need two more letters to be the same length as his. Ms. Alvarez summarizes and concludes the conversation by pointing out that "everyone else's name is in the middle."

Ms. Alvarez glances at the clock in the back of the room. She informs the children they will now transition to the meeting area in the back of the room to watch a video about national symbols. The children calmly move to their new location, some eagerly anticipating the video.

To outside observers who are not familiar with what kindergarten looked like twenty-five years ago, the series of events that unfolded within the vignette might give the impression that productive learning is happening in Ms. Alvarez's classroom. Indeed, Ms. Alvarez is a good teacher and finds very positive ways to manage behavior and engage the children in the tasks she must cover according to her district's AC.

What might be questionable, however, is whether the children saw connections in counting and comparing quantities to other learning experiences or in their daily lives outside of the classroom. The word problem they solved at the beginning of math time was structurally similar to the mathematical content they explored in the counting and comparing name activity they did immediately afterward. The big idea underlying both activities—how to figure out quantitative differences between two sets of objects—was never explored in depth, such as how you could count forward from the smaller number or backward from the larger number. Instead, both activities occurred relatively close together with little reflection as to how they were related or connected. Perhaps the word problem wasn't necessary, which would have allowed the children to have more time exploring the topic outside of the large-group time during individualized centers. As the children played the games independently, Ms. Alvarez could have been available to assist those who were struggling to understand the comparison concept or have differentiated materials accessible to make accommodations for those ready to use more sophisticated strategies to determine the quantitative differences.

In addition to the unnecessary redundancy of content presentation that occurred in this classroom vignette, another notable place to reconsider was the immediate transition from one subject area (mathematics) to another (social studies). Perhaps there is no real connection between these two subject areas. However, the failure to help children see how what they are learning in one domain is connected to other aspects of their lives (*Integrating content areas*) gives the impression that school is a place where you accumulate information and facts with no other purpose than to be more knowledgeable. It is important for children to see that what they learn can be applied or transferred to other situations.

Teachers like Ms. Alvarez and Ms. Melching are hardworking professionals interested in helping their students learn and be successful, and they find themselves in an unfortunate dilemma with no outside support to go beyond the high-stakes content they must teach. They do not have the support to consider an alternative, more liberating pedagogy that allows them to meet the individual, developmental, and cultural needs of students. In the section that follows, we attempt to provide examples of those teaching in ways that are more representative of the RIGOROUS DAP framework within their highly structured teaching environments.

Rethinking Surveillance, Shovedown, and Silos through RIGOROUS DAP

We now turn to the work of Ms. Demling and identify some of the ways she exemplified aspects of RIGOROUS DAP in her teaching of the mandated curriculum and content standards within her classroom. As we do this, we also identify some growth areas within her instruction that could improve her interactions with her students.

Ms. Demling's school is a few blocks from the center of a large urban city. Its student population is primarily Latinx, with recent influx of refugees from various African countries. Most of the children are bilingual and qualify for free or reduced lunch. The school has five pre-K classrooms: three bilingual (English–Spanish) and two taught in English. Ms. Demling is a teacher whom others within her school admire. For example, her assistant principal, a former pre-K teacher who once taught with her, said, "I just love everything about her. If I could clone her, I would. I love how all her centers are play based, and all the academics are taught through play. She does it all so appropriately." When asked what she believes are the skills an effective early educator in a high-stakes teaching context needs to possess, Ms. Demling noted,

> You have to be very confident in yourself as a teacher, which can take time to develop. You need to be even keeled. Your personality needs to be very calm. You

need to be a flexible person. I think that goes with any age you're teaching—you just need to be flexible. You need to be a team player because you soon learn that you don't have all the answers and you can't do this by yourself.

We agree that being confident, flexible, and a team player are essential characteristics for early educators to possess so that they can engage in RIGOROUS DAP. We would add that you also must be knowledgeable about the content and be community driven, meaning you not only reaching out to your colleagues but also to the families and members of your community. These additional traits will assist you in *Pushing every child forward* in a manner that *Integrates content* and allows you and your students to *Grow as a community*.

MS. DEMLING'S ACTIVITIES THAT REFLECT RIGOROUS DAP

These notions of confidence, flexibility, and teamwork that Ms. Demling used to describe an effective pre-K teacher were also exhibited in her practice. Let's look at an example of a transition activity that took place midway through the year in her classroom.

In the middle of the morning, Ms. Demling and the children transition from a literacy focus (making a story chart about The Three Billy Goats Gruff, *and then acting it out) to a math lesson on patterns and numbers. Ms. Demling uses this transition time, which is only a few minutes long, to reiterate a key literacy goal for that week as identified on the AC—children can produce a word that begins with the same sound as a given pair of words. She does this through singing "This Old Man." She introduces the song to her twenty students by saying, "I am going to sing a song that you've probably heard before." She then begins to pat her thighs and clap her hands in the rhythm of the song. She sings, "This old man, he played one, he played knick knack on my thumb" and so on. Luke says, "I've heard that song before."*

Ms. Demling continues, "Now, I am going to sing it in a sleepy voice," and repeats the first line in a sleepy voice that several children begin to impersonate. She asks, "If I were to add one more, what would be next?" Several children say, "Two." She says, "Yes, two, and when we get to two, we are going to pat our what? What rhymes with two?" Several children say, "Shoe." She then shows them how to pat their shoes, and they then sing the line.

She sees a little girl starting to take off her shoe and says, "We don't need to take off our shoes to pat them. Just pat them on your feet, and if you're sitting crisscross, your shoe is where it needs to be. You should be able to pat your shoe easily." Then she shows them how to pat their shoe with two fingers. They then sing the line.

Ms. Demling then asks, "What comes next?" Several children say, "Three." She asks, "What rhymes with three?" Again, several students say, "Knee." She then shows them how to pat their knees, and the class continues with the song up through ten.

Ms. Demling asks the children if they noticed anything mathematical about the song they just sung. While some children appear to be a little lost by this question, Maria says, "We counted." Ms. Demling replies, "Yes, we did count, which is something we do in math. Nice observation, Maria. Is there anything else we did mathematically in that song?" The class pauses, and then José quietly says, "Patterns." Ms. Demling puts a hand up to her ear and says, "I think I heard an answer to my question, but it was very soft. I have a hard time hearing soft answers, so I would appreciate it if that person might say his answer a little louder." José repeats his answer with a little more volume, and Ms. Demling responds, "José, that's a very interesting answer. Please explain what you mean." José says, "It sounds like there's a pattern to the song. We say, 'This old man, he plays one' and then another number over and over till ten." Ms. Demling replies to José and the whole class by stating, "José thinks there's a pattern in the song we just sung. What do you think about that?"

The class discusses José's answer, and then Ms. Demling uses José's response to lead the class into a math lesson where the students will use two colors of Unifix cubes to practice counting to ten and create and document patterns (for example, red and blue).

Ms. Demling engaged in a range of teaching behaviors that not only reflect our conception of RIGOROUS DAP but also exemplify characteristics found on Bredekamp and Rosegrant's continuum of instruction. This transition activity began with a directive, moved into a demonstration of the song, and offered chances for coconstruction. The children then reflected on how their singing connected with math. Ms. Demling designed this lesson in response to the AC to foster her students' academic skills (rhyming, beginning sound recognition, counting, patterns, and so on). At the same time, the lesson bridged the three literacy centers the students just participated in to the math lessons through a song that asked them to use both literacy and mathematical skills. Almost everything Ms. Demling planned and implemented for this activity reflects her response to district- and state-generated policy documents that seek to standardize and align what takes place in all the pre-K to grade five classrooms in her district.

Conceptually, this lesson is an age-appropriate song that requires Ms. Demling's students to use their cognitive, physical, and social-emotional skills—*Seeing the whole child* while *Integrating content areas*. Moreover, clearly, Ms. Demling expects all her students to succeed at this task and includes each of them in the activity—*Reaching* and *Pushing every child forward*. Still, high-stakes reforms have led to policies, curricula expectations, and instructional recommendations that Ms. Demling is expected to follow so she produces learners who can succeed in elementary school. When examining her teaching at this moment as well as across the day, it is neither an act of resistance nor one of contrition in which she must decide between teaching either the curriculum or the children. Rather, she addresses both the AC and her students through a range of developmentally appropriate and culturally responsive and sustaining practices.

TEACHING AND THE AC

Ms. Demling knows that for children to be prepared academically for elementary school, they need to know the skills and knowledge outlined in the AC:

> The alphabet; the sounds that the letters make. They need to be able to write their first and last names. In math they need to have one-to-one correspondence, counting skills, recognizing the numerals from one to ten, counting up to twenty. In science they need more knowledge about the natural world around them. They need to know simple cycles: the cycle of their day, the life cycle of the plants. Socially, we're working on being able to get along with others. I call it being a respectful citizen. Physically, they need be in control of their bodies, having some coordination, being able to hop, skip, and jump. We don't have physical education classes, but being able to do all those things helps them have a coordinated body.

While these academic and developmental skills are age appropriate and can be found in these teachers' AC and the state's pre-K content standards, they are also seen in Ms. Demling's transitional activity. In many ways, the skills Ms. Demling outlines represent the strange coupling of power found in policy makers' high-stakes SBA education reforms. It seems natural to list what children need to know to be ready for what lies ahead in kindergarten. Knowing such information is necessary so Ms. Demling can push every child forward. Yet in making such a list, the onus of being ready for school is placed on the child. Such a political act not only diminishes the role of government but also the role of the teacher and the larger community in the education process, which is an unfair and unjust expectation for the children.

THE AC AND MS. DEMLING'S TRANSITIONAL ACTIVITY

The tightly organized system of instruction implemented by Ms. Demling and the other teachers we've explored in this chapter differs from how others have documented their struggles with mandated content standards and from traditional ECE practices that pivot curricular decisions off topics of interest to the children in the classroom. The AC and the assessments these teachers are expected to implement do not reflect who they are as professionals or who the children are as learners.

The activity described in the previous vignette took place during the twentieth week of school (a short week due to the Martin Luther King Jr. holiday). The AC for that week (see figure 5.2) provides instructional focal points for all the district's pre-K teachers to use that match the content areas of literacy, math, science, and social studies. It shows how they can teach these skills each day, which includes using the state-approved DLM Early Childhood Express curriculum the district has provided for each teacher. Additionally, each week the AC provides pre-K teachers with guidelines for assessment that align with the district's pre-K assessment rubric that all pre-K teachers use to assess the children for the standardized pre-K report card. The AC also offers clarifying activities for intentional, purposeful, and focused instruction. Finally, at the bottom of figure 5.2, the AC provides teachers with suggestions for differentiated instruction, aspects of what they term the "principles of learning" to address each week, and special features they can integrate from either a previous learning experience or across content areas.

FIGURE 5.2

The AC for Week 20

Integrated Content Areas: Literacy/Math/Science/Social Studies

Weekly Pre-K Guideline Focal Points	Assessment	Clarifying Activities for Intentional, Purposeful, and Focused Instruction
LANGUAGE AND COMMUNICATION DOMAIN • **II.D.2** Child demonstrates an understanding of terms used in the instructional language of the classroom. **EMERGENT LITERACY—READING DOMAIN** • **III.B.7** Child can produce a word that begins with the same sound as a given pair of words. • **III.D.1** Child retells or reenacts a story after it is read aloud. • **III.D.2** Child uses information learned from books by describing, relating, categorizing or comparing and contrasting (*e.g., identifies characters and predicts events, plot, and the resolution of the story*). **EMERGENT LITERACY—WRITING DOMAIN** • **IV.D.1** Child uses some appropriate writing conventions when writing or giving dictation.	**LANGUAGE ARTS** ***Ongoing Assessment:*** • To assess **Pre-K Guideline III.B.7**, refer to the activities listed at the top of p. 3 of the 3rd Nine Weeks Assessment Rubrics. • Refer to the top of p. 2 of the 3rd Nine Weeks Assessment Rubrics to determine which elements of storytelling you should be looking for as you assess. **Pre-K Guidelines III.D.1** and **III.D.2.** **MATHEMATICS** **SCIENCE** • ***Interactive Notebook:*** After students make their tornado bottles (see the Special Feature section for details), assess **Pre-K Guideline VI.A.1** as suggested on p. 10 of the 3rd Nine Weeks Assessment Rubrics. • ***Work Sample:*** Use the *Estimating* sheet located on pp. 32–33 of the *Assessment SPSI.* **SOCIAL STUDIES**	**LANGUAGE ARTS** • You can address **Pre-K Guideline II.D.2** by inviting students' families to share traditional tales from their own native cultures. It is fun to point out similarities and differences between these stories and ones typically shared in the United States. For shared writing, make a chart to document and keep track of the various tales that are shared. (See **Pre-K Guideline IV.D.1**.) • Use a Venn diagram as a graphic organizer to compare two versions of the same traditional tale. Cut out pictures from the stories and place them in the diagram to make the graphic organizer accessible and readable for young learners. Model strategies for retelling stories **(Pre-K Guidelines III.D.1** and **III.D.2)** as you compare the tales. ***Vocabulary:*** *Retell, Sequence, Characters, Plot, Resolution* **MATHEMATICS** **SCIENCE** • For **Pre-K Guideline V.A.2**, refer to the Blocks Activity on p. 67 of the DLM TE-C. In this activity, students create various building projects (bridge, raft, cottage, and castle) with unit blocks. Place pictures of these structures in the block center to help generate ideas on what and how to build.

FIGURE 5.2 *(continued)*

Weekly Pre-K Guideline Focal Points	Assessment	Clarifying Activities for Intentional, Purposeful, and Focused Instruction
MATHEMATICS DOMAIN **SCIENCE DOMAIN** • **VI.A.1** Child describes, observes, and investigates properties and characteristics of common objects. • **VI.A.2** Child investigates and describes position and motion of objects. • **VI.C.3** Child observes and describes what happens during changes in the earth and sky **SOCIAL STUDIES DOMAIN**		• The children will address **Pre-K Guideline VI.C.3** as they engage in Activity 1 on pp. 275, 281 and p. 63 of the DLM TE-C. The children will be investigating tornadoes/hurricanes, condensation, and gravity through these three activities. • Incorporate **Mathematics Pre-K Guideline V.D.1** as you do Activity 1 on p. 53 of the DLM TE-C. Here the children explore the different lengths of two paper bridges, which they will build. ***Vocabulary:*** *Gravity, Condensation, Precipitation, Evaporation* **SOCIAL STUDIES**

Differentiated Instruction	POL—Academic Rigor	Special Feature: Science
ELL Accommodations: To address **Mathematics Pre-K Guideline V.C.3**, provide opportunities throughout the day for students to physically act out position words (*under, on, beside, in,* etc.) with their bodies as well as with toys. This instructional strategy, referred to in ESL as *Total Physical Response*, is especially effective for teaching non-English speakers English vocabulary.	Circle time, story time, and learning centers provide specific opportunities for teachers to engage students in higher-level questioning strategies, such as analysis, synthesis, and evaluation. For an example of higher-level questions for the story, *The Three Little Pigs*, refer to the questions listed under the section *One Way to Develop the Lesson* on p. 36 of the DLM TE-C.	You can integrate last week's emphasis on weather into this week's Traditional Tales theme by retelling various stories about significant weather events—e.g., floods and tornadoes. The activity described on pp. 275 of the DLM TE-C suggests discussing tornadoes and hurricanes as well as having students make a tornado in a water bottle. You can subsequently assess **Pre-K Guideline VI.A.**1, by following the format of the Scientific Process Vocabulary charts—Investigate (see **Addendum**)—as the children begin to investigate tornadoes. **Addendum**: Estimating pp. 32–33, *Assessment SPSI* **Literature Connection:** *I Like Weather* (Fisher), *Rain* (Kalan), *Down Comes the Rain* (Branley)

In figure 5.2, we provide information only for language arts and science. For math that week, some of the expectations include "Child counts one to ten items, with one count per item"; "Child demonstrates that the order of the counting sequence is always the same regardless of what they counted"; and "Child recognizes and compares heights or lengths of people or objects." The math lesson Ms. Demling transitioned into after singing "This Old Man" addressed many of these skills.

The AC divides language arts into the domains of language and communication, reading, and writing. The focus for week 20 was on traditional tales—see the top of the AC where the DLM curriculum is noted. In science the focus was on examining the properties of common objects, positioning such objects, and changes in earth and sky. The AC specifies which state's pre-K content standards these objectives address, and it often cites pages in the DLM where one can find activities. Furthermore, in science it provides suggestions for how to link to conversations that were to occur the previous week: in this case, linking the weather to an activity in which the children make a tornado using a pair of two-liter bottles filled with water which when spun correctly makes a funnel that looks like a tornado.

HOW MS. DEMLING USED THE ALIGNED CURRICULUM

In responding to and addressing the official curriculum in her teaching, Ms. Demling and her pre-K colleagues read the AC and translated it into a series of lesson plans. Some of those lesson plans might match the AC word for word, or they might substitute another learning activity. As Ms. Demling commented,

> I see the AC as a document that provides suggestions on the activities we should be doing with our children, which are also attached to all the state's pre-K content standards and the DLM. For me, it's this big picture. When we meet as a team, we've each looked at the AC for that upcoming week. Then we choose the different state content standards from the AC that we are going to hit. We also look to see what assessments the children will be doing at the end of the nine weeks to make sure that we are putting in activities that will help the children succeed or move forward on those assessments. We use the AC as best we can to fit the needs of the children in the classroom, but we sometimes will divert from it quite a bit.

Ms. Demling did not try to resist teaching the AC. Rather, she saw it as

> a general guide that is good for all the content areas. And it always has suggestions for differentiation. We're blessed. I've heard from different teachers at other grade levels, and they don't have such a positive opinion about the AC. We have an actual pre-K department, and they, with some of our pre-K teachers, created the AC. So it reflects an early childhood viewpoint of teaching and learning.

Having the AC developed by administrators and teachers who are part of the district's pre-K program appeared to have helped Ms. Demling buy into the document. She felt it provided good suggestions for taking the first step in creating their lessons. Additionally, because it created curricular coherence across the school year, she and her colleagues could consider amending or changing it rather than worrying whether they were covering all the content found in the state's pre-K content standards. Ms. Demling did not see the AC as "the way" to teach pre-K. Rather, she saw it as a tool she had to respond to in her instruction. She did so in two ways. First, she used the AC to craft her official response to the expectations placed on her by school, district, and state policy makers and administrators. Second, she saw this document as a first draft in considering what she might cover in her instruction for each week. In both responses, Ms. Demling recognized that the AC organized the state pre-K content standards in a way that helped her understand what children need to know and do to be ready for kindergarten. From there, she employed her understanding of each learner to create a set of lessons that attempted to *Reach all children* by *Integrating content areas*, *Offering choices and challenges*, *Differentiating instruction*, *Revisiting new content*, and *Assessing constantly* so she could *Push every child forward* in her learning.

LINKING THE AC TO THE STATE'S PRE-K CONTENT STANDARDS

In the twentieth week of school, Ms. Demling and her colleagues planned lessons examining traditional tales in language arts, but for science they substituted the study of water for the examination of the properties of common objects. As a pre-K team, Ms. Demling and her colleagues decided to create a unit of study around water for several months. They chose water because this was an area of inquiry children seemed to enjoy and wanted to learn more. Knowing the pre-K curriculum, they could align the pre-K science standards with this unit of study through a lesson that Ms. Demling felt "worked best for the kids."

Once they decided what to use and not use from the AC, they spelled out the exact pre-K content standard they would address every week. These content standards became the objectives they planned to cover over the course of the week in their proposed lessons. For language arts, they typed up and copied all the state's pre-K content standards for week 20 for each teacher's planning files. The state's pre-K content standards covered that week came from the domains of Language and Communication, Emergent Literacy Reading, and Emergent Literacy Writing. These state-based pre-K content standards can be seen in figure 5.3.

FIGURE 5.3
State's Pre-K Content Standards for Week 20

1. ELL (English Language Learners): Child increases listening vocabulary and begins to develop vocabulary of object names, actions, and common phrases in English.
2. Child demonstrates understanding of terms used in the instructional language of the classroom.
3. Child can produce a word that begins with the same sound as a given pair of words.
4. Child retells or reenacts a story after it is read aloud.
5. Child uses information learned from books by describing, relating, categorizing, or comparing and contrasting (such as identifies characters and predicts events, plot, and the resolution of the story).

Using the state's pre-K content standards as their proposed objectives, Ms. Demling and her colleagues developed a set of lesson plans for each content area. In Ms. Demling's school, like Ms. Alvarez's kindergarten team, each of the four pre-K teachers was responsible for developing the plans in one of the four content areas. Ms. Demling oversaw science, which included lessons using classroom technology such as computers, interactive whiteboards, and iPods. Ms. Demling noted, "We outline our goals for that week in every single subject, reflect on those in our team meeting, and go toward that in our lessons."

Ms. Demling and her colleague's plans for reading on Thursday, January 21, are outlined in figure 5.4 and exemplify how they addressed the state's pre-K content standards through a range of reading activities. Across that school day, teachers planned to develop the children's reading skills by engaging them in read-alouds, phonological awareness development, phonics instruction, and differentiation for ESL students.

POSITIONING THE AC AS A FLEXIBLE DOCUMENT

Ms. Demling didn't see the lesson planning process as rigid. "We look at the AC, but we make sure we keep going back to the state's pre-K content standards and use them to set our goals, all while thinking about how it works best for the kids." You can see part of this flexibility in her incorporation of the science center during her literacy period. On the morning of January 21, Ms. Demling had three assistants helping her (two practicum students from the local university and an AmeriCorps volunteer), so she let them run the three literacy centers outlined above. At the fourth center, she worked with students to examine how water moves, which was part of a larger unit of study on water that she designed for the pre-K team to work on over a four-week period. This unit was not part of the AC.

FIGURE 5.4
Pre-K Reading Lessons for Thursday of Week 20

Fiction: *The Three Billy Goats Gruff* by Paul Galdone. Read the story and make a chart featuring title, characters, setting, beginning, middle, and end.

Nonfiction: *A Cool Drink of Water* by Barbara Kerley.

Shared Reading: *Mrs. Wishy-Washy* by Joy Cowley. Students list and discuss what happened in the beginning, middle, and end of the story. Students complete a story map.

Phonological Awareness: Words that start with the same sound.

Nursery Rhyme: "The Queen of Hearts"

Songs: "Goodnight, Irene"—Practice the song echo style and sing along with the CD. Practice "Go in and out the Window"—echo read the lyrics line by line with the children, and then sing the song.

Phonics:

Rhyme Cards: Repeat the rhyme cards introduced to date.

Song: "Gabby Gorilla" song of *Phonics and Friends* series big book. Sing along with flute, and students chime in and find words that begin with *G* using classroom texts.

ESL: Continue to work on the "I like . . ." and "I don't like . . ." sentence stems with the different food categories, like meats, fruits, and so on.

Vocabulary/Oral Language: goats, tool names, better, worst

Before the week of January 18, the students had already examined how water can change when it's exposed to temperatures below freezing, and this week they planned to examine how water moves. Specifically, the students were to explore the following concepts: water can flow; water can pour; water can drip; water can spray; water can be absorbed; some things float in water, and some things sink; and all things need water to live. Ms. Demling's plans for science on Thursday, January 21, are outlined in figure 5.5. They describe the way she planned for her and the children to examine how water can be moved in both a large-group and small-group lesson. Ms. Demling followed the small group component of this lesson during the literacy centers.

This lesson demonstrates how Ms. Demling and her colleagues not only had a solid understanding of what the state and district expected them to teach, but also a strong sense of the content they were planning to teach. Incorporating documents such as the AC into one's teaching in an authentic way that reflects your students and their communities requires you to have knowledge in "the conventional subject areas and [to become] so familiar with the key content ideas shaping each area" (Schwartz and Copeland 2010, 29). Part of the reason these teachers could create and implement the Water Movers unit, which allows

FIGURE 5.5
Science Lesson for Thursday of Week 20

Thursday: Water Movers

Vocabulary: water movers, tool names, better, best, worst, title

Materials: eyedroppers, spoons, basters, straws, tubing, buckets, jars, funnels, sponges

Activities: Some tools work better than others for moving water from one place to another. Certain tools work best for specific tasks. They drop or lose water precisely. A cup moves a greater volume than an eyedropper. Water movers allow the students to learn for themselves the attributes of each tool.

Large Group: Use a tub or water table to show students how you can use a cup to take water from the tub to another container. Show each of the other items that can be used to move water. Do not demonstrate how they work, but say that each can be used to move water from one container to another. Tell the students that their job is to figure out how they can move water.

Small Group: Spend time observing students as they engage in water play. Take pictures and make anecdotal notes to share later. Ask, "Can you count the number of times it takes this tool to move water from one container to another? Which containers hold a little water? Which containers hold a lot of water?"

Reflection: Students share water play experiences.

for the exploration and discussion of scientific principles, was because they had a good understanding of the content they wanted their children to learn.

Finally, the "This Old Man" activity was a short lesson that introduced what the children would be studying in math that day. The proposed objectives Ms. Demling was to cover in math included having children learn to predict what comes next when they extend patterns. Using this song was a practical way to connect the traditional tales they had been studying in their literacy centers to the tower-building and pattern activities they would be completing during math time. In figure 5.6 we provide the specific math lesson Ms. Demling's pre-K teammate created.

The lesson outlines the objectives, vocabulary, and introductions. Furthermore, it cites a page in the DLM that uses a traditional tale to teach patterns. Interestingly, this math lesson is not part of the traditional tales theme found in the DLM. Choosing this math lesson exemplifies how Ms. Demling and her teammates were more concerned about providing children with math activities that they believed *Integrated content* and *Pushed each child forward* in their learning. Their bridge-like actions demonstrate how they saw it as their responsibility to manipulate as well as connect the AC and DLM so that it met children's learning experiences, extended their thinking, and challenged each of them.

FIGURE 5.6
Math Lesson for Thursday of Week 20

Student expectations:

- Begin to predict what comes next when patterns are extended.
- Vocabulary: pattern, pattern core

Activities:

- Sing "This Old Man." Call attention to the N=1 pattern.
- Reintroduce building stairs. Make steps connection cube towers containing one to ten cubes.
- Show children the steps that range in height from one to five connecting cubes laid out in random order. Ask the children to help you put them in order. How many cubes would we need for the next step to continue the pattern? Then lay out the towers containing six to ten cubes and challenge the children to keep going. DLM p. 256, Book B
- Sponge activities: Invite the children to order the dot cards from 1 to 5. Challenge the children to continue N+1 pattern while making steps with more than ten connecting cubes. Encourage children to make their own patterns with paper blocks or building blocks. Have the children review copying and extending pattern strips.

SCHOOL READINESS AND THE AC

As you can see, Ms. Demling is expected to teach her students a detailed set of knowledge and skills that will hopefully prepare them for success in elementary school. But this press for school readiness has led many school districts across the United States to create and implement a standardized, aligned curriculum that all early educators are to follow without accounting for the developmental variance and individual needs of children. What is interesting about the expectations outlined in such documents as the AC is that they imply that by simply following a standardized curriculum children will be successful in kindergarten and beyond. However, as you might expect, the work of Ms. Demling and her colleagues demonstrates that such documents are not enough for them to be successful at their job. Ms. Demling and her colleagues tweaked the AC into proposed objectives that they could use to help the children meet state and district learning expectations. They also added topics that students would enjoy—such as the exploration of water in their science instruction.

GROWTH AREAS FOR MS. DEMLING

Many of Ms. Demling's instructional decisions reflect numerous practices found in RIGOROUS DAP. For example, because she and her colleagues understood each of their students as well as saw the whole child as a part of the learning process, they did not allow the AC to dictate their teaching. However, we also recognize there are many opportunities for growth in her teaching. For instance, much of her and her colleagues' instruction appears to be teacher directed, and while numerous occasions are provided for the children to learn the mandated context through a variety of learning experiences, it is not clear how her instruction offers children choices in their learning. For example, incorporating dramatic play into her literacy instruction can provide the children a chance to offer their interpretations of stories/songs they are learning or create new narratives on their own.

Furthermore, how Ms. Demling and her colleagues differentiate their instruction to support the developmental needs of all children is unclear. For example, with the counting and patterns activity with Unifix cubes, there were students who struggled with counting to ten and others who had mastered this skill. The same could be said for creating and extending A/B patterns using two colors. Some easy steps she might have employed to *Push every child forward* include simplifying the task for those struggling with counting to ten by asking them to count to five or working with a more knowledgeable peer to help scaffold their counting. For those who already knew how to count to ten, she could have asked them to count to twenty or higher or backward from ten or twenty. With the patterns, she could have added a third, fourth, or fifth colored cube or asked them to create a new line to the "This Old Man" song that extended the pattern past ten.

Finally, Ms. Demling and her colleagues must consider how the AC may be shaping their visions for *Pushing every child forward* in their learning. Their goals ultimately appear to align with the goals of the AC, and thus they may unknowingly forgo the goals and interests of the children in the classroom, their families, and/or the local community, which are essential components in understanding each learner. One way they could address this issue is by reflecting on the lessons they taught from the standpoint of their decision making rather than simply noting whether students met the learning objectives for the lessons. Ms. Demling and her colleagues would need to think about whether the practices they engaged in during the lesson were in tune with the children in their classrooms, and if they were not, why not? Were they misinterpreting their students' knowledge and skills, or was there a lack of connection to other things they were studying in the classroom? Perhaps they failed to consider students' sociocultural worlds, or did they perhaps fail to grasp the underlying concepts that define the knowledge and skills they were hoping to teach?

Nevertheless, Ms. Demling's teaching provides insight into how teachers can begin to incorporate the practices found within RIGOROUS DAP.

Reexamining Why Knowing Your Context Is Important

- Discuss with your colleagues what you are expected to teach your students on a daily, weekly, monthly, and yearly basis. Then discuss the following questions:
  1. Where and from whom (policy makers, administrators, families) do these expectations come?
  2. How do these expectations reflect your conceptions of teaching young children? If you could change or tweak them, how would you?
  3. How do these expectations reflect your students? How might they be altered to be more reflective of your community of students' cognitive, sociocultural, emotional, and physical development?
- In this two-part activity, first discuss with your colleagues the instructional decision-making of two of the teachers in this chapter, Ms. Melching and Ms. Demling. Discuss how they described how their teaching does and does not reflect the principles of RIGOROUS DAP. How might they extend their thinking to better align their visions of early childhood education with these principles? Second, talk about their teaching. In the examples provided in this chapter, identify the ways their teaching does or does not align with RIGOROUS DAP. In those instances where it does not align with RIGOROUS DAP, how might they change and/or improve their teaching practices?

Extending Your Learning

- The following three books might be helpful in considering how you can engage in RIGOROUS DAP within a range of teaching contexts.
  — A kindergarten teacher employs her students' interests to teach her math curriculum in *Little Kids—Powerful Problem Solvers* by Angela Andrews and Paul Trafton.
  — Mariana Souto-Manning's book *Multicultural Teaching in the Early Childhood Classroom: Approaches, Strategies, and Tools, Preschool–2nd Grade* provides numerous examples across a range of teaching contexts of early educators engaging in multicultural teaching practices that not only address children's worlds but also the context in which teachers are expected to teach.
  — Vivian Gussein Paley's important work frames the process of teaching through the context of children's lives. She has published numerous texts that explore her teaching. *The Girl with the Brown Crayon: How Children Use Stories to Shape Their Lives* is a good place to start. In it she highlights the importance of letting children take the lead in their learning. In a more recent text, *A Child's Work: The Importance of Fantasy Play*, she makes a strong case for the need for fantasy play in the early childhood classroom.

- Much of what the teachers in this chapter are responding to is the impact of policy makers' reforms on their teaching. The National Education Policy Center (http://nepc.colorado.edu) provides a range of publications, blogs, and reviews that examine what is known about current educational reforms (such as accountability policies or vouchers). It also includes position papers by a range of political organizations that can help you better understand what is and is not known about the impact of particular policies on teaching and learning.
- Defending the Early Years (www.deyproject.org) is an organization that strives to get educators to take action on policies that affect the education of young children. They do so by promoting appropriate practices, tracking the impact of policies on teachers, and mobilizing the ECE community to speak out against inappropriate standards, assessment, and classroom practices.

Steps You Can Take toward Change

- If you are in a teaching situation like Ms. Alvarez, where you must post your daily teaching objectives for all to see, take a step back and think about what these objectives really mean for you and your students. Try to see how you might expand them in such a way that they consider who the children are in your classroom and what you want to accomplish in your teaching. You may even want to use a graphic organizer such as the one below to help you translate such statements into actionable practices that reflect you and the students you teach.

The Standard(s) I Have to Post in My Classroom	What This Means for Me and My Interactions with Children

6

Monitoring Students' Achievement

In general, there are four purposes of assessment in early childhood education: accountability reporting, identification of special needs, program evaluation and monitoring trends, and educational planning. The first three tend to require teachers to use a standardized assessment. The last, educational planning, is primarily rooted in teachers' informal and formal assessment measures, but standardized tests can be a part of this process as well. For example, Ms. Garcia, a prekindergarten teacher, wanted to ensure that Louis understood the mathematical terms of *more* and *less*. She could find this information informally by observing Louis during choice time, which he usually spends in the blocks center, and see if he uses this or any other mathematical vocabulary and record it using an anecdotal note. Using a formal assessment, Ms. Garcia could pull Louis aside with her class checklist in hand and ask him a series of questions using two piles of counting bears to see if he understands *more* and *less*. Finally, using a standardized assessment for pre-K math, such as Tools for Early Assessment in Math, Louis, along with the rest of his class, might be asked to locate the picture on the computer screen that has the fewest number of grapes.

All three methods assess the same knowledge and skill, but the process of gathering the information is quite different and affects Ms. Garcia's instructional planning in different ways. With the informal assessment, Ms. Garcia may or may not observe Louis using the terms *more* or *less* in the block center. However, she will be able to observe multiple students at the same time and have the chance to document a range of skills for Louis and his classmates that extend beyond this single mathematical concept. She can use any or all of this information to inform her future instruction with her prekindergarteners. With the formal assessment, Ms. Garcia will get the information she needs in a controlled setting only with Louis, and she can ask every child to complete the same task when she needs to collect that information. Again, she can use that information to plan for her future interactions with children. Finally, with the standardized assessment, depending on who administers it, where they administer it, and when they score the test, Ms. Garcia may or may not have immediate access to how Louis performed on the assessment. She will not know if Louis understands how to use this terminology in a real-world situation. While she will eventually have a standardized score for Louis and all the students who took the test, this information may not come when it is relevant to her as she makes her instructional plans.

Standardized Assessment

In almost every early education program across the United States, standardized assessments touch the lives of teachers and children in multiple ways. Standardized assessments compare children to other children who are similar in some way—developmentally or in their level of schooling. Such assessments require teachers to follow the same procedures for conducting the test with each child, using a testing manual. Each child is asked to do the same thing in the same way. Their performance usually generates a score that is either compared to the scores of a specific population of people or compared to a set of knowledge and skills the child is to know at a particular point in his life.

There are three types of standardized exams in early childhood settings. *Standardized achievement tests* measure what children have learned in school in general or in specific content areas like reading or math. *Standardized aptitude tests* are designed to predict future performance (like the SATs). *Individualized screening* or *diagnostic tests* are used to identify whether a child has a developmental delay or is at risk for a possible learning issue—these are often the first step in a sequence of assessments that might identify a child as having a special learning or developmental need.

Across all three of these assessments is the assumption that the same test for every child is appropriate and will provide the required information needed to make an educational decision. Such an understanding of assessment fails to account for the variation that exists among children—cultural, familial, linguistic, socioeconomic, and so on. Moreover, there appears to be an underlying belief that everyone thinks about the children's achievement in the same way, which is not the case.

VARYING CONCEPTIONS OF STUDENT ACHIEVEMENT

One of the biggest challenges for early educators teaching in high-stakes contexts is that under SBA reforms student achievement is considered differently than it typically is in the early childhood field (Brown 2011). Under these reforms, student achievement is thought about in absolute rather than developmental terms. When stakeholders talk about student achievement, they typically define it as a set score a child must get on a criterion-referenced standardized exam. This definition of academic achievement does not reflect what children have learned or how they have developed since entering an early education program. Rather, it reflects whether the children have obtained the skills and knowledge policy makers have prioritized in their SBA reforms.

But in early childhood settings, the goal is to support each child working toward her developmental and educational goals. While teachers are to have end-of-year or end-of-program goals for every child, the process and timetable to achieve those goals varies. Thus, the expectation is not for all children to achieve the same level of performance at the same time. Rather, teachers assess and monitor children's achievement to adapt their instruction and provide children with learning experiences that develop their individual skills and knowledge in relation to empirically based norms of development.

Early educators working in high-stakes environments must recognize that a conceptual mismatch over the construct of student achievement more than likely exists within their teaching context (Brown 2009b). Early educators must make sure that they and those with whom they work understand the purpose of the assessment being given and what the students' test scores are to display. For example, is it a score all children must attain, or should the teacher expect to see a range of scores, which would suggest varying levels of conceptual/skill attainment? Early educators and their colleagues must also ensure that they view student achievement appropriately. If all children are to attain a specific standardized score, they must work toward ensuring that all children attain that score. They cannot employ a developmental understanding of student achievement whereby they expect some children to fail to attain that score. Moreover, early education teachers, administrators, and other colleagues must come together and explicitly discuss how their assessment measures are connected to their varying conceptualizations of student achievement and what this means for their students' education. These conversations must be meaningful and ongoing, allowing educators time to reflect and revise their curriculum, teaching strategies, and learning experiences.

How Constant Assessment Affects Instruction

To engage in RIGOROUS DAP, early educators must ensure their practices align with the sociocultural, individual, and developmental needs of the children in their classrooms. To do this, we need to assess our students constantly. To define ongoing assessment, we turn to the work of Joanne Weiss and her cycle of instructional improvement. Weiss (2007) offers five steps involved in this cycle.

First, early educators need to set their instructional goals and then align their resources to them. To do this, teachers should possess a professional knowledge base that includes information about how children learn and develop, as well as recognize the importance that children's culture plays in their lives and learning. It also requires early educators to understand their individual students' learning process and experiences, strengths, needs, preferences, and interests. Early childhood educators must have positive relationships with students and their families to learn more about children's lives and experiences, as well as understand parents' expectations and sociocultural practices.

With all this in mind, early educators plan and set instructional goals, and then the second step within Weiss's cycle of instructional improvement is for them to interact with their students to teach and facilitate these goals they've set. Third, they collect data and share what they find with their students to help them monitor their learning. After the learning activity, the fourth step is for early educators to analyze and reflect on the data they collected.

The last step involves them using the information they've collected to create plans of action—possibly to move forward, reteach/revisit, or take a step back because the children lacked the required experiences or background knowledge to engage in the planned learning experience effectively. For example, Ms. Garcia first wanted to see what Louis (and his classmates) knew about *more* or *less*. With this in mind, she revisited the concept by discussing and graphing students' responses to a survey question they answered as they arrived in the classroom—"Do you like pepperoni pizza?" She continued to monitor whether students grasped this idea through documenting children's conversations across the next few days using anecdotal observations. These anecdotal observations were brief written descriptions describing scenarios in which the students made comments about *more* or *less*, and based on that information, Ms. Garcia planned for future instruction.

Weiss's cycle demonstrates how assessment is a central part of teaching young children. Across each day, teachers who engage in RIGOROUS DAP observe, document, and reflect on their students' development and learning. In other words, assessment is a constant process. Because of this, you will see a range of performance levels among your students across all their developmental domains. For example, you may see children who can read but don't know how to interact in a small group, and you must try to provide instruction that will move all your children forward in each domain.

We know many of you are in teaching contexts like Ms. Melching and Ms. Demling, where a range of policies constrict your instruction—be it at the school, district, or state level. Moreover, these reforms often frame children as lacking in some way, which can lead to using assessment tools to find out what's missing. We think one of your primary goals should be to remember that children are brilliant and capable, and they come to school with a range of assets that will help them learn and thrive in your classroom.

Additionally, assessing your students constantly assists you in knowing whether you are reaching all of them and pushing them forward in their learning. For example, as we pointed out in chapter 4, when working with English language learners, you need to monitor their development in their first and second languages on a consistent basis. Doing so will allow you to plan for instructional activities that are aligned to the children's levels of proficiency in both languages and target specific areas in which they may need additional support.

Teachers often conduct informal assessments either to quickly check whether children are learning certain concepts, such as sink or float, or to document a specific skill or domain that appears on their students' report cards; for example, asking a child to count as high as she can. Both formal and informal assessments are important and can provide information to help you with your teaching. Still, these moments of capturing children's skills and knowledge are often isolated events that do not tap into your daily instruction and interactions with children. One way you can develop your understanding of your students' knowledge and skills is to take some time after a lesson or at the end of the day and ask yourself two questions: (1) what did you learn about your students that day, and (2) how effective were your instructional ideas in helping students achieve the goals you set for them? In our work with preservice teachers, asking these questions helped them gain insight into children's academic, social, and emotional skills and needs, as well as the effectiveness of their instruction. For example, after Ms. Reynold's social studies lesson, she commented that several students were excited to talk about family travel. She decided to talk to these students about the places they had visited outside of their home with their families (be it a local hardware store or a different city) to see if she could incorporate some of their expertise and experiences into her future lessons.

IMPORTANT ISSUES TO CONSIDER WHEN ASSESSING CONSTANTLY

The purpose of assessment is to improve instruction so you are *Pushing every child forward*. To do that, you must discover what your students know, the learning standards or the curriculum goals of your program, and the expectations of children's families. You are always assessing in relation to something—that something can be an immediate, short-term, or long-term goal. It can be academic, developmental (physical, social, emotional), or personal, which includes the needs and wants of children's families. It is important to be familiar with the assessment procedures you may be required to use or implement across the school year: What does this data offer you, and when might you receive it? Remember, by implementing RIGOROUS DAP your goal is to create an environment that engages children in learning experiences that reflect who they are as learners, while at the same motivating them to strive to know more.

Second, when assessing children, you must recognize that what you know about them is incomplete. You must reach out to others in their lives to get to know your students better—be it family members, previous teachers, or other members of their communities. Moreover, when you start to assess children's development and learning, you must frame your conceptions of children as fluid. Carlina Rinaldi (2006) reminds us that when documenting student learning you are capturing your ideas of the children; you gather the information you are looking for in your attempt to make sense of children as learners. Thus, you must ensure that you are sensitive to children's linguistic and sociocultural differences. For example, many cultures hold teachers in high regard (such as Korean culture), and therefore children may be shy, quiet, or nonverbal when first interacting with you. If your school or program requires you to assess children's skills and knowledge on the first few days of class, the data you collect may not reflect what children know, because they are not yet comfortable interacting with you.

You also cannot hold on to preconceived notions of children while ignoring what you find through the assessment process. For instance, we have found for ourselves and through discussions with our colleagues that getting beyond our first impressions of children can be very difficult, particularly when we start to assess them academically. You must be honest with yourself and recognize your inherent biases when collecting and analyzing data. As you collect data about your students, you must be ready to accept or reject ideas based on your analysis of the data you collect, not based on your personal (and often superficial) opinions or beliefs. To help avoid these biases, we suggest that you check in with colleagues, the child's family, and in some cases, the child herself, to discuss what you notice in the child's learning and development. By conferring with others, you keep your biases in check and hold yourself accountable.

Third, you will need to decide how to organize and collect the data necessary to be an effective teacher; you will use this information to plan for your day-to-day instruction as well as your monthly and yearly goals. Many teachers develop portfolios. These portfolios can be paper-based or digital. Review any information from previous teachers or families. Set aside time each day to organize, analyze, and reflect on the data you collected from your students.

You must think about how to organize information to document and evaluate children, be it for a report card or end-of-the-year summary, as well as share this information with families and others. Some schools or programs have formal report cards that dictate what you specifically need to document on a regular basis. If not, children's development is typically organized by some mixture of developmental domains and specific academic skills/content domains; for instance, personal/social development, language and literacy skills, mathematical thinking, scientific thinking, social studies, the arts, physical development, and so on. Be aware of these requirements as you document children's learning.

If you are purposeful and well organized in your assessment of your students, you will be better able to carefully and thoughtfully analyze your students' performance and development. Doing so will help you recognize which of your instructional strategies are most effective in general and specifically for each student. Furthermore, monitoring student achievement will help you become aware of when there are mismatches between the curricular content and the instructional strategies you are using and children's differing levels of development, learning styles, or cultural knowledge.

Fifth, we must consider the type of feedback we want to give children based on the data we collect and analyze in relation to their performance in our classrooms. Within a dynamic understanding of children's development and learning, we must understand the purpose of assessing children. Accordingly, we should provide feedback on children's learning to improve their conceptual understandings of the content, skills, and knowledge covered. Encourage your students to consider how and why they were successful at something, not just the fact that they were successful. Your goal is to teach children how to offer process-oriented feedback rather than person-oriented feedback (such as "Your drawing of this dog included details showing it is a Boston terrier, and I know that you worked hard on this" versus "You're a good artist"). Our goal as teachers and for our students is to focus on the process, which includes effort and strategy, rather than the product.

Finally, we must consider how to include children in the assessment process—in relation to themselves as learners and in relation to their interactions with classmates. Children can self-assess by helping us select the work they want us to share with their families. Research has shown that children who are involved in their own assessment have improved levels of performance and empowerment (Goldhaber and Anthony 2007). We also need to teach students how to offer their classmates feedback on their learning. For instance, in Ms. Tily's second grade classroom, the students engage in a writer's workshop activity where children share their stories and their classmates respond to these stories. Ms. Tily gives them sentence stems, which she has posted on the wall near the author's chair to help students give feedback to their classmates. Some of these stems include I appreciate how you . . . ; I noticed that you . . . ; I am wondering what you mean by . . . ; How did you come up with . . . ; and Have you thought about . . . Ms. Tily's goal is for her students to learn to talk with one another about their work in a constructive and supportive manner.

Tools You Can Use to Assess Children Constantly

You can use a range of tools to assist you in *Reaching all children, Revisiting new content, Offering challenges, Understanding each learner, Differentiating instruction, Assessing constantly,* and *Pushing every child forward.* Each tool provides limited information about the child as a learner, and thus varied learning situations require different tools. With any assessment, consider your objectives and goals, be it the goals of the program, mandated curricula, or state standards. Knowing what you are looking for when you assess children is essential. Again, your goal should be to collect information on children using several different sources and organize them in a way that helps you interpret as well as reveal the strengths and growth areas of each child.

To help you consider how to investigate, capture, and reflect on children's learning, we have organized these tools so you can easily recognize what each offers regarding your learning about the children in the classroom, as seen in table 6.1.

TABLE 6.1
Tools for Observing and Documenting Children's Learning

Capturing and recording children's learning

- anecdotal observations
- learning videos
- learning photos
- note taking/running records
- frequency counts
- time samples
- checklists

Collecting evidence reflecting children's learning

- work samples

Inquiring into children's learning

- documenting conversations with children
- eliciting specific responses

Reflecting on children's learning

- reflection notes

We supply you with so many tools because each one provides certain information, which may or may not align with what you need to document. For instance, figure 6.1 is a learning picture of Chris's youngest daughter, Lucille, reading a book. Think about what this learning photo tells us. What doesn't it tell us?

When looking at the picture, we see that Lucille appears to have an interest in this book, is holding it the proper way, and is engaged with the physical

FIGURE 6.1
Lucille reading a book

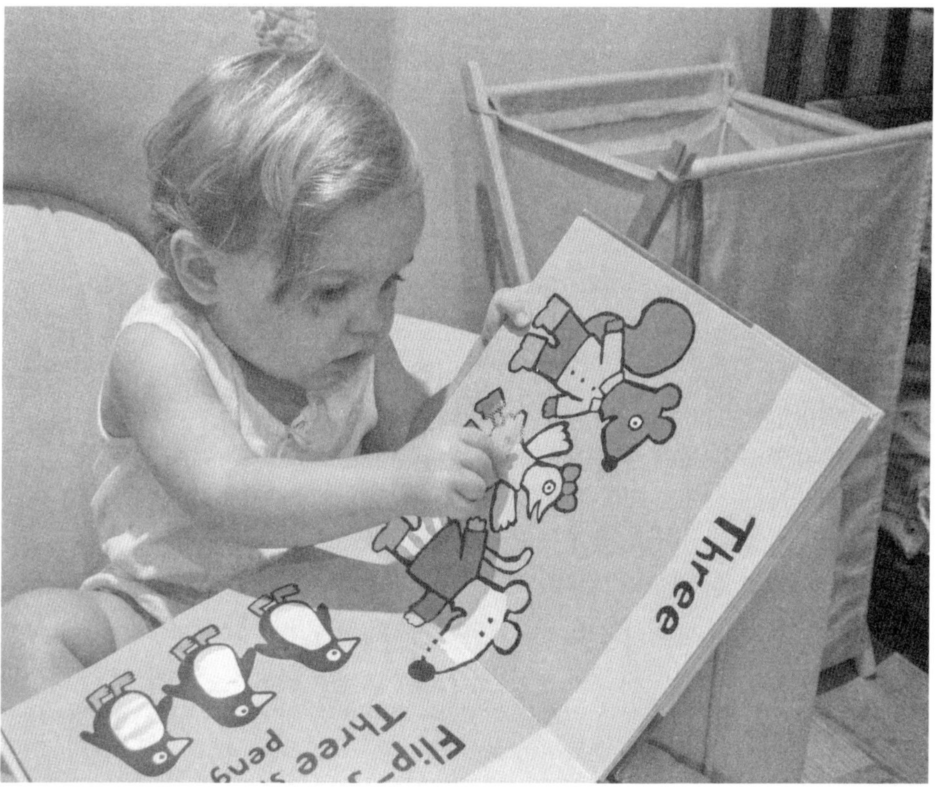

materials (a pink skirt) for children to interact with as they read. Still, the picture cannot tell us if she is reading, whether someone placed the book in her hands in the correct manner, or whether she stayed engaged with the text. To assess constantly, we need to have the right tools for the job.

The focus should be on learning behaviors rather than uniqueness, beauty, or entertainment. Capturing cuteness is not the purpose of these tools. The purpose is to learn from watching children, so your focus needs to be on what the children are doing and what this tells you about them regarding knowledge, skills, and experience. Your purpose as their educator is to deepen your knowledge and understanding of each child as a learner, and with this knowledge and understanding to improve your teaching and increase your students' growth and development.

CAPTURING AND RECORDING CHILDREN'S LEARNING

Part of coming to understand the children you work with as learners requires you to document and record that learning as it occurs. Maximize your chances for seeing a particular behavior by knowing when or possibly how a child might display the skill at certain points across the day or in specific learning situations.

Other times children will display their knowledge and skills in an unexpected manner, and thus you must be ready to document that event.

Anecdotal Observations

One tool often employed by early childhood educators is anecdotal observations. Here is an example of one:

> CHILD'S NAME: Stephanie (a kindergartener)
>
> DATE: 5/4/21
>
> The students were working in small groups using two different colors of blocks to make A/B patterns using alternate colors—red, green, red, green. Stephanie immediately used her blocks to show the pattern I asked for. Once she made the pattern, she had some extra green blocks and did not use them. When I asked her about it, she said she did not have any more reds, so she couldn't make the pattern longer. This example shows how Stephanie is meeting the pre-K standard that asks children to create, recognize, and build on patterns.

Anecdotal observations are written descriptions of your students either making a statement or engaging in an incident or situation that provides insight into their development and learning. Such observations allow you to record and share with parents, students, and other stakeholders meaningful learning experiences and children's emerging skills. They also provide you with important information about future learning goals. In the above example, we provide an anecdotal observation about Stephanie's understanding of patterns. You would include this information in her learning portfolio to demonstrate that Stephanie is meeting academic expectations for understanding patterns in math for pre-K.

With anecdotal observations, teachers record these incidents in various ways (on sticky notes, tablets, note cards, clipboards, laptops, and so on) with as much information as needed to capture the moment and discuss what it reveals about the child as a learner. By having this information, teachers are not only documenting what children can know and do, but they are also planning for future instruction in the classroom. The teacher considers what is next for Stephanie's mathematical learning in relation to grade-level expectations from the above note and might offer her opportunities to create more complex patterns (such as ABC or ABCD patterns).

To use anecdotal observations effectively requires that you pay attention to what is going on in your classroom and know what is of significance. Maintain an attitude of readiness because you cannot predict when something significant might happen. Anecdotal observations are most helpful when they are written down as soon as possible after an incident occurs, which helps you capture and record direct quotes of children's own language and specific, meaningful details.

How do you know something is significant? The significance is dependent on the child, the curriculum, the program, and your interests as their teacher. For example, it is significant to note a child's developing understanding of specific academic concepts, such as Stephanie's explanation of how patterns work. It's also significant to document social, emotional, physical, and cultural/community growth, such as a child sharing a personal item with a classmate for the first time.

When doing an anecdote, be sure to include as much detail as possible (you'll be surprised by how much you forget). Capture the child's words or actions as precisely as you can, and then provide a brief discussion of what this anecdote reveals about the child as a learner, which can mean discussing her actions in relation to grade-level, class, or familial expectations.

Learning Videos

In the past decade, advances in digital technology, such as digital cameras, smartphones, and tablets, have altered the teaching, learning, and assessment process with young children. These devices allow teachers to capture a significant amount of data with relative ease. When using these devices, remember that your goal is to gain insight into children's learning. While capturing and sharing performances or special occasions with children and their families helps build community, it may not necessarily help you in planning for effective instruction with young children.

With learning videos, you can capture children in real-life situations in your classroom. For instance, recording Louis building with blocks in the block center shows him applying his cognitive skills in a real-life situation, such as using the terms *more* or *less* or other mathematical terms like *under, above,* or *next to*. It also allows you to see how he fosters relationships with his classmates as they build together, and how he uses his fine- and gross-motor skills to create his structure. Unlike anecdotal records, you can capture most of the details of an interaction in a learning video.

Other ways you can use learning videos are to capture the children performing such academic skills as reading a book or having a conversation with their classmates about why they think a feather will float and a penny will not.

Learning videos can provide insight into many different aspects of children's growth and development, but you must be careful when using them. You should have an intended purpose when taking any video, and most often the best time to use such videos is during child-directed learning experiences, such as free choice or independent work time. Using a learning video when you are providing direct instruction or leading a lesson often does not provide the information you are looking for. Moreover, when you pull out a video camera, children notice—so be prepared for some canned performances (like making silly faces or being overly dramatic) the first time you use this tool. Being spontaneous and inconspicuous when using this tool to document student learning can be difficult, and recording can disrupt children when they are doing their work. Still, the more you document student learning by using videos, the more comfortable children will become with you recording in your classroom.

You will need to record why you took that video on some other form of documentation—a sticky note, digital note, or piece of paper. Remember, you want to record what the video tells you about the children as learners. Also, be sure to date (either in the video or on your documentation) when the event occurred. That will allow you to make comparisons across the school year.

With any digital documentation, you must consider two key issues. The first is whether you have permission from families to document learning through these devices. Each program is different, and if you work in a public-school setting, your school, district, or program more than likely will have specific policies you must follow to collect this type of data. Second, consider how you are going to store as well as share this information in a safe and secure way. Again, many early learning environments already have rules and equipment in place, but if not, these are decisions you will need to make.

Learning Photographs

Like a learning video, a learning photo shows the child involved in the process of learning—meaning the focus is on the action and not the product. If your focus is on the product, the photo becomes a work sample. Moreover, if the picture is of the child sharing the work rather than doing the work, it is no longer a learning photo and is simply a performance. A learning photo depicts a child working hard on a project, and a work sample depicts the finished project.

To use learning photos, the teacher must be aware of what children are engaged in and take advantage of those moments, which technology makes easy. Like learning videos, a key drawback with learning photos is that because a picture captures a single moment, teachers need to typically record what the photo demonstrates and why they took that photo on some other form of documentation. Again, the goal in using this tool is to gain insight into the child as a learner, and thus this is what you need to record alongside the photo.

We want to make one last point about learning photos and learning videos. While we present these tools as vehicles that help you document children's learning, we want you also to recognize that you should be sharing this information with families on a regular basis—not just during conferences. In our experience, families truly enjoy being kept up to date on their child's learning, and it can be quite easy to share what you're documenting without much effort. Doing so will further develop the bond you are trying to establish with families and their children.

Note Taking or Running Records

The process of note taking or writing running records is somewhat similar to the process of recording anecdotal observations, but rather than focusing on one primary event, you document learning as it occurs over a period of time. It begins with selecting a child to watch and an observation period (say, three minutes or ten minutes). Watch the child and write down everything the child is doing during the observation period.

Record what the child is experiencing, doing, and saying within that designated period. Say you want to document how the child engages with materials, the curriculum, and other children. To find this information, pay attention to the child's facial expressions, movements, tone of voice, interactions with peers, adults, materials, and so on.

In some cases, you may simply be interested in how the child does things. You may be curious as to what Lupe does during math centers or what Nicholas does during recess. With note taking or writing running records, you simply document the child's experience. By doing so, you have data you can go back to and analyze to possibly change your instruction, offer children specific support or guidance, or just be aware of how children interact with one another on a particular activity. Taking such notes or running records can be done during the learning encounter or right after the encounter has occurred. To take notes or complete a running record, you will need to use a recording system—either a notebook, laptop, or tablet. You will also need to plan to observe the children in your classroom on a regular basis, in a variety of settings, during different times of the day, and on different days.

Note taking helps you focus on what students are learning through the various activities they engage in across the day. Moreover, when rereading and analyzing your notes, you will learn about each student in relation to the goals you have set for them over time, be it for the day, week, month, or year. Speaking to the learning process within the note or record is essential.

Frequency Counts

At times in your teaching it feels a like a child is engaging in a particular behavior on a constant basis: "Why is Joanna always interrupting the other children as they play in the block center, even when she's not working in that center?" or "Why is Kelli always out of her seat during writer's workshop?" A frequency count provides you a tool to document how often a particular behavior is actually occurring. Such data is easy to collect and quite convincing to you, the child, and the family. You may also find out that what you think is *always* or *often* may not be the case. Either way, documenting the behavior is a first step in addressing the issue at hand. If Kelli is getting out if her seat during writer's workshop as much as you think, you then need to figure out why. You may also need to discuss this issue with her and her family to gain insight on how you can support Kelli during this activity. Remember, Kelli's behavior—getting out of her seat—is telling you that something is not working for her during the workshop. You, with Kelli, need to address that issue for her to attend to the task at hand.

Begin by identifying a child and behavior that you are interested in understanding and assessing. Use a set period (circle time, nap, free play—whenever you think the behavior is frequently happening). Make a tally mark on paper or a digital document every time the behavior occurs. You do not need to write any details or explanations of what is occurring. Simply focus on counting the observable behavior. As you do these counts, be sure to label your document with the observable behavior, the date you observed the behavior, and the child's name. Store the information with your other observation tools.

Time Samples

Sometimes you will have questions about how children in the classroom spend their time during choice time or when you've asked them to complete a work activity or a project with their classmates. Time samples are a means for tracking and documenting those experiences. Time samples help reveal the regularity and frequency of a given behavior in a specific time slot. By documenting such behaviors, you will see how the child is using his time, whether he can stay on task, and whom he interacts with during a period of small- or whole-group work.

To do a time sample, you will need to create a form for recording information—either on paper or digitally.

Student:

Date:

Time of day sample was taken:

Time	Child's Actions
9:00	
9:05	
9:10	
9:15	

To begin a time sample, select a child, a time period (circle time, nap, free play) for your observation and an interval for observing (three, five, or ten minutes). Check on the child at every interval and record what he is doing in the appropriate box on the form. Date and label the information. Store the information with your other records. This process can be time and labor intensive and difficult to use while teaching, so you may wish to use this tool when you know you will have others in your classroom to help you.

While time samples and frequency counts are similar tools, a time sample is documentation that is prompted by the clock. During the allotted time, you write down what is happening, even if it does not connect to what you are hoping to assess. Frequency counts are prompted by the child's behavior; if the child demonstrates the designated behavior, you write it down. Time samples and frequency counts allow you to chart your data in different ways—particularly using different types of software on computers. For instance, you can turn your counts into a bar graph or a pie chart. This graphical representation allows you to display your data in a way that helps you monitor and understand what the child is doing as a learner within your classroom.

Each tool gives you a different view of the child. Time samples allow you to check in with the child every certain number of minutes over a period of time and document what he's doing. With note taking, you watch the child constantly for a specific period and document everything you see. Time samples are a little less labor intensive, but they do not give a clear indication of what the child is doing in between those time intervals.

COLLECTING EVIDENCE REFLECTING CHILDREN'S LEARNING

Coming to understand the children you work with as learners requires you to collect evidence that reflects children's learning. Unlike capturing and recording children's learning, this process requires you simply to collect data as children generate it across the day and then document what that data shows regarding children's learning.

A work sample is a piece or picture of a child's work that documents student learning and offers insight into the student as a learner. Such work not only captures the knowledge and skills of the child but also provides guidance on where your instruction should be headed with this child. Children generate work samples from the activities they do every day in your early learning setting. These samples could be a writing activity, structure, or pattern children generate during play. Such work samples help you see how children apply their skills and knowledge to real-world challenges in the classroom. We often take pictures of children's work because they want to take their work home or the work they are completing is temporary—for example, a block structure or a performance.

When selecting work samples, look for evidence that demonstrates student learning. These work samples may not be children's best work, and as often is the case, they will not capture all the skills or gaps in children's learning; that's why it's necessary to collect multiple examples.

Figure 6.2 is an example of Camille's writing in her first month of kindergarten. In the sample, we can see how she is learning to write her name as well as Amber's. She uses upper- and lowercase letters interchangeably, and with her drawing, she has created a representation of herself and Amber. These are

FIGURE 6.2

A work sample of Camille's writing, 09/02/2021

"headwalkers," meaning they have no bodies, just legs, have clear faces and rather large arms with no hands. The picture does not show how well she understands individual letter sounds, but it is clear she knows that words have meaning and contain letters. She uses this drawing to represent text—herself and Amber. Finally, her fine-motor skills seem to be on grade level, and she can form letters and draw images that represent her thinking. As Camille's teacher, you might begin to talk with her more about how to improve her illustrations—drawing the entire body—as well as introducing how to use capital and lowercase letters in her writing.

While collecting work samples is a relatively easy form of documenting children's learning—you are simply selecting a piece of a child's work—the goal of capturing a child's learning is more difficult than it sounds. When choosing a work sample, ask yourself, what does this sample reflect in relation to the child's learning? If you cannot answer that question, do not pick that sample. If you decide to pick the sample, be sure to write the date and what the sample reveals about the child's learning on the back of the piece, on a sticky note, or on a digital document.

We want to be clear that work samples are not informal assessments, such as a checklist of how many numbers a child knows or a spelling test. While that information is important to your instruction, it provides a different type of information and occurs in teacher-directed and tightly structured learning scenarios. When thinking back to our example of Ms. Garcia at the beginning of the chapter, such tools provide a different type of insight into your students as learners.

Work samples help make children's learning visible to you, to the child, and to others. Having such documentation of children's learning allows you not only to plan for your instruction but to have the chance to share students' growth with children and their families. This documentation allows you to help them see the importance of children's work and include them in the curriculum. Finally, by sharing this information with them, you provide an opportunity for both the child and the family member to think about the work the child is producing.

INQUIRING INTO CHILDREN'S LEARNING

The third way you can understand your students as learners flips the script in that instead of simply observing or collecting evidence reflecting children's work, you discuss the children's learning directly with them. To do this effectively requires you to have a good relationship with your students so they feel you are trying to learn about them rather than interrogate them.

Documenting Conversations with Children

We know there are many times across your day when you may not understand how a child is thinking about his work or how he is attempting to solve a problem or complete a task. In other instances, a child may make a statement that causes you to wonder where it came from, or perhaps you see a child responding to a statement in a way you don't understand. It's these moments when you should consider engaging in a conversation with the child about his thinking. Systematically documenting your conversations with children about an issue you are curious about or a topic you're studying with them can be very useful.

Begin by asking a question about what the child is thinking, and then document his answer with audio or video, or by writing it down. To be clear, these conversations should be brief. You are working with young children, so keep your exchange short and to the point. For instance, simply ask a child to explain his thinking about a problem he has solved.

Documenting conversations with children is the only way you can incorporate the child's explanations and beliefs about his own learning into your understanding of the child. By talking with him in an intentional manner, meaning you have a question about his learning you want answered, you include the child's voice into your conceptions of teaching.

Eliciting Specific Responses

In certain situations, it's perfectly fine to elicit a specific response from a child about a particular issue. For instance, you may want to know whether a child understood the ending of a story you read in a shared reading activity with the class. Thus, as you transition into the next activity, you pull the child aside and ask for her to tell how she thought the story ended. Other types of questions you might ask include yes or no questions, sentence extensions (such as, "The sound the letter *B* makes is . . . ?"), and so on. No matter what you ask, consider how you document these responses.

Note that this type of assessment is not an endorsement of quizzing or putting children on the spot. Instead, you may need to document moments across the day that demonstrate particular areas of learning for a progress report or report card. For instances like these, the most efficient way to get what you need and move on in your instruction may be to elicit a specific response. Still, be cautious when using this tool. Remember, you do not want the child to feel as if you are interrogating her, and if a child does not respond to your question or complete the task, it may not be because she doesn't know but rather that she didn't want to respond.

REFLECTING ON CHILDREN'S LEARNING

The final practice we want to discuss in this chapter is the process of reflecting on children's learning. We know you may already do this on a regular basis, but we want to show you how to document such reflection to include it in the cycle of instructional improvement. As you reflect, you often have insights, ideas, or questions about your students, and a reflective note allows you to put down your insights and ideas either on paper or digitally for future reference.

Reflective notes, as shown in figure 6.3, are meant to be descriptive, rich, and thoughtful. Your goal is to generate ideas, ponder issues, and think hard about the child and the situation. With this, as with any documentation tool, it is essential that your notes are dated so you can see how your ideas and understandings develop over time. By documenting this thinking, you are providing an evidence trail of children's learning within your classroom, as well as recording how that child's thinking changes as you work together across the school year.

Reflective notes are *your* thoughts about what is happening in the classroom. These notes differ from anecdotal observation in that those observations are a record of something the child did specifically. Because reflective notes are your own thoughts, they do not have to be about a specific incident. Rather, they are a tool that systematically documents your thinking about each child in your classroom on an individual basis across the school year.

FIGURE 6.3
A reflective note

Reflective Note:

1/22/2019

After looking at the paper Michelle had been writing, I noticed she worked very hard and filled the entire page with developmental writing. I wonder if she remembers what she wrote. I wrote the word *sorry* for her, which she asked me to do, and then she started writing for her own purpose. Will she choose writing as an activity if she has other options or only when it is the expected activity? I wonder what might happen if we add some new stationery to the writing center. Also, she is still grasping the pencil with all her fingers laying across her palm, so I need to continue helping her to develop her fine-motor skills to improve her finger strength.

Your goal should be to incorporate this, or any of the tools described, into your teaching practice to develop a complete picture of each child as a member of your learning community. Remember that while each tool has a specific purpose and gives a different view of the child as a learner, all these tools can help you with your instruction. You will use these tools to focus in on the child as a learner, and the information you gather throughout the various assessments can be used to help you improve your instruction so that it meets the needs of your students.

Assessment within the Cycle of Instructional Improvement

The purpose of assessing children constantly is to ensure you meet children's needs as learners. You need to use the information you collect to plan for learning opportunities that support children's continued progress and development in the classroom. Moreover, good assessment creates a vivid portrait of each child as a learner. This picture is more meaningful and informative than a checklist or report card. It captures what makes the child unique and special, and demonstrates how well you know the child and how much you care about teaching him as effectively as possible.

Beyond coming to know the children in your program more closely, documenting student learning also helps you make instructional decisions within your classroom. It lets you know what is and is not working within the curriculum so you can make changes to better meet the needs of your students, such as eliminating an expected prekindergarten unit on primary colors because all your students already know and understand their primary colors. These tools also help you understand whether your instructional practices are effective with the children with whom you are working. As you know, just because an activity or teaching strategy worked with children in the past does not mean it will automatically work again in the future. Finally, monitoring student achievement provides you with the documentation you need to communicate effectively with children and their families about the child's learning. Such communication is essential for your learning community to grow in a positive manner.

Pushing Your Own Learning Forward

As you go about assessing children's learning with these tools, you will have to experiment and find what works for you. We each have our preferences, and while each tool provides a different insight, we know that the realities of your teaching context may also influence which tools are more or less accessible. Moreover, as you observe and document children using these tools, ask yourself: Why is this important? How does it connect to what I saw early in the day, week, year? What action should I take next to change or improve either my instruction or the curriculum we're covering?

Establish a routine or find common points across the week when you can intentionally focus on student learning and record observations. That means planning for assessment in the classroom, moments to reflect on the information you collect, and moments to organize and arrange this data in a useful manner.

It's also important as you collect data using these different tools that you set aside time weekly to go back and reflect on what you observed. Collecting data from three or four children each day ensures you can plan for students' emerging needs. If you have a portfolio system, going through the work you've collected for five or six students at the end of each week will allow you to be aware of how your students are learning, growing, and struggling on a consistent basis.

No matter how you decide to systematically document children's learning in your classroom, take the time to step back from the daily practice of teaching and reflect on what's happening. While this takes time away from the other tasks that demand your time and attention, this time is well spent. Thinking intimately about, planning for, and even questioning how particular students are learning in your classroom will help you make better planning, pedagogical, and assessment decisions in the future.

Reexamining Why We Should Monitor Students' Achievement

- When you hear the word *assessment*, how do you feel? Why do you think that is, and how do your thoughts influence your teaching of young children?
- Discuss with your colleagues how to document student learning within your early education setting. Describe your goals in relation to engaging in these assessment practices. What areas would you like to improve on?

Extending Your Learning

- Resources that examine a range of assessment practices with young children include the sixth edition of *Assessing and Guiding Young Children's Development and Learning* by Oralie McAfee, Deborah J. Leong, and Elena Bodrova and the second edition of *Alternative Approaches to Assessing Young Children* by Angela Losardo and Angela Syverson.
- NAEYC provides a range of position statements on key issues affecting early childhood. They have position statements on curriculum, assessment, program evaluation (www.naeyc.org/files/naeyc/file/positions/StandCurrAss.pdf), and assessing English language learners (www.naeyc.org/files/naeyc/file/positions/WWSEnglishLanguageLearnersWeb.pdf).
- Herbert P. Ginsburg wrote a text on how to interview young children called *Entering the Child's Mind: The Clinical Interview in Psychological Research and Practice*. While the book is academic in nature, it provides a detailed description of how to talk with children so that you understand how they are cognitively constructing their worlds. Ginsburg provides insight into the state of mind a teacher should have when talking with children about their learning, as well as provides examples of how to discuss their learning so the teacher can identify what the child does and does not know.

Steps You Can Take toward Change

- Draw two columns on a piece of paper. On one side, create a list of all the assessment strategies listed in this chapter that you engage in with your students on a regular basis. On the other side, develop a list of assessment strategies you would like to implement in your classroom and what it would require to do so.
- Take time to learn about why your program or school implements specific standardized assessments of children's learning and development. Find out what specifically these tools are designed to measure and whether the information collected from them is used in a way that reflects what these tests are designed to do.
- Several free apps are available to facilitate formative assessment using a phone or tablet within your classroom. Flipgrid (https://info.flipgrid.com) is a tool for student engagement and formative assessment. Recap (https://letsrecap.com) allows teachers to gather video evidence of student learning. Kiddom (www.kiddom.co) helps teachers plan, analyze, and assess learning. Nearpod (https://nearpod.com) offers teachers the freedom to create, engage, and assess through a mobile device. Peergrade (www.peergrade.io) is a tool to facilitate peer assessment. Select a few to try out with you colleagues, test them, and see if they might help you with assessing and teaching your students.

7

Integrating Content Areas through Quality Educational Experiences

Ms. Saunders began her investigation into seeds and plants with her kindergarteners by going on a neighborhood walk on a warm spring morning. Two parent volunteers accompanied her and her class. She had the students bring the class digital camera, science journals, and pencils. She began the walk by reminding the class they were scientists going on an exploration to investigate and document the plants living in their community. She also asked them to pay attention to these plants and think about whether they were similar to or different from the plants they read about earlier that week in Eric Carle's The Tiny Seed *or Lois Ehlert's* Planting a Rainbow.

As the students walked through the neighborhood, Ms. Saunders occasionally stopped and pointed out specific plants and trees to the students. "This is an oak tree—check out the horizontal grooves in its bark and the shape of the leaves." "This is a dandelion—you can tell by its flower." "This is a prickly pear cactus—notice it's long needles and pear-shaped leaves." She asked the students if the trees and plants they saw around their school looked like what they saw around their homes.

Josephine said that at her house, her mother had planted a garden, and Juan said that his father had to cut down a big tree because it was dead. Ms. Saunders extended these points by asking Josephine what types of plants her mother had in her garden and asking Juan if he knew what caused the tree to die and what his dad had done with all the dead branches and the trunk of the tree. As she used this vocabulary, she reminded the children that the trunk of a tree is like their bodies, the branches are like their arms and legs, and the bark is like their skin.

Halfway through the walk they came to a park, and Ms. Saunders had the students stop and draw and/or write in their science journals about some of the seeds, plants, and trees they noticed. She asked them to capture the characteristics, features, and details of the plants. She also reminded them she and the parent volunteers were there as resources to help them. As the students worked in their science journals, Ms. Saunders visited with several students and recorded some anecdotal observations in her teaching notebook. For instance, Luke told Ms. Saunders that plants can grow in cracks in the sidewalk, and he wondered if there is soil under the sidewalk. Becca wrote in her journal, "THE TRES R TL." Ms. Saunders noted that during future read-alouds with the students, she would emphasize how authors use capital and lowercase letters in their writing so Becca could start to make the connection to her own writing.

As they began their walk back to school, retracing their earlier steps, Ms. Saunders asked her students to compare what they had drawn or written to what they were seeing again for the second time. She reminded them that scientists must confirm that the data they've collected matches what they actually see. But in doing so, she also noted that often when you see something a second time, you notice things you did not see before, so it's okay to add more to your writing and drawings.

After the walk, Ms. Saunders came back to the class meeting area and asked the students to share what they noticed. She wrote their statements on a large piece of chart paper. Drakar said he saw red and yellow flowers on the walk. Suzie said she saw a squirrel living in an oak tree. Ms. Saunders said, "Oh, that's interesting. So are other living things dependent on plants and seeds to live?" Suzie nodded her head, and Zack added, "We all need plants to live." Ms. Saunders asked Zack what he meant. He said, "You know, like we eat plants, and we need them to live. Like I eat salad, and my mom says I need salad to live a healthy life." Ms. Saunders said, "Oh, so you eat lettuce, which is a plant, and your mom, who cares about your health, said you need to eat healthy things like lettuce to live." Zack replied, "Yep."

After the students shared their statements with Ms. Saunders and helped her write words such as red, yellow, *and* plants, *she asked the class to reread them with her. Once finished, she noted, "I can tell that each of you knows quite a bit about plants and seeds. I am wondering if you might have some questions about plants and seeds that we should investigate further." Several children nodded their heads. Ms. Saunders continued, "I'd like you to think about those questions. In a minute or so, I am going to ask you to pair up with a neighbor and share your questions. After each of you shares your ideas, we'll come back together as a whole group and generate a class list of questions that we'd like to investigate."*

We start this chapter with Ms. Saunders's introduction to a thematic investigation into seeds and plants with her students to examine what it means to engage in RIGOROUS DAP on a regular basis with children. We'll revisit Ms. Saunders's thematic unit exploration throughout this chapter to illustrate how early educators can engage in lessons rooted in RIGOROUS DAP across their day, in a manner that integrates multiple content areas, and that reflects the sociocultural worlds in which children live. We also examine how Ms. Saunders differentiates her instruction and offers multiple types of learning experiences so children can have varied opportunities for experiencing and processing new information. By developing and fostering a learning environment that integrates academic domains through a range of instructional activities, Ms. Saunders reinforces the varied aspects of the curriculum she teaches across the day and gives her students the chance to develop the skills and knowledge necessary for future success. Our goal in this chapter is to bring together all the other chapters and put these strategies into action to give you a better understanding of how to engage in RIGOROUS DAP on a consistent basis within your instruction.

Applying RIGOROUS DAP to Ms. Saunders's Class

When we apply our conception of RIGOROUS DAP to Ms. Saunders's teaching, we notice that she initiated the class investigation into seeds and plants by sharing a collection of stories. These stories introduced the children to a range of vocabulary words and images about seeds and plants. In Eric Carle's *The Tiny Seed,* the children learned what environmental factors seeds need to grow into plants, flowers, and trees—soil, the sun, and water. This shared vision and vocabulary helped the students interact with one another and the investigation in a productive manner.

By taking the children on a neighborhood walk, Ms. Saunders offered them the chance to explore the seeds and plants that grow in their immediate community. Ms. Saunders wanted to ensure the knowledge and skills she is expected to cover in her curriculum reflects the world in which her students live, and throughout the walk she pushed the children to make connections between what they were seeing and the plants that grow where the children themselves live. The statements made by Josephine and Juan demonstrated how these children were making such connections. Moreover, a neighborhood walk offers children a multisensory learning experience that asks them to use their whole bodies to investigate this topic.

Additionally, Ms. Saunders began to introduce tier two words. Tier one words (like *cat, house,* and *girl*) rarely need to be taught and often have easy-to-understand meanings. Tier two words (like *patiently, maintain,* and *fancy*) are used frequently by fluent speakers across a variety of literacy experiences—such as reading a book or having a conversation. When Ms. Saunders asked the children to try to capture the characteristics of plants in their writing and drawing, she connected language the children will come across in reading and other science explorations. Teachers who use complex vocabulary in their interactions with children create a learning scenario that has lasting benefits to children's reading comprehension well into elementary school.

Ms. Saunders also integrated science into her instruction. This walk introduced children to how scientists study the natural world through making observations, drawing conclusions from the data they collect, and generating new questions based on what they've seen. Scientific investigations like Ms. Saunders's neighborhood walk offer children the chance to develop such skills as exploring, observing, questioning, describing, recording, using simple tools, explaining, and working collaboratively.

Across this introduction to seeds and plants, Ms. Saunders's children generated a range of work samples that demonstrated what they noticed and understand about seeds and plants. In several instances across this investigation, Ms. Saunders could use learning photos and videos to document student learning. She did generate anecdotal observations about Luke and Becca, as well as other students, to document their learning, but as always, there is room for her to grow in her instruction.

THE IMPORTANCE OF CHILDREN'S VOICE IN INSTRUCTIONAL DECISIONS

While there are many more examples of how Ms. Saunders engaged in RIGOROUS DAP with her students, we want to highlight two points. First, throughout this walk, Ms. Saunders emphasized the role of each child in his or her learning. Ms. Saunders asked the students on the walk and in the classroom to share what they were noticing, thinking about, and questioning. Such acts attempt to level the playing field within the classroom by using students' interests and questions as a guide for their investigation. Ms. Saunders also asked the children to think and then share their hypotheses in pairs before having to share with the large group. This allowed the children to test their hypotheses in a safer environment and develop relationships that fostered coinvestigation with their peers.

Finally, while the topic of seeds and plants originated from the curriculum Ms. Saunders was expected to teach, she did not allow state and district content standards to silence her students. Instead, she took this content, tied it directly to their worlds, and then asked them to generate a list of questions they wanted to investigate. By empowering her students, Ms. Saunders ensures every child has choice and voice in his learning so that he can move forward in his growth and development.

Employing Dewey's Ideas to Foster Learning

For John Dewey, the primary purpose of education is to develop children's capacity for learning. His ideas can help educators offer children choice and voice, just as Ms. Saunders did. By combining Dewey's ideas with recent brain development research, we argue that children are hardwired to learn. Dewey framed this hardwiring through what he termed *four impulses*. First, children are hardwired to be social, which includes their ability to communicate with their peers and adults, and while Dewey did not discuss this, these social actions and knowledge are rooted in children's sociocultural worlds. Second, children are hardwired to construct their understandings of their worlds through play and other cultural practices. Third, children are also hardwired to investigate those worlds. Finally, children tend to be expressive about their learning, which includes the desire to tell and represent their understandings of the world around them.

It is your responsibility to notice and foster these impulses so children develop the skills and knowledge needed to be successful in school. To do this, Dewey contended that teachers need to draw from their knowledge and insight about learning, child development, the sociocultural practices of the learning community, and the content they are expected to teach and build a bridge that connects the child to the curriculum. One way to do this is through the language we use when communicating with children. For example, in the following scenario Ms. Clements, a pre-K teacher stated, "Andy, I noticed you matched the cubes you counted to each finger on your hand. How many fingers do you have on your hand?" Andy replied, "Five." Ms. Clements continued, "So if you have five fingers and one cube for each finger, how many cubes do you have?" Andy replied, "Also five!" Ms. Clements concluded the conversation by saying, "Wow! Your finger-matching strategy really works to help you know you have exactly five cubes! That's what good problem solving looks like." In this example, Ms. Clements noticed that Andy was making use of his informal understanding about numbers (that he has five fingers) to help him keep track of and represent the cardinal value (there are five cubes altogether) of a discrete set of objects.

In our interactions with young children, we must notice what they are doing and ask them questions that extend or require them to explain their learning; for example, asking children how they found a solution or figured out a new word. Early educators need to remind children about how far they have come in their learning. During the neighborhood walk, Ms. Saunders asked the children what types of seeds or plants they noticed, which helped them focus on the purpose of the activity. Additionally, Ms. Saunders could have asked a child to explain how she drew a particular plant or seed or to describe any difficulties she had in either drawing or writing about a particular observation. The point being, it is the teacher's responsibility to be present within the learning process with children and demonstrate that presence through conversations and questioning.

Striving for Balance

A teacher's key goal is to strive for balance in her instruction. The teacher tries to incorporate the needs of the children in her classroom with the knowledge, skills, and dispositions she wants them to attain while interacting with one another. Dewey noted that teachers cannot emphasize the child's interests at the expense of the curriculum, and teachers cannot emphasize the curriculum at the expense of the child's interests and experience. Thus, the instructional opportunities you offer children must be of the highest quality, which for Dewey meant that each learning experience should be chosen with care and have meaning and purpose. Such experiences consider each child's previous experiences, present needs, and future goals, which includes his sociocultural understanding of learning. To do this requires you to be present within the learning process, actively engaged in a narrative of learning, conversing with and questioning the students, and pulling from your understandings of their sociocultural practices to help you and your students grow together as a dialogic learning community. Furthermore, it requires you to think about the types of instructional strategies you use across the day to *Push every child forward* in gaining the skills and knowledge needed to succeed in school, in the larger community, and in life.

Remember, teachers must take the long view about the learning process. View your instruction as a continuous process that builds off the past and directs the child toward future investigations. Thus, when integrating continuity into the lesson planning process, start from the children's experiences in and out of school and move forward in a thoughtful and organized way.

Finally, to know where you are leading your students, Dewey argued you must know what direction you wish to take with your instruction. For Dewey, the process of education must move the learners toward desired end states, which reflect the integration of your goals as an early educator, the goals of your school/program/learning community, and the goals of the students and their families. Your goals for your students, both short and long term, should guide your decision-making.

In sum, it is your responsibility to create learning-centered classrooms that balance the curriculum with the child's personal experiences. This insight from Dewey helps us to theoretically orient our conception of RIGOROUS DAP— it is your responsibility to ensure the direction of your instruction (*Offer choices* that *Push every child forward*) creates a continuous link between prior personal, sociocultural, and learning experiences (*Understanding each learner*) and current learning demands (*Revisiting new content* and *Integrating content areas*).

Continuing to Employ RIGOROUS DAP across the Day

As early educators who understand the importance of hearing children's voices in the rising demand for improved academic achievement, we want to spend the remainder of this chapter examining how Ms. Saunders addressed content throughout her teaching of seeds and plants. It is important not only to position your instruction in relation to the content you are expected to teach, but also in regard to how children develop and learn within their sociocultural worlds. As we examine Ms. Saunders's teaching, we pull from a range of content areas to help you recognize how her instruction taps into what we know about how children develop and learn.

TEACHING LITERACY THROUGH RIGOROUS DAP

Ensuring children develop their early literacy skills continues to be a primary focus of many early education policy makers in the United States. Our goal is for children to become logographic readers, meaning they read words rather than individual sounds or phonemes. To help children achieve this goal, we must help them first become aware of phonemes within our language system and then build on this awareness. Our goal as instructors is to develop children's phonological awareness (an awareness of units of speech such as syllables), then build phonemic awareness (manipulating individual sounds/phonemes), and then see them become phonological, and hopefully, logographic readers.

Breaking Down Language

To put children on a trajectory to become logographic readers, begin by helping them develop their listening skills so they can make distinctions in general sounds (Adams et al. 1998). You can help them develop this skill by sharing interesting objects that make different noises, or change the volume in your speech, which helps make children aware of the listening process. Next, you want to develop their rhyming skills, which helps them distinguish between sounds that are similar and different. An easy way to do this is to share poems, sing silly songs, and play games using rhyming words. From there you want to help children become aware of sentences and words. Many teachers use oak tag and sentence strip holders to help children see the individual words in a strand of poems or verses in songs. Again, provide many rich literary experiences to help children recognize the difference between sentences ("Let's make up a sentence about this picture of a dog and write it down on this sentence strip") and words (cutting up that sentence about the dog into individual words). Once students can recognize sounds (both similar and different) and have an understanding that our language system consists of sentences made up of words, we then want children to become aware of syllables. You can develop this skill by playing games, such as a version of Head, Shoulders, Knees, and Toes in which children touch one body part for each syllable they hear, or reading poems that have many multiple syllabic words. From there help children become aware of beginning and ending sounds by doing all the above, as well as using word families and other word-building activities that allow children to manipulate the sounds at the beginning and end of words. Next, address phonemes, cultivating the child's ability to match letters to individual sound units. An effective program for developing this skill is *Words Their Way* (Bear et al. 1996). The letter sorts in this program are extremely helpful in developing children's ability to distinguish between different sounds.

Building Up Language

Once you've broken down the alphabetic nature of our language, the next step is to build it back up by creating words through programs such as *Words Their Way*; providing a range of writing experiences, such as shared writing and journals; and so on. Of course, you continue helping children read words throughout this process.

We cannot overemphasize your role in these literacy experiences. You are the children's guide in so many ways. To help children develop language skills, talk to them and extend their thinking across the day. For example, notice posters or flyers announcing events, work together to determine the number of syllables in new complex words in a shared reading, emphasize the beginning sounds of the days of the week or the end of sounds in poems read in class, have students predict what a word may be as you sound it out, and so on. Try to spend as much time as you can thinking out loud and talking with your students about what you are doing.

We notice in a lot of classrooms we visit that such talk is disappearing. Rather, teachers are simply directing their children from one learning experience to the next and not engaging them in rich, meaningful conversations about what is occurring across the day. Moreover, we see fewer teachers reading poems, singing silly songs, playing language games with children (such as beginning sound bingo), and so on. Such activities truly offer children important opportunities to play with as well as better understand how language works. For instance, in Ms. Saunders's classroom, she and her students read and learned several poems about seeds and plants. One such poem was "My Garden":

This is my garden.
I will plant it with care.
Here are the seeds
I will plant in there.
The sun will shine.
The rain will fall.
The seeds will sprout
and grow up tall.

This poem provides a brief explanation of how seeds become plants and offers Ms. Saunders and her students the opportunity to engage in a range of phonological skills. These skills include listening for rhyming words, seeing sentences and words strung together to explain the life cycle of plants, drawing a clear distinction between one-syllable words and the only two-syllable word in the poem, *garden*. The poem offers opportunities to manipulate beginning and ending sounds (what happens if I change the "s" in "sun" into an "r"), and children can even identify particular phonemic sounds such as short and long vowel sounds.

By reading such poems, children come to understand how they, as writers, can communicate ideas to readers. For instance, one aspect of Ms. Saunders's teaching we find to be quite powerful is that she always wants the students to see how to improve their work as authors. With this poem and many others they read across the school year, she asks the children to add a stanza that extends the author's ideas in a new direction. In this case, they came up with the following:

Now that there are plants
We have to keep out the ants.
And in just over a week,
We'll have plenty to eat.

By extending this poem, not only does Ms. Saunders help children develop their emerging literacy skills, which vary among the students, but she also builds their confidence as writers, which helps push every child forward.

TEACHING MATH THROUGH RIGOROUS DAP

After their morning recess, Ms. Saunders's students came back to the classroom to see groups of seeds placed at each of their tables. Ms. Harrison, a parent volunteer, had come in during recess and deposited three piles of seeds at each child's seat. One pile of pinto beans, another of sunflower seeds, and a third of corn kernels. No pile was greater than six seeds, and none had fewer than three.

After the students took a drink of water and washed their hands, they took a seat on the carpet. Ms. Saunders asked the students what they had noticed when they came in the classroom. Gregory raised his hand and said, "I notice that my mom is here." Chantelle commented, "I see seeds at our seats." Jared said, "One of those seeds is corn because that's how my Nana makes what she calls 'real popcorn' on her stove." Ms. Saunders acknowledged and thanked each child for his or her observations and restated Jared's point, "Yes, Jared, there are kernels of corn at your seats, and I really enjoy eating what your Nana calls 'real popcorn.' I am going to write 'kernel of corn' on the board so we know how to write these words. Who knows what letter kernel *starts with?" With Heather's help, she spelled out the words. Then she continued, "I am also wondering if anyone saw a different type of seed at your seats." Ms. Saunders called on Hannah, who had her hand up. "I saw sunflower seeds, like the ones my dad likes to eat when he's outside working in the yard." Ms. Saunders said, "Nice observation, Hannah. Have you ever eaten a sunflower seed?" Hannah nodded her head. Ms. Saunders asked, "How do they taste?" Hannah said, "Seedy and salty." Ms. Saunders replied, "Yes, they do taste seedy, and many times people add salt to make the seedy part taste better." Again, she asked the students to help her spell "sunflower seed." After writing on the board, she noticed that Nick still had his hand up, so Ms. Saunders called on him and asked what he wanted to share. Nick said, "You forgot the beans." Ms. Saunders replied, "Oh, you mean you saw that there were pinto beans at your tables." Nick said, "Yes, those are the types of beans we eat at home. They're yummy. I especially like them mashed up on the tortillas my grandma makes." Ms. Saunders said, "That sounds delicious," thanked Nick for pointing out the last type of seed, and again asked for help spelling out "pinto beans" on the board.*

After asking the class to help her read the names of the seeds on the board, Ms. Saunders continued, "Now that you've shared what you noticed to be different about our classroom and how these seeds are connected to your own lives, which is so interesting to hear about, we are going to use these seeds in multiple ways to help our minds grow as learners. First, we are going to use these seeds to help us with our math skills. Then tomorrow we are going to use these seeds to help us learn more about our communities and our understanding of science. For today we are going to do several activities that help us with subitizing, counting, adding and subtracting, and graphing. Remember, subitizing is looking at a group of objects and instantly knowing how many are there without counting. When I call your name, come up and get your math journal and a pencil. Then on the carpet open your journal to the next clean page, write the date at the top, and draw three circles on the page. Then put one seed name under each circle so that each seed has its own circle."

After Ms. Saunders and Ms. Harrison helped the students draw their circles and write the seed names, which for some children simply meant writing the first letter for each seed (C, S, and P), she then told them what they would do next. "Children, I now want you to go to your seats and look over each of your piles and write in the circle the number of seeds in each pile. So if you see three kernels of corn, you'll write the number 'three' in the circle above the word corn. *Or if you see five pinto beans, you'll write the number 'five' in the circle above the words* pinto bean. *When you are finished subitizing for each group, I want you to put down your pencil and notebook and count the seeds by touching them and counting. Once you're done counting the seeds one by one, I want you to write that number under the name of each seed. It's okay if the numbers are different. Remember, we are still learning how to subitize, and the only way to get better at it is to practice. Okay, so let's go to our seats, subitize, and then check our work. Remember, Ms. Harrison and I are both here if you need some help."*

In the above example, Ms. Saunders integrates a range of academic skills and knowledge into this activity, such as writing, reading, decoding, observing, sharing, and community building. She is also trying to assist children in developing subitizing, a skill that many early education programs focus on in their math instruction. There are two types of subitizing: perceptual and conceptual. Perceptual is what Ms. Saunders is asking these children to do—look at each pile of seeds and know how many seeds are in each pile. This activity may sound simple, but it's more complicated than it looks. It requires children to perceptually see each seed as its own unit in the pile. Conceptual subitizing is a more complex process of recognizing a pattern that is made up of separate parts—for instance, seeing a pile of three seeds and a pile of four seeds and knowing that there are seven seeds altogether.

Children may use perceptual subitizing to begin to make up units for counting. Conceptual subitizing, such as looking at a domino and knowing how many total dots are on it, helps children develop their ability to recognize patterns as well as estimate. Moreover, it helps children begin to recognize how to compose (two 10s and one 1 makes twenty-one) and decompose (breaking twenty-one into two 10s and one 1), which also helps children develop their ideas about addition and subtraction (Clements 1999). For example, seeing a domino with four dots on one side and two on the other helps them see how these two sets of dots combine to make six. In fact, during the remainder of the lesson, Ms. Saunders had the students add all the beans together. She then asked them to subtract the kernels of corn from their totals, and then the pinto beans, and so on.

Developing a Positive Attitude toward Math

Beyond helping children develop their ability to subitize, Ms. Saunders is cultivating a positive disposition in the children toward learning and using math. This includes helping children understand and appreciate the importance of math and providing them with experiences that engage them in the process of mathematics. To foster such understanding requires helping children see the connection between school-taught numbers and symbols and their everyday lives. It also requires teachers to help children understand how different mathematical ideas are related (such as the relationship between subitizing and addition and subtraction). To facilitate this type of learning environment requires educators to encourage exploration into mathematical concepts and provide children with the space to experiment, manipulate, play, reflect, self-correct, and extend their mathematical thinking. Early educators must be present to help children with this process and intervene when they are stuck.

To help children develop a positive attitude toward mathematics, the activities educators engage in need to be purposeful, meaningful, and inquiry-based. In the case of Ms. Saunders, she touches on these points, but her investigation is more teacher directed and artificial than inquiry based. While manipulating the seeds is a hands-on experience, Ms. Saunders does not examine why the children need to know how many seeds each of them has or why knowing such information would be important. Math should be a part of children's everyday learning experiences, with educators offering children numerous learning opportunities to practice and explore mathematical concepts, responding to their questions, and engaging in such activities as games or songs that offer meaningful experiences. While Ms. Saunders tries to connect the seeds to the children's lives, the activity itself is driven by developing a specific skill, which is not necessarily bad, but the intent behind the activity or its connection to children's everyday lives is not clear. Meaningful learning experiences are those in which the teacher builds off children's informal math experiences and helps children see mathematical concepts as pattern in their everyday lives.

Connecting Math to Students' Experiences

To help her students connect math to their everyday lives, Ms. Saunders could have had the children compare who is and is not at school, count how many students are buying lunch, look for triangles in the classroom, or predict how many students brought fruit for snack. Inquiry-based instruction means early educators provide children with opportunities to explore mathematical conceptions through investigations, projects, and thematic teaching that offer children choice and voice in their learning. During these events, teachers should encourage dialogue among the children and push them to reflect on their learning rather than simply provide feedback (Baroody and Li 2009). While this math lesson is rooted in the current theme Ms. Saunders and her students are investigating, the activity itself could have been altered in such a way that gave children the seeds and allowed them to generate their own mathematical explorations and share and record their findings.

Still, Ms. Saunders's use of seeds within the mathematical exercise shows the tension early educators face in constructing learning activities that reflect RIGOROUS DAP. Again, we see critique as an essential component in pushing ourselves forward in our instruction. Let's do that by examining how Ms. Saunders continued her math lesson with the children:

Ms. Saunders had the children help her complete a seed bar graph that was made on chart paper and placed in the front of the room for everyone to see. The graph already had the name of the seeds on the x axis in ABC order, and Ms. Saunders had premade columns and lines on the y axis, with each division marked off by 5s up to 150. Three students came up one at a time and worked with her and the class to fill in the number of seeds. As the last group came up, she had the entire class see how many seeds were distributed among the 20 kindergarteners. Combined, there were 135 kernels of corn, 120 pinto beans, and 102 sunflower seeds. After completing the graph, Ms. Saunders asked the children which column had the most, which had the least, and which was in the middle. She planned to revisit the column the next day with the students and discuss how to estimate differences using the premade lines on the y axis that counted by 5s.

At the end of the lesson, Ms. Saunders asked her students to put their kernels of corn and their pinto beans into two separate large plastic bags, each labeled. She stated that they would use both sets of seeds later in the week. She also asked the students to eat or taste their sunflower seeds and share with their neighbor how the seeds tasted. After sharing with their neighbors, Ms. Saunders had them share their descriptions with the class. Students provided such descriptions as salty, seedy, tiny, round, *and* small, *which Ms. Saunders listed on the front board. Then Ms. Saunders said, "Let's see if we can make up a quick rhyme to remember this taste. I'll try to think of one, and I want you to think with your neighbors about one. We'll check back with each other in two minutes."*

After two minutes, Ms. Saunders had written the following on the front board, "Sunflower seeds taste salty and seedy. My auntie shares them with me and calls me her sweetie. Oh, how I love those round little treaties." After she had shared it with the class, she asked for some groups to share. One group shared, "Sunflower seeds, salty and sweet, oh what a treat." Another said, "Eat your sunflower seeds. They're salty and sweet, and they'll give you big feet." This poem made the entire class laugh, even Ms. Saunders.

NCTM's Five Strands

In the remainder of this math lesson, Ms. Saunders employed both mathematical and literacy knowledge. Let's focus on the math aspect of the conclusion of this lesson, using the National Council of Teachers of Mathematics' (NCTM) five strands of content that students should learn in school to help unpack Ms. Saunders's math lesson.

The NCTM's first strand is number and operations. For young children, developing an understanding of numbers and operations involves being able to count whole numbers, compare quantities, develop an understanding of the base-ten number system, and perform as well as explain computations in different ways. Across this lesson, Ms. Saunders engaged in several activities that asked the children to identify and use numbers (identifying how many kernels of corn each child has) as well as number operations (comparing and contrasting groups of seeds).

Before children can perform complex operations that describe change—how a quantity increases or decreases—they need to be able to count objects meaningfully. Meaningful object counting is an effortful process that requires children to recite the counting sequence of numbers from memory and synchronize those words to their object pointing—a skill commonly referred to as *one-to-one correspondence*. Finally, once children finish one-to-one counting, they must understand that the last number they say in the count tells how many objects there are in the set. This concept is known as the *cardinal principal of number*, which many state standards call *cardinality* in their student outcomes.

The NCTM's second strand is algebra. Skills that fall under this strand for young children included being able to sort, classify, and order objects by size, number, and other properties. They should also be able to recognize, describe, and extend patterns, including numeric patterns, and translate a pattern from one representation to another. Finally, children should be able to analyze how both repeating and growing patterns are generated. In this lesson, Ms. Saunders had her students classify the seeds by type. She could have had them create patterns using the three seeds, but that would have been a different lesson.

The NCTM's third strand is geometry, which includes the ability to describe shapes and space. Children need to be able to identify, name, and describe a variety of two- and three-dimensional shapes presented in a variety of ways. For instance, children should be able to recognize a triangle is a triangle even if the lines on one side of a triangle are longer than the lines on a different triangle. They also need to understand and use vocabulary that locates and directs objects within their environment—*above, below, next to,* and so on. Finally, they need to be able to develop their understanding of spatial relations, which includes spatial reasoning and orientation; for example, recognizing whether they can put a small square block through a round hole or putting puzzle pieces together. In this lesson, Ms. Saunders brought in vocabulary that assisted them in developing the spatial reasoning needed to locate the correct number on the graph. Specifically, she introduced the children to the coordinate system (X, Y) as organized on a quadrant. By having the children identify the number on the graph, the children engaged in the geometric skill of reading the left to right orientation of the number on the x axis, which identified the type of seed, and the top to bottom directionality of the y axis, which identified the number of seeds for that type.

The NCTM's fourth strand is measurement, which includes being able to use measurable attributes, such as length, and being able to solve problems by comparing and ordering objects. Children begin to make sense of measurable attributes by first making direct comparisons between two objects to determine which is longer, shorter, taller, wider, and so forth. Once children see how this relationship can be applied to make indirect comparisons with other objects, they will be able to use units. First, they will use nonstandard units (such as cubes) and then standard units (like inches) to count and assign a numerical value that tells how much of that attribute (length, height, or weight) the item they are measuring has. For example, Ms. Saunders had the students compare the lengths of columns in their seed bar graph.

The final NCTM strand involves data analysis. The NCTM states that to analyze data, children must classify and organize it, represent it, and then interpret and apply data to answer a question or solve a problem. Again, the seed bar graph addressed this strand by allowing the students to organize and classify their data, compare the amount of each seed on the graph, and interpret the similarities and differences in the amounts of seeds.

When examining the entirety of this math lesson, Ms. Saunders's students engaged in a range of hands-on and mental math activities. Much of it was teacher directed, which could be modified to provide children more choice and voice. Nonetheless, Ms. Saunders brought together a range of strands of mathematical knowledge into a lesson that provided the children an opportunity to manipulate and organize data through a variety of activities that they can then apply to many different learning situations. The key components of her lesson that align with RIGOROUS DAP are that she offered her students a range of mathematical learning experiences that provided them with multiple opportunities to engage in these concepts through play, small groups, and whole groups, as well as individualized learning experiences. In this way, she is *Integrating content areas* (math and science) by *Offering the children choices* (through hands-on manipulation via different activities) to *Revisit new content* (sorting, graphing, and classifying).

TEACHING SOCIAL STUDIES THROUGH RIGOROUS DAP

As part of their social studies curriculum, Ms. Saunders's kindergarteners were to learn about production, distribution, and consumption. She planned to incorporate this information into her seeds and plants investigation by discussing with the students where the seeds they investigated came from and how farming was an important part of their community.

While Ms. Saunders had already turned the pretend and learn center in her classroom into a farm, which would soon be followed by a grocery store, and had planned for children to plant some of the seeds, she wanted to stimulate a conversation around farming using the book Farm Crops! Plants That Grow on Farms. *Before reading the text, she asked the children where they might find the seeds they've been investigating. After Tony said, "The science center," which forced Ms. Saunders not to smile so Tony would see she took his answer seriously, Ms. Saunders added, "Where might we find these seeds outside of our classroom?" Lakeya noted, "I have sunflower seeds at my house." Ms. Saunders again acknowledged this answer and realized that she and her students were thinking about seeds differently. She continued, "Students, while you have been giving me terrific answers, I've been asking some misleading questions. I guess what I am trying to ask is who might use seeds as part of their work? Who needs seeds to produce the food we eat?"*

With this question, most the children's hands went up, and Terrance answered, "Farmers." Ms. Saunders replied, "Yes, Terrance, farmers use seeds to plant crops that they will grow and then sell—either to grocery stores or at famers' markets. Have any of you been to a farm before?" Nick blurted out, "My grandpa is a farmer." Ms. Saunders said, "Oh, that's so interesting, Nick! What does he grow on his farm?" Nick said, "Beans, corn, cows, chickens, watermelons, pigs, pumpkins, goats, and a whole bunch of other stuff." "Wow," Ms. Saunders replied, "that's a lot of things your grandpa grows and raises on his farm." After a few other children shared their own stories, Ms. Saunders said, "I was ten years old before I ever had the chance to go to a farm and see what happens there. I am wondering, since y'all are only five and six years old, if some of you are like me and have not been to a farm yet?" Several children nodded their heads in agreement with Ms. Saunders. She continued, "Well, remember, you are young and have a whole lot of adventures still to come, so hopefully, if you want to, you'll get to visit a farm someday."

Ms. Saunders then said, "I want to share a story with you today that examines how farmers grow their crops on their farms. It's important to understand how food, which is something we consume every day, is produced. When we talked earlier in the year about our community, we talked about the idea of production, which is making things for others to consume or buy; distribution, which is how products, like ears of corn, are brought to stores; and consumers, who are the people that buy what was made or produced. What I hope is that after we read the story, you use some of these ideas in our pretend-and-learn farm area. As we move into science, I want you to see the connection between what farmers do and our planting of seeds in our class. So let's read the story."

As Ms. Saunders read the text, she worked with the class to decode and define such terms as crops, labor, *and* harvesting. *She also made connections to the crops they saw in the book, such as corn to the seeds and food they've explored in their class.*

As the story came to an end, Ms. Saunders reminded the students of the role of farmers in producing crops that get distributed to grocery stores and markets, which their families then buy for them to eat. She also mentioned that in the next few days they'd take a historical look at who had farmed in their community, including Native peoples, and what and where they farmed these crops.

EXAMINING TEACHING THROUGH RIGOROUS DAP

On the surface, it's quite clear that Ms. Saunders employed the thematic unit of seeds and crops to explore the constructs of production, distribution, and consumption with her students through a shared reading. These are constructs found in the state content standards that she is expected to teach her kindergarten students. Nevertheless, she tried to approach teaching this content through two learning experiences: one, this shared reading, and two, inviting children to play with the constructs and vocabulary introduced in the text in their pretend and learn center.

Ms. Saunders tried to guide the students into this content by asking them where they might find the seeds they've been exploring, but soon realized that her questioning did not guide the students where she hoped they would go. Still, this mistake was an important learning opportunity for her and the students. She admitted her mistake, corrected it, and moved on. By doing so, she revealed to her students how to address their mistakes while at the same time *Pushed her children forward* in their learning.

Ms. Saunders asked if any students had ever visited a farm, but because she understood who her learners were, she knew that not all had. Thus, she knew that she needed to position this question in her own history of not visiting a farm until she was ten years old. Doing so let the children know that it was okay if they had not visited a farm yet and that they may get the chance as they grow up, which further exemplifies how Ms. Saunders is trying to instill a growth mindset in her students. If she had the time and resources available, Ms. Saunders could take the children on a field trip to a farm—maybe even Nick's grandfather's farm. However, taking such field trips has become more difficult for teachers in this time of standardization, academic achievement, and limited resources.

Once she had a sense of who in her class had and had not been to a farm, Ms. Saunders was able to examine the constructs of production, distribution, and consumption through the shared reading. By the end of the discussion and reading, she had offered the children multiple opportunities to hear and read about the big ideas she was trying to get across in this lesson. Moreover, when the reading was over the lesson was over. Because Ms. Saunders knew she had and would continue to revisit these ideas over the course of the year, she did not fall into the "Introduce, Teach, Worksheet" routine that teachers often fall into in their high-stakes teaching context. Instead, she tried to "Connect, Discuss, Allow for Exploration and Incorporation," which aligns more with what we know about how children develop and learn.

Finally, she primed the children for follow-up investigations into who has farmed in their community and what and where they farmed. Such investigations create opportunities to pursue discussions around colonization, map making, and, depending on the context, slavery. The point being that to engage in RIGOROUS DAP within the domain of social studies means finding the moments within your instruction to make clear connections between children's worlds (*Understanding each learner*), the world they currently live in (*Revisiting new content*), and the world they have inherited (*Growing as a community*).

Examining the Social Studies in This Lesson

Children are constantly trying to make sense of their social and physical worlds. The key for early educators is to move beyond the content/processes dichotomy, which can lead to teachers isolating social studies from other content areas. Instead, teachers can focus on generating thematic learning opportunities built on what children know, and develop these concepts and processes through culturally and personally relevant hands-on learning experiences that capitalize on children's interests and histories (Mindes 2005). With her lesson, Ms. Saunders is trying to assist the children in seeing how essential seeds are not only to their lives, but also to the larger community.

To integrate rather than isolate social studies from your curricular experiences with young children, look to the National Council for Social Studies (NCSS). This organization defines the aim of social studies as promoting civic competence among students so that they can become engaged participants in public life. Part of our job as early educators is to help children become who they want to be, and social studies plays a key role in this process. To assist teachers in achieving this goal with their students, the NCSS have published ten themes for organizing strands of social studies programs from pre-K through grade 12:

- culture
- time, continuity, and change
- people, places, and environments
- individual development and identity
- individuals, groups, and institutions
- power, authority, and governance
- production, distribution, and consumption
- science, technology, and society
- global connections
- civic ideals and practices

Ms. Saunders noted in her lesson that the students had already examined the importance of family and community (people, places, and environments), which quite naturally fits with developing a sense of self in relation to others (individual development and identity). The lesson also touched on the roles and responsibilities of members of a community (civic ideals and practices). The current investigation into farming tied directly to the production, distribution, and consumption theme. If Ms. Saunders goes more deeply into the science of farming by discussing such ideas as fertilizer and organic farming, she can make a nice connection to the science, technology, and society theme.

Social studies can naturally be woven into the everyday early childhood curriculum. For example, by offering play-based learning experiences, early educators help children learn how to become members of a social community (Seefeldt, Castle, and Falconer 2013), which ties directly into culturally relevant and sustaining teaching practices. By paying attention to children's understanding, misunderstanding, and questions about their social worlds, educators can formulate inquiry-based investigations that help children better understand how to be active participants in their learning community and the social worlds that exist beyond the classroom.

Finally, being a guide for children as they come to understand the larger social world and the history that has shaped it requires an awareness of their narratives (both historical and current) within the classroom and the curriculum they enact. You need to ask yourself, "Am I sharing an understanding of the world that is told almost exclusively from a Western, white perspective?" When you discuss other ethnicities or cultures, are you simply "adding" them to that dominant narrative? Or, particularly in the case of stories around Native people, are you making it sound as if they and their culture exist only in the past, or that the structural and social racism that discriminated against a range of sociocultural groups no longer exists? We know these are tough questions to consider, but we as teachers of young children need to be aware of how we approach these issues so that we no longer perpetuate historical inaccuracies. We need to be aware of the limited perspectives we are sharing with children about history and should strive to incorporate their voices and their sociocultural histories within our teaching across all content areas, not just social studies (Sleeter 2011).

TEACHING SCIENCE THROUGH RIGOROUS DAP

Scientists study the world around them and beyond, and propose explanations based on evidence from their investigations—be it an experience or observation. The willingness to propose, experiment, and make conclusions based on the data collected is how most children live their lives every day. The job of early educators is to tap into, foster, or rekindle children's inquisitiveness and connect this to learning throughout the day—not just science.

Nevertheless, when thinking about science education, the National Research Council (NRC) outlined the key domains early educators should take into consideration within their planning and instruction. These domains include science as inquiry, physical science, life sciences, earth and space sciences, science and technology, and science in personal and social perspectives, which includes discussions and activities about such things as conserving resources (NRC 2012).

Furthermore, the National Science Teachers' Association (2014) position statement on early childhood science education identified three key principles to guide the learning of science among young children. The first is that children can engage in and develop an understanding of scientific practices and principles at a conceptual level. Early educators need to be aware of the underlying scientific concepts found within children's investigations. For instance, some of the underlying scientific concepts for an investigation into seeds and plants fall under the life sciences, which include developing an understanding of the characteristics of living things, what is required for them to grow and reproduce, and the importance of a healthy environment for plants and humans to grow.

A second key principle is that adults perform an important role in helping children learn science. Providing age-appropriate materials and resources and spurring children's investigations forward by asking "I wonder" questions is important for children to develop their scientific knowledge and skills.

Finally, children need multiple and varied opportunities to participate in science activities. Doing so helps them develop science knowledge and skills through experiential learning over time in both formal and informal learning settings. Early educators should provide children with the opportunity to explore their world, raise questions about it, and try to answer those questions through careful observations and investigations. During such observations and investigations, children need to be taught how to work collaboratively and record what they are observing and learning, develop the vocabulary as well as an understanding of the skills needed to describe, compare, sort, classify, and order the information they collect. Students will more than likely learn how to use a range of simple tools. Children then need to identify and recognize patterns and relationships so that they can develop and explain their ideas and tentative explanations about what they are investigating. These ideas all align directly with what we mean by *Revisiting new content* in our conceptualization of RIGOROUS DAP.

Ms. Saunders purposely designed several activities for her students to develop their scientific skills within the seeds and plants thematic unit. For instance, she shared Gail Gibbon's (1991) *From Seed to Plant* with the class to start a conversation around what seeds need to become plants and what plants need to survive.

After sharing the story, Ms. Saunders asked the class if they remember what plants need to live. Tony said, "Sun." Hannah said, "Air." Rachel added, "Water," and Clemente said, "Earth." Ms. Saunders asked Clemente what he meant by "earth." He said, "You know, earth, the dirt, rocks, and stuff." Ms. Saunders said, "Oh, you mean the soil the plants need to grow in?" Clemente said, "Yes."

Ms. Saunders then asked, "Do plants have to grow in the earth? Or are there other places they can grow and live?" Jaralyn asked, "You mean, like on another planet?" Ms. Saunders said, "No, I mean, here on Earth, are there other things plants can grow in besides being outside as a part of the earth?" The class was stumped for a second, and then Lucy, looking toward Ms. Saunders's desk, commented, "Oh, I know, you mean, like the plant on your desk that's growing in a pot." Ms. Saunders said, "Yes, Lucy, plants can grow in pots, and I noticed that you used your environment to help you answer the question. That's a great strategy we can use when we're stuck with a question." Ms. Saunders continued with another question, "And when a plant is in a pot, what does it need to grow?" Lucy said, "Dirt and soil and water and sun." Ms. Saunders replied, "Yes, they need dirt, which is also called soil, and water, and the sun."

She continued, "Do y'all remember the three parts of the seeds we've been examining under the microscope in our science center?" Terrance replied, "There's coat—you know seeds need coats to protect the baby plant and the food to help it grow." Ms. Saunders agreed and then asked, "Can anyone remember what we call the baby plant and food supply?" Ms. Saunders called on Becca, who said, "The baby plant is called an embryo*, which is a word we can use for people, like the baby in my mommy's belly." "That's right," Ms. Saunders replied. "And how about the food in the seed?" Drakar said, "Coyotedon." Ms. Saunders responded, "Close, it's* cotyledon*, which sounds a lot like coyotedon."*

At this point, Lakeya, a very precocious kindergartener, had her hand up, and Ms. Saunders called on her. "Ms. Saunders, I think most of us know how to grow seeds." She pointed to a class-made poster of "How Seeds Grow" and said, "Soil, water, sun. And what makes up a seed—the coat, the embryo, and the coyote . . . cotyledon. But we've been talking about corn kernels, beans, and sunflower seeds for a while now. And for two of those seeds, you just eat—beans and sunflower seeds. But with corn kernels, you have to cook 'em to make them pop. Who figured that out? Like, you know, who had the idea to heat them up so they would pop and then eat them? And why does cooking a kernel make it pop out like that?"

Ms. Saunders paused for a moment and responded, "Lakeya, that's a great question. So why don't we do this? Today, during our afternoon center time, I want our class to plant some of our corn kernels, beans, and sunflower seeds in soil. Then we will make some predictions about how quickly and how large they will grow and begin to document how we planted them so we can have a starting point to record, analyze, and evaluate our predictions over the next few weeks. Then tomorrow, why don't we investigate how to make popcorn. How does that sound?"

Lakeya responded, "Okay, popping corn sounds fun, but that still doesn't answer all my questions. I still want to know who figured out popping corn." Ms. Saunders replied, "Okay, again, that's a great question. Let's do this. Today we'll plant seeds. Tomorrow we'll examine how to pop corn, and tonight I want you and your classmates to investigate with your families who figured out how to pop corn. Part of being a scientist requires you to do research on what's already known, so tonight I want you to research with your family and find out who figured out how to pop corn. How does that sound?" Lakeya said, "Okay, you've got a deal."

In this example, Ms. Saunders provided the children the opportunity to revisit the content they had discussed about the essential elements seeds require to grow into plants, and as Lakeya pointed out, she feels that she and her classmates understand this. Ms. Saunders wanted to provide her students with the opportunity to explore how seeds grow into plants, collect data about this process, and eventually reflect on what they had learned. Ms. Saunders has created a learning community that has grown together in such a way that the power among her and her students is leveled enough that Lakeya can openly question not only the material and the processes by which they are learning that material, but also feel empowered enough to let Ms. Saunders know if her learning needs are not being met. Rather than feel threatened or inadequate, Ms. Saunders capitalizes on Lakeya's questioning and offers to amend the curriculum to meet her and her classmates' needs. Doing so ensures Ms. Saunders is attending to two dimensions of RIGOROUS DAP: First, she takes responsibility for *Reaching all children* by connecting the dots for classmates to see the relationship in the content of Lakeya's questioning to the learning objective. Second, Ms. Saunders *Offers challenges* by encouraging the children to take responsibility for their learning in and outside the classroom. By asking the students to research who figured out how to pop corn, Ms. Saunders is *Integrating* the science content into social studies.

Children's inquisitiveness about the world needs to be nurtured and fostered within and outside your classroom. We know that what and how much you must cover in your early education setting can distract you from taking advantage or even noticing children's questions about the content. However, to encourage children to grow as learners, we recommend that you make every effort to *Push them forward* in the process of building their knowledge through the principles we have outlined in this book and this chapter. Moreover, following these recommendations will allow you to continue to pursue your hopes, dreams, and aspirations as a teacher.

ADDRESSING THE WHOLE CHILD THROUGH RIGOROUS DAP

Up to this point, we've examined how Ms. Saunders addresses children's cognitive learning in specific subject areas. Embedded within these activities, Ms. Saunders is attending to children's social (working as a learning community), emotional (regulating one's self in small- and whole-group learning activities), and physical development (taking a nature walk). Still, we want to point out that across the day, Ms. Saunders provides opportunities for her students' bodies and minds to breathe. Fostering children's learning requires teachers to engage children's whole bodies, with both active and calming activities.

For example, within any thematic unit or project-based learning activity, Ms. Saunders has the students engage in silly dances that tie the content they are exploring to physical activity. Sometimes these dances are to songs she's made up, such as a song she calls "Plant Man." This song is sung to the tune of the old *Batman* TV show and includes a range of body motions tied to how a plant grows from seed to flower, as well as silly Batman moves (saying, "Ka-pow" while punching her hand forward, opening her fingers, and saying, "My hand just transformed into a flower"). Other times she finds songs related to the theme or project on YouTube.

Furthermore, throughout the year, she has at least two to three body-breathing stations in her classroom that children can visit during their center time or playtime. For large-motor development, she always has a Nerf basketball hoop attached to her door that students can play with for two-minute intervals. She often has a large-motor center available where children can engage their whole body in movement, either by watching a tablet containing body-moving videos to mimic, or by following an exercise card she has made. Ms. Saunders also has a calming station available for the children year-round that is designed to help children settle their bodies down. At this station, children have videos on a tablet and teacher-made cards available that cover such exercises as belly breathing and yoga. Finally, dancing is an activity her kindergarteners really enjoy because Ms. Saunders fully engages with her students as they dance and because she asks family members to come in across the year and share their favorite dances—be it cultural or a popular dance. There are moments throughout the day, week, and school year where Ms. Saunders and the children dance to favorite songs simply to take a break from the everyday routine. Doing so demonstrates to the students that physical activity is fun and enjoyable and can be done in and outside of school.

Reexamining Why It's Important to Integrate Content Areas through Quality Educational Experiences

- Using Dewey's ideas, discuss how you take responsibility for creating a learning-centered classroom that balances the curriculum with the child's personal experiences. Second, discuss how you try to create a continuous link between children's prior experiences and current learning demands. Finally, discuss where Ms. Saunders engages in a balanced set of instructional practices with her students.
- Discuss with your colleagues how you might edit or rearrange Ms. Saunders math lesson so the children have more choice and voice in their learning.
- Think about Ms. Saunders's response to Lakeya's insistence to know who figured out how to pop corn. Would you have responded differently? If so, how? If not, what additional steps might you take to address Lakeya's desire to learn more about seeds and plants?

- Throughout this chapter, we gave several examples of Ms. Saunders's teaching to demonstrate how her practices reflect the principles of RIGOROUS DAP. Still, there are several areas within her teaching that could be improved. Pick any of our examples, and use the practices that define RIGOROUS DAP to think about how you might improve Ms. Saunders's teaching.

Extending Your Learning

Literacy

- Susan Neuman and her colleagues (2007) published a text that examines ways in which teachers can extend children early literacy skills across all content areas titled *Nurturing Knowledge: Building a Foundation for School Success by Linking Early Literacy to Math, Science, Art, and Social Studies.*
- The website www.readingrockets.org offers strategies for assisting young children in their development of literacy skills. For example, to learn about developing preschoolers' literacy practices, visit www.readingrockets.org/article/preschool-language-and-literacy-practices. To examine different words you might use in your teaching (such as tier two words), check out www.readingrockets.org/article/choosing-words-teach.

Mathematics

- *Young Children's Mathematics: Cognitively Guided Instruction in Early Childhood Education* provides insight into the development of children's mathematical thinking and provides counting and problem-solving strategies.
- The National Council of Teachers of Mathematics has websites dedicated to the five content standards that explain each standard in detail and what it means in terms of teaching children from preschool through grade twelve:
  1. Number and Operations: www.nctm.org/Standards-and-Positions/Principles-and-Standards/Number-and-Operations
  2. Algebra: www.nctm.org/Standards-and-Positions/Principles-and-Standards/Algebra
  3. Geometry: www.nctm.org/Standards-and-Positions/Principles-and-Standards/Geometry
  4. Measurement: www.nctm.org/Standards-and-Positions/Principles-and-Standards/Measurement
  5. Data Analysis and Probability: www.nctm.org/Standards-and-Positions/Principles-and-Standards/Data-Analysis-and-Probability
- The What Works Clearinghouse under the Institute for Educational Sciences provides a practice guide that details how early educators should instruct young children in math (https://ies.ed.gov/ncee/wwc/PracticeGuide/18). The guide provides a developmental progression for teaching young children

mathematics. Like NCTM it begins with numbers and operations and provides insight as to where a child might be developmentally and what she needs to display to demonstrate that she's ready to move on to the next concept.

Social studies

- One resource worth mentioning is *Black Ants and Buddhists: Thinking Critically and Teaching Differently in the Primary Grades* by Mary Crowley.
- The National Council for the Social Studies' website www.socialstudies.org/positions/elementary explores what it means to teach social studies from preschool through elementary school.

Science

- Teachhub.com (a website dedicated to sharing resources among K–12 teachers) has an article on how to integrate science across the curriculum: www.teachhub.com/integrate-science-across-curriculum.
- Another resource for thinking about how to teach young children science is Jacqueline Brooks's *Big Science for Growing Minds: Constructing Classrooms of Growing Thinkers.*

Physical Activity

- Healthy Kids (www.healthykids.nsw.gov.au/default.aspx) is a teacher-friendly resource designed by the New South Wales (NSW) Ministry of Health, NSW Department of Education, Office of Sport and the Heart Foundation of Australia.
- Spark (sparkpe.org) is a research-based program out of San Diego State University Research Foundation that offers teachers resources that promote lifelong wellness for children.

Steps You Can Take toward Change

- Look back to the eleven actions that define RIGOROUS DAP. Think about what your strengths are as a teacher in relation to implementing these actions in your classroom. What are your growth areas? Then develop a plan of action to address these growth areas in your teaching and interactions with children across your day. Within your plan, identify those actions you can change immediately and those that will take more time. For those that will take more time, set some deadlines to reevaluate your teaching. If you find you're not making the progress you hoped to achieve, you might want to identify other resources (such as colleagues or professional development) that can help you meet your goals.

8

Moving Forward to Ensure All Children Engage in RIGOROUS DAP

Throughout this book, we've provided you with steps you can take toward change—be it change in your practice, your teaching context, or early childhood education in general. In this chapter, we revisit and extend many of these ideas so that you can develop a plan of action to promote RIGOROUS DAP in your classroom, school, and the larger community. In essence, our goal is to provide you with not only a plan of action for your immediate teaching context but also a reminder of all the things we are trying to help you achieve with this book.

What This Means for You

By now, you should have a clear vision of what it means for you to engage in RIGOROUS DAP on a regular basis. Something we ask preservice teachers we work with to do to help them embody their vision is to create an artistic representation, such a class crest, tattoo, slogan, or rhyme/tune. For example, a group of preservice teachers in one of Chris's former classes put together the following rhyme (the class was put in groups that day based on farm animals, which is why they refer to themselves as hens):

The Hens' Rap
We are the hens and we're here to say
When you start to teach, this is the way
Every single student is unique,
So the lessons . . . they gotta be tweaked
The curriculum should accommodate
Something all cultures can appreciate
The dignity of risk is bliss
Otherwise we got learned helplessness
Every time they come in the door,
Don't teach less, let's teach more!

By creating such a vision, be it the "Hens' Rap," a rhyme, tattoo, or slogan, you give yourself a gentle prompt that will remind you what you are trying to accomplish every day in your interactions with your students. Do not make decisions in your teaching that will disrupt your progress toward achieving your goals. We also tell our students that teaching is an act of hope for a better future. By having a concrete vision of what you want that future to look like, this image has the power to keep you focused on what you want to accomplish in your classroom with the students and families with whom you work.

We have created an image (see figure 8.1) that we think will help you carry the principles that shape RIGOROUS DAP forward in your learning environment. We see the process of RIGOROUS DAP being cyclical and expanding—starting with the children in our early learning setting and expanding out into the larger learning community. We move forward in our practice through critique and reflection, and with each new cycle, our knowledge, skills, and understanding of the children in our classroom and how to support them, their families, and the larger learning community increases.

Finally, in regard to what this means for you in relation to enacting the principles of RIGOROUS DAP in your classroom, we hope that you see being a part of the early childhood education profession means you have the power to change it. While we know our construct is not the only skill required to accomplish change in the field, we hope it gives you direction in incorporating such practices in your classroom as well as becoming an advocate for RIGOROUS DAP with others.

Sharing Your Vision with Others

In our introduction, we made the case that RIGOROUS DAP is a framework for early childhood instruction that educators can use to inform families, colleagues, administrators, and policy makers about what is and should be occurring in early learning classrooms. This framework helps children enter and

FIGURE 8.1
The Cyclical and Expanding Vision of RIGOROUS DAP

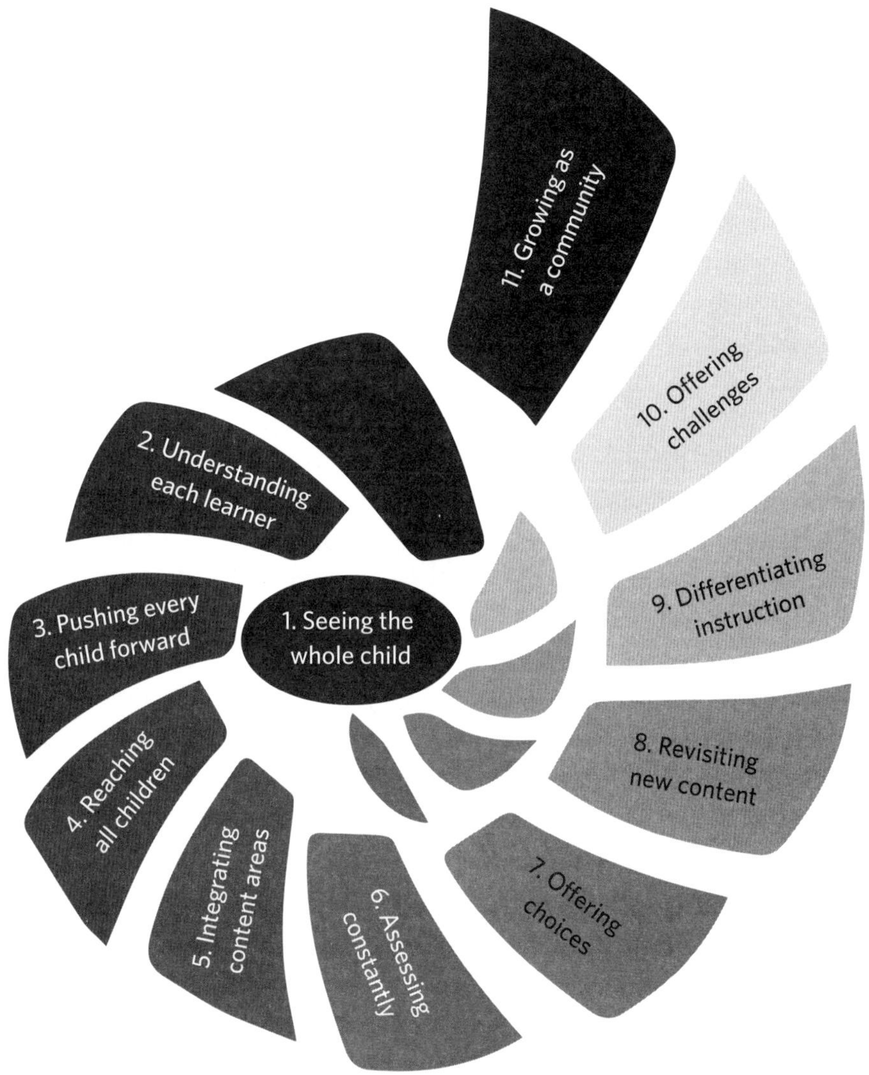

proceed through elementary school prepared and confident in their abilities to meet the academic and social demands that await them.

The intensity in political discussions over preparing children to perform has led many teachers across the various fields of public education to consider simply retreating to their classrooms and shutting their doors (Madaus, Higgins, and Russell 2009). Refusing to acknowledge this dilemma, however, will not make it disappear. Rather, we believe early childhood teachers should confront this issue by being advocates for what they do. They should inform others about how their practices with children build on each child's individual, sociocultural, and developmental strengths and prepare him for the rigor of elementary school (Brown, Feger, and Mowry 2015).

TALKING TO COLLEAGUES AND ADMINISTRATORS

When talking to early childhood and elementary school colleagues and administrators about RIGOROUS DAP, remind them that young children grow and develop differently than their older schoolmates. Young children also have limited attention spans and are just beginning to develop a level of intentionality in their learning. Additionally, learning new content is not a seamless process (even for adults). To that end, help colleagues and administrators understand that children will be inconsistent in demonstrating their newfound skills and will need multiple opportunities to internalize new information into their thinking. Because of this, consider letting people unfamiliar with developmentally appropriate practice know that creating a RIGOROUS DAP early learning environment requires children to experience a complex set of multimodal learning activities based on their individual, sociocultural, and developmental knowledge. Some of the teaching strategies they might see in such classrooms include whole-group, small-group, and center-based instruction; child-initiated activities; indoor and outdoor play-based learning activities; loud and quiet learning activities; and depending on the length of the school day, they will see children eating snacks and possibly taking a rest. Furthermore, discuss how these various activities tie into the learning goals set for children across each day, week, and month, and across the school year.

Some additional topics of conversation include the skills and knowledge preschoolers will bring with them to kindergarten and kindergarteners to first grade, and how such learning is monitored. Almost every state has a set of early learning standards, and all have kindergarten through grade three content standards. Familiarize yourself with these standards and show how such content is touched on across the day. Doing so will help elementary school or grade-level counterparts understand what is occurring in your classroom on a daily basis. Also, consider talking with elementary school colleagues about how to work together to help children and their families succeed in school. Finally, reach out to other teachers and program directors in your community to strengthen the coalition of committed educators working toward change within your local early education environment. Locate other early educators in your community through such organizations as your local NAEYC affiliate (www.naeyc.org/affiliates/offices) or other professional early educator organizations like Child Care Aware (www.childcareaware.org), the National Association for Family Child Care (www.nafcc.org), the Association for Childhood Education International (www.acei.org), the National Black Child Development Institute (www.nbcdi.org), the National Head Start Association (www.nhsa.org), and the American Federation of Teachers (www.aft.org/earlychildhood). For those of you working in programs that also serve infants and toddlers, Zero to Three (www.zerotothree.org) is an organization that can help you build alliances locally and nationally and gain information about policy and research affecting your work.

INFORMING FAMILIES

When talking with families, consider including many of the same topics we suggested when discussing with elementary school colleagues and administrators about what occurs in the classroom. However, when talking about RIGOROUS DAP, we have found there is a tendency to overemphasize children's cognitive and academic development. It's easy to forget to discuss all the important things you do to help children develop their social-emotional skills and ignite their passion for learning. We think touching on the affective aspects of teaching and learning in these conversations with families will help them see how much you care about their children. Moreover, to ensure we are *Reaching all children, Growing as a community, Understanding each learner, Seeing the whole child,* and *Pushing every child forward,* building strong relationships with children's families is essential. Failing to do so makes it seems as if we are simply trying to get children to assimilate to our values and understanding of schooling.

To do this, we must recognize that families lead complex lives. Reaching out to families in as many ways as possible is our responsibility; for example, using newsletters, postings outside your classroom door, maintaining a class blog with photos and videos, using web-based portfolio programs like Seesaw (http://web.seesaw.me) or ClassDojo (www.classdojo.com), sending home copies of the children's work, and using word of mouth informs families about what you do with their children and why. Such activities provide children's families with easy access to information about what the children are doing daily in the classroom, and your communication helps foster an environment of informed advocates who can communicate to others in the larger community why the practices found within RIGOROUS DAP are essential.

An example of what this looks like in practice comes from Chris's work as a kindergarten teacher. As the year progressed, Chris would share weekly newsletters with families that detailed many of the practices he would engage in with the children during the week. Within those explanations, he provided references and web links to research or citations that explained why such practices assisted children in their learning and development. As he gained more experience within the school community, he informed families about upcoming school or district meetings that involved curricula or pedagogy issues that supported or challenged the goals he, the children, and their families were trying to attain within their classroom community. In private conversations, he made suggestions to families concerned about certain issues to either contact school board members or write a letter to the editor of the local newspaper about district or state policies that made it difficult for them and their children's teachers to engage in appropriate practices.

Chris had these conversations in private and outside of school time. He was working in a public school at that time, and in many states, teachers cannot speak in favor or against public policies or state policies. If you are a public employee, you need to know what your rights are and how you can engage politically in a manner that will not affect your standing as a classroom teacher. For example, in Chris's newsletters, he would merely inform parents about upcoming policies and explain how it would affect children's lives in school. He would not advocate for or against a policy.

In saying this, we recognize the easier thing to do is to say nothing about policy or politics and their impact on your teaching, but we believe that decision goes against RIGOROUS DAP. The goal should always be working with others, be it your colleagues, administrators, families, or policy makers, to design, develop, and implement RIGOROUS DAP classrooms.

TALKING TO POLICY MAKERS

A former administrator for Wisconsin's Department of Public Instruction had this advice for how advocates for education can achieve change:

> The press want a headline. That's their focus. So you have to talk to them that way. Policy makers want to be reelected. That's their big issue. So you need to talk to them that way. The teachers' union primary job is to make its constituents better; better benefits, that's their primary goal. If you approach each of those groups with their primary goal in mind and try to meet them where they're at, then you're successful. When you try to fight them, then you get conflict.

Essentially, what this administrator is saying is that to promote change at any level, you must know your audience. For policy makers, that means knowing what issues are of primary importance during that current policy session. For instance, in Texas, school funding and school choice dominate much of the political discussions surrounding education. Even with the focus on these two issues, pre-K expansion and kindergarten readiness have been part of policy discussions. There is space for a range of policies to emerge on the agenda of a governing body, be it local, state, or national, and getting to that point takes organization by those, like you, who can advocate for their issue.

Thinking broadly about early education policy and RIGOROUS DAP, for any issue to take hold within the policy arena requires that it have constant support and advocacy by groups of constituents. Over the past decade, such issues as expanding access to early education programs, improving the professionalism of the field, improving the quality of early education programs, and aligning early childhood systems both horizontally across the varied types of programs that exist within the field and vertically with elementary and secondary education systems have emerged on local, state, and national policy agendas. Such change has occurred because early childhood educators and other stakeholder groups became vocal advocates for these policies.

Thus, if you want to ensure the principles of RIGOROUS DAP are an accepted part of your teaching, you must reach out to others in the larger community. You must help them come to understand that early education is more than an issue of access and affordability. It is an issue of the principles early educators engage in to support the development and learning of all children. Broaden your audience beyond those who work in early childhood education, and connect with the larger education and political communities in your area. A resource that will help you feel more confident in your ability to advocate for these principles is NAEYC's Public Policy page (www.naeyc.org/policy). Here you'll find resources to effectively advocate for issues you care about (www.naeyc.org/policy/advocacy), as well as more information about the legislative process, working with the media, and developing coalitions. Other organizations, such as the National Association for Family Child Care (www.nafcc.org/Public.Policy) and Child Care Aware (http://usa.childcareaware.org/advocacy-public-policy), also have public policy advocacy pages. Furthermore, both NAEYC (www.naeyc.org/policy/action) and Child Care Aware (www.usa.childcareaware.org/advocacy-public-policy/take-action) have pages that include ways to take immediate action on current federal legislation.

Next, talk with your educational and political leaders (school board members and locally elected officials) about their positions on early childhood education and your vision of early education. Your expertise might persuade them to consider the issues in a new light, and you may even be able to assist them in developing appropriate policies that strengthen the field. It is through these interactions that you can help educational and political stakeholders recognize how early education is a necessary component in fostering a healthy democracy.

While it can be easy to become stuck in your immediate environment, it is important to reach out to the larger world. Become aware of what's happening in early childhood education policy across your town, state, region, and the nation. The history of education reform demonstrates that most local and state education policies are simply the retooling of another state or community's reform. To learn what's happening across the United States, sign up for NAEYC's Children's Champions policy update email list at www.naeyc.org/policy. You might also want to visit sites like the Association for Childhood Education International's Center for Education Diplomacy (www.educationdiplomacy.org), which provides insight into what issues are important and how you can develop the skills to advocate for them on a broader level. To read about current early childhood education policy issues and how well solutions are grounded in research, you can find articles and reports at the National Institute for Early Education Research (www.nieer.org), the Foundation for Child Development (www.fcd-us.org), the New America Foundation (www.newamerica.org/education-policy/early-elementary-education-policy), RAND (www.rand.org/education.html), the Brookings Institute (www.brookings.edu/topic/early

-childhood-education), The Future of Children (www.futureofchildren.org), The New America Foundation (www.newamerica.org/education-policy/early-elementary-education-policy), and the Alliance for Early Success (http://earlysuccess.org). Each organization produces newsletters offering insight and access to policy and research issues that affect early childhood education, and many of these groups either evaluate and analyze early childhood education issues or put forward a policy plan they feel will improve the status of early childhood education. You can also gain a more global perspective on early care and education through the World Forum on Early Care and Education at www.worldforumfoundation.org.

However you decide to become an advocate for RIGOROUS DAP or other issues tied to early education, it is important to recognize that being a strong advocate requires that you continue to grow and develop as a learner. Such learning must go beyond what takes place in your immediate early education environment and encapsulate an understanding of how policies from all levels of government affect what you and the larger early childhood community do. For example, to become active in your community, you can work with local advocacy groups around the many issues that affect you and the children you work with—be it early education in general, public schooling, community access to health care, homelessness, abuse, being a refuge in the United States, and so on. Numerous advocacy groups are always looking for volunteers. Enrich your professional knowledge by seeking out a professional development course through your school district or a local chapter of professional organization such as NAEYC or AFT. You could also create your own learning group with colleagues to study books or investigate a specific curricular topic with the children in your classrooms (Brown, McMullen, and File 2018). Depending on your level of education, you could enroll in a local community college or graduate program. Finally, you can simply become an informed citizen by reading up on the legislative process of your state. Almost every state legislature has a webpage that lists its members, committees, policies, and so on. Most states have print and online media that follow the working of state and local governments. By beginning to examine these processes, you'll soon come to understand the structure of governance in your state and who appears to be dictating policy and reform.

Using the knowledge gained through reading this book and engaging in some of the activities outlined above, you can work with members of the field, the families you serve, and other local education and political stakeholders to advocate for changes that respect the uniqueness of each child, their learning, and our interactions with them. Such involvement will lead to early education programs that ensure the provision of the essential components of RIGOROUS DAP.

Upward and Onward

We know that the slogan most often heard is "onward and upward," but Chris tends to say, "I'll see it when I believe it." When he does this, he knows his audience notices the slight difference, and in fact, it often further engages them in the conversation. We know this text can easily be seen as just one more argument for practices that continue to be pushed out of the early education classroom by a range of policy makers, families, and others who expect tougher or more rigorous instruction in the early years. Such statements simply become like everyday sayings as "onward and upward."

Thus, to move forward it's time to flip these ideas around and become an advocate for what you believe in about educating young children—it's time to move upward and onward. Throughout this text, we have advocated for what we see as some of the essential components required to be an effective early childhood educator. The principles of RIGOROUS DAP marry academic rigor and developmentally appropriate practices. Remember, by concentrating on academics, an academically rigorous learning environment allows all children to learn at high levels by addressing the whole child through hands-on learning experiences that connect the child to his or her world in and out of school. By concentrating on developmentally appropriate practices, an appropriate early learning environment considers the children's developmental, cognitive, social, emotional, and physical development, including their linguistic and cultural talents. This aspect of the construct points to the significance of learning being a whole child process that requires the child to engage with her or his mind, body, and heart as she learns to construct new knowledge with you and her classmates. Engaging in RIGOROUS DAP reflects a process in which early educators, such as yourself, expect children to learn and demonstrate the knowledge and skills across their developmental domains needed for school success through practices that consider what is known about development and their children's individual and sociocultural needs. Additionally, the content of your instruction and expectations for children should increase as the year progresses. To ensure children are receiving an appropriate level of support, you should consistently and constantly monitor children's development.

To be able to do all of this as an effective early educator means that you are going to get messy—both literally and figuratively. Children will enter your classroom with a multitude of experiences (involving education, health, emotions, and so on) and talents (cultural, linguistic, personal), and thus it is your job to work with the child where she is at so that she can be successful in school and life. Don't forget that teaching is a complex act and that many of the solutions to the problems you will face are dependent on the context in which you will be working and the families and administrators with whom you are working. To meet young children's needs will require you to employ a range of instructional practices that weave together what we know about how children learn and develop across all developmental domains. You will also need to know the curriculum you are expected to teach, a range of instructional and assessment practices, the hope/dreams/wishes of the child and her family, and your personal and professional goals as an early educator. Essentially, you'll want to create a classroom community rooted in RIGOROUS DAP.

To engage in RIGOROUS DAP daily will also require you to be able to explain why what you do assists all the children in your classroom to grow as individual learners and become members of a democratic learning community. You will need to inform families, colleagues, administrators, and/or elementary school colleagues about the practices you engage in with the children in your classroom. You will also have to help them see the cultural, linguistic, academic, social, emotional, and physical strengths each child in your classroom possesses. You must do this while explaining to them how they can help you facilitate children's learning and development in your and their classroom/program. By discussing with them how the intentionality of your instruction offers children meaningful choices, opportunities to experiment with new ideas in a safe and comfortable setting, and time to revisit new knowledge and skills, they will better understand how the academic rigor embedded in developmentally appropriate practice builds off of what children know and can do. They can then develop the skills and knowledge needed to be successful in school and beyond.

In sum, RIGOROUS DAP is an actionable response to the challenges early educators face in this age of standardization, academic achievement, and limited resources. By engaging in these eleven principles/actions daily in your interactions with children, you can help them become the people they and their families want them to be.

References

Adams, Marilyn Jager, Barbara Foorman, Ingvar Lundberg, and Terri Beeler. 1998. *Phonemic Awareness in Young Children: A Classroom Curriculum.* Baltimore, MD: Paul Brookes.

Anderson, Patricia, Kristin Butcher, and Diane Whitmore Schanzenbach. 2011. "Adequate (or Adipose?) Yearly Progress: Assessing the Effect of "No Child Left Behind" on Children's Obesity." *Education Finance and Policy* 12 (1): 54–76. doi:10.3386/w16873.

Anyon, Jean. 2010. "Critical Pedagogy Is Not Enough: Social Justice Education, Political Participation, and the Politicization of Students." In *The Routledge International Handbook of the Sociology of Education,* edited by Michael W. Apple, Stephen J. Ball, and Luis Armando Gandin, 389–95. New York: Routledge.

Barcelona, Jeanne Marita. 2017. "Investigation of the effects of physical activity on executive function in the early childhood setting" (Doctoral Dissertation). Retrieved from www.lib.utexas.edu.

Baroody, Arthur J. and Xia Li. 2009. "Mathematics Instruction that Makes Sense for 2 to 5 Year Olds." In *Informing Our Practice: Useful Research on Young Children's Development,* edited by Eva Essa and Melissa Burnham, 119–35. Washington, DC: The National Association for the Education of Young Children.

Barufaldi, Jim. 2002. "The 5E Model of Instruction." Presented at the Eisenhower Science Collaborative Conference, July 2002.

Bassok, Daphna and Sean F. Reardon. 2013. "'Academic Redshirting' in Kindergarten." *Educational Evaluation and Policy Analysis* 35 (3): 283–97. doi:10.3102/0162373713482764.

Bassok, Daphna, Scott Latham, and Anna Rorem. 2016. "Is Kindergarten the New First Grade?" *AERA Open* 2 (1): 233285841561635. doi:10.1177/2332858415616358.

Bear, Donald R., Marcia Invernizzi, Shane Templeton, and Francine A. Johnston. 1996. *Words Their Way: Word Study for Phonics, Vocabulary, and Spelling Instruction.* Upper-Saddle, NJ: Merrill.

Berger, Kathleen Stassen. 2009. *The Developing Person through Childhood.* New York: Worth.

Braun, Eric. 2011. *Trust Me, Jack's Beanstalk Stinks!* Mankato, MN: Capstone.

Bredekamp, Sue, and Teresa Jane Rosegrant. 1995. *Reaching Potentials: Transforming Early Childhood Curriculum and Assessment.* Washington, D.C.: National Association for the Education of Young Children.

Bronfenbrenner, Urie. 1979. *The Ecology of Human Development: Experiments by Nature and Design.* Cambridge, MA: Harvard University Press.

Bronfenbrenner, Urie and Pamela A. Morris. 2006. "The Bioecological Model of Human Development." In *Handbook of Child Psychology: Theoretical Models of Human Development,* edited by Richard M. Lerner and William Damon, vol. 1, 793–828. 6th ed. Hoboken, NJ: Wiley.

Brooker, Liz. 2002. *Starting School: Children Learning Cultures.* Buckingham, England: Open University Press.

Brown, Anthony L. and Keffrelyn D. Brown. 2010. "Strange Fruit Indeed: Interrogating Contemporary Textbook Representations of Racial Violence towards African Americans." *Teachers College Record* 112 (1): 31–67.

Brown, Christopher P. 2005. Creating Opportunities. *Contemporary Issues in Early Childhood* 6 (2): 112–27.

——. 2007. "Unpacking Standards in Early Childhood Education." *Teachers College Record* 109 (3): 635–68.

———. 2009a. "Pivoting a Pre-Kindergarten Program off the Child or the Standard? A Case Study of Integrating the Practices of Early Childhood Education into Elementary School." *The Elementary School Journal* 110 (2): 202–27.

———. 2009b. "Being Accountable for One's Own Governing: A Case Study of Early Educators Responding to Standards-Based Early Childhood Education Reform." *Contemporary Issues in Early Childhood* 10 (1): 3–23.

———. 2011. "Searching for the Norm in a System of Absolutes: A Case Study of Standards-Based Accountability Reform in Pre-Kindergarten." *Early Education and Development* 22 (1): 151–77.

———. 2013. "Reforming Preschool to Ready Children for Academic Achievement: A Case Study of the Impact of Pre-K Reform on the Issue of School Readiness." *Early Education and Development* 24 (4): 554–73.

———. 2015. "Conforming to Reform: Teaching Pre-Kindergarten in a Neoliberal Early Education System. *Journal of Early Childhood Research* 13 (3): 236–51.

Brown, Christopher P., Beth Smith Feger, and Brian Mowry. 2015. "Close Early Learning Gaps with RIGOROUS DAP." *Phi Delta Kappan* 96 (7): 53–57.

Brown, Christopher P. and Yi-Chin Lan. 2015. "A Qualitative Metasynthesis Comparing U.S. Teachers' Conceptions of School Readiness Prior to and After the Implementation of NCLB." *Teaching and Teacher Education* 45 (2015): 1–13. doi:10.1016/j.tate.2014.08.012.

Brown, Christopher P. and Jae-Eun Lee. 2012. "How to Teach to the Child When the Stakes Are High: Examples of Implementing Developmentally Appropriate and Culturally Relevant Practices in Prekindergarten." *Journal of Early Childhood Teacher Education* 33 (4): 322–48.

Brown, Christopher Pierce, Mary Benson McMullen, and Nancy File. 2018. *The Wiley Handbook of Early Childhood Care and Education*. Hoboken, NJ: John Wiley & Sons.

Brown, Christopher P. and Brian Mowry. 2016. "Using Testimonio to Bring Children's Worlds into a Standardized Teaching Context: An Example of Culturally Relevant Teaching in Early Childhood Education." *Childhood Education* 92 (4): 281–89.

———. 2017. "'I Wanted to Know How They Perceived Jail': Studying How One Early Educator Brought Her Students' Worlds into Her Standardized Teaching Context." *Early Childhood Education Journal* 45 (2): 163–73.

Brown, Christopher P., Natalie Babiak Weber. 2016. "Struggling to Overcome the State's Prescription for Practice: A Study of a Sample of Early Educators' Professional Development and Action-Research Projects in a High-Stakes Teaching Context." *Journal of Teacher Education* 67 (3): 183–202.

Brown, Christopher P., Natalie Babiak Weber, and Yeojoo Yoon. 2015. "The Practical Difficulties for Early Educators Who Tried to Address Children's Realities in Their High-Stakes Teaching Context." *Journal of Early Childhood Teacher Education* 36 (1): 3–23. doi:10.1080/10901027.2014.996925.

Bullough, Robert V., Kendra M. Hall-Kenyon, Kathryn L. Mackay, and Esther E. Marshall. 2014. "Head Start and the Intensification of Teaching in Early Childhood Education." *Teaching and Teacher Education* 37: 55–63. doi:10.1016/j.tate.2013.09.006.

Carle, Eric. 2009. *The Tiny Seed*. New York: Little Simon.

Carlo, María S., Diane August, Barry Mclaughlin, Catherine E. Snow, Cheryl Dressler, David N. Lippman, Teresa J. Lively, and Claire E. White. 2004. "Closing the Gap: Addressing the Vocabulary Needs of English-language Learners in Bilingual and Mainstream Classrooms." *Reading Research Quarterly* 39 (2): 188–215. doi:10.1598/rrq.39.2.3.

Castro, Diana C., Linda M. Espinosa, and Mariela M. Páez. 2011. "Defining and Measuring Quality Early Childhood Practices That Promote Dual Language Learner's Development and Learning." In *Quality Measurement in Early Childhood Settings* by Martha J. Zaslow. Baltimore: Paul H. Brookes, 2011.

Castro, Dina C., Cristina Gillanders, Donna Bryant, and Ximena Franco. 2011. "Nuestros Ninos: Promoting School Readiness of Dual-Language Learners." *PsycEXTRA Dataset*. doi:10.1037/e684922011-001.

Castro, Dina C., Ellen Peisner-Feinberg, Virginia Buysse, and Cristina Gillanders. 2010. "Language and Literacy Development of Latino Dual Language Learners: Promising Instructional Practices." In *Contemporary Perspectives on Language and Cultural Diversity in Early Childhood Education* by Olivia N. Saracho. Charlotte, NC: Information Age.

Centers for Disease Control and Prevention (CDC). 2017. Milestone Tracker. Atlanta: U.S. Department of Health & Human Services.

Chang, Yu-Kai, Yu-Jung Tsai, Tai-Ting Chen, and Tsung-Min Hung. 2012. "The Impacts of Coordinative Exercise on Executive Function in Kindergarten Children: An ERP Study." *Experimental Brain Research* 225 (2): 187–96. https://doi.org/10.1007/s00221-012-3360-9.

Charity, Anne H., Hollis S. Scarborough, and Darion M. Griffin. 2004. "Familiarity with School English in African American Children and Its Relation to Early Reading Achievement." *Child Development* 75 (5): 1340–356. doi:10.1111/j.1467-8624.2004.00744.x.

Clements, Douglas H. 1999. "Subitizing: What Is It? Why Teach It?" *Teaching Children Mathematics* 5: 400–05.

Clopton Kerri and Katheryn East. 2008. "'Are There Other Kids Like Me?' Children with a Parent in Prison." *Early Childhood Education Journal* 36: 195–98. 10.1007/s10643-008-0266-z.

Conboy, Barbara. 2013. "Neuroscience Research: How Experience with One or More Languages Affects the Developing Brain." In *California's Best Practices for Young Dual Language Learners: Research Overview Papers* by Child Development Division, California Department of Education (CDE). Available online at www.cde.ca.gov/sp/cd/ce/documents/dllresearchpapers.pdf.

Conboy, Barbara T., and Patricia K. Kuhl. 2011. "Impact of Second-language Experience in Infancy: Brain Measures of First- and Second-language Speech Perception." *Developmental Science* 14 (2): 242–48. doi:10.1111/j.1467-7687.2010.00973.x.

Cooper, Patsy. 2018. "The Enduring and Evolving Nature of Early Childhood Care and Education." In *The Wiley Handbook of Early Childhood Care and Education*, edited by Christopher P. Brown, Mary Benson McMullen, and Nancy File, 403–25. Hoboken, NJ: John Wiley & Sons.

Copple, Carol, and Sue Bredekamp. 2009. *Developmentally Appropriate Practice in Early Childhood Programs*. Washington, D.C: National Association for the Education of Young Children.

Corsaro, William A. 2015. *The Sociology of Childhood*. Los Angeles: SAGE.

Corsaro, Willliam A., Luisa Molinary, and Katherine Brown Rosier. 2002. "Zena and Carlotta: Transition Narratives and Early Education in the United States and Italy." *Human Development* 45 (5): 323–48. doi:10.1159/000064646.

Cowley, Sue. 2006. *Getting the Buggers to Behave*, 3rd ed. New York: Continuum.

De Lissovoy, Noah. 2013. "Pedagogy of the Impossible: Neoliberalism and the Ideology of Accountability." *Policy Futures in Education* 11 (4): 423–35. doi:10.2304/pfie.2013.11.4.423.

Deci, Edward L., Richard Koestner, and Richard M. Ryan. 1999. "A Meta-Analytic Review of Experiments Examining the Effects of Extrinsic Rewards on Intrinsic Motivation." *Psychological Bulletin* 125 (6): 627–68, discussion 692–700. https://doi.org/10.1037/0033-2909.125.6.627.

Deci, Edward L. and Richard M. Ryan. 2002. "The Paradox of Achievement: The Harder You Push, the Worse It Gets" in *Improving Academic Achievement: Impact of Psychological Factors on Education* edited by Joshua Aronson. New York: Academic Press.

Dee, Thomas, and Brian Jacob. 2011. "The Impact of No Child Left Behind on Student Achievement." *Journal of Policy Analysis and Management* 30 (3): 418–46. https://doi.org/10.1002/pam.20586.

Denton, Paula. 2007. "Open-Ended Questions: Stretching Children's Academic and Social Learning" from *The Power of Our Words* by Paula Denton. Northeast Foundation for Children.

Dutro, Elizabeth, and Makenzie Selland. 2012. "'I Like to Read, but I Know I'm Not Good at It': Children's Perspectives on High-Stakes Testing in a High-Poverty School." *Curriculum Inquiry* 42 (3): 340–67. doi:10.1111/j.1467-873x.2012.00597.x.

Dweck, Carol S. 2006. *Mindset: The New Psychology of Success*. New York: Ballantine Books.

Edwards, Susan, Mindy Blaise, and Marie Hammer. 2009. "Beyond Developmentalism? Early Childhood Teachers' Understandings of Multiage Grouping in Early Childhood Education and Care." *Australasian Journal of Early Childhood* 34 (4): 55–63.

Farrington, C.A., M. Roderick, E. Allensworth, J. Nagaoka, T.S. Keyes, D.W. Johnson, and N.O. Beechum. 2012. *Teaching Adolescents to Become Learners. The Role of Noncognitive Factors in Shaping School Performance: A Critical Literature Review.* Chicago: University of Chicago Consortium on Chicago School Research.

Fowler, Laura T. Sanchez, Tachelle I. Banks, Karla Anhalt, Heidi Hinrichs Der, and Tara Kalis. 2008. "The Association between Externalizing Behavior Problems, Teacher-Student Relationship Quality, and Academic Performance in Young Urban Learners." *Behavioral Disorders* 33 (3): 167–83. doi:10.1177/019874290803300304.

Freire, Paulo. 1970. *Pedagogy of the Oppressed*. New York: Continuum

Frey, William H. 2011. "A Demographic Tipping Point Among America's Three-Year-Olds." Brookings Institute: *State of Metropolitan America*, 26. Retrieved from www.brookings.edu/opnions/2011/0207_population_frey.aspx?p=1.

García, Ofelia, Jo Anne Kleifgen, and Lorraine Falchi. 2008. "From English Language Learners to Emergent Bilinguals." *Equity Matters: Research Review No.1*. New York: Teachers College, Columbia University.

Gibbon, G. 1991. *From Seed to Plant*. New York: Holiday House.

Gichuru, Margaret, Jeanetta G. Riley, Jo Robertson, and Mi-Hwa Park. 2015. "Perceptions of Head Start Teachers about Culturally Relevant Practice." *Multicultural Education* 22 (2): 46–50.

Gillanders, Christina, Dina C. Castro, and Ximena Franco. 2014. "Learning Words for Life: Promoting Vocabulary in Dual Language Learners." *The Reading Teacher* 68 (3): 213–21. https://doi.org/10.1002/trtr.1291.

Goldhaber, Dan, and Emily Anthony. 2007. "Can Teacher Quality Be Effectively Assessed? National Board Certification as a Signal of Effective Teaching." *The Review of Economics and Statistics* 89 (1): 134–50. doi: 10.1162/rest.89.1.134.

Goodwin, A. Lin, Ranita Cheruvu, and Celia Genishi. 2008. "Responding to Multiple Diversities in Early Childhood Education: How Far Have We Come?" In *Diversities in Early Childhood Education: Rethinking and Doing*, edited by Celia Genishi and A. Lin Goodwin, 3–10. New York: Routledge.

Gopnik, Alison. 2012. "Scientific Thinking in Young Children: Theoretical Advances, Empirical Research, and Policy Implications." *Science* 337, no. 6102: 1623–627. doi:10.1126/science.1223416.

Green, Elizabeth. 2015. *Building a Better Teacher: How Teaching Works (and How to Teach It to Everyone)*. New York: W W Norton & Company.

Hatch, J. Amos. 2002. "A Special Section on Personalized Instruction Accountability Shovedown: Resisting the Standards Movement in Early Childhood Education." *Phi Delta Kappan* 83 (6): 457–62. doi:10.1177/003172170208300611.

Healthy Children. 2017. "Ages and Stages." www.healthychildren.org.

Heckman, James, Seong Hyeok Moon, Rodrigo Pinto, Peter Savelyev, and Adam Yavitz. 2010. "The Rate of Return to the High/Scope Perry Preschool Program." 2009. *Journal of Public Economics* 94: 114–28. doi:10.3386/w15471.

Helm, Judy Harris and Lilian G. Katz. 2015. *Becoming Young Thinkers: Deep Project Work in the Classroom*. New York: Teachers College Press.

Hyson, Marilou. 2008. *Enthusiastic and Engaged Learners: Approaches to Learning in the Early Childhood Classroom*. New York: Teachers College Press.

Hyson, Marilou, and Jackie L. Taylor. 2011. "Caring about Caring: What Adults Can Do to Promote Young Children's Prosocial Skills." *YC Young Children* 66 (4): 74–83. www.jstor.org/stable/42731285.

Jerome, Elisabeth M., Bridget K. Hamre, and Robert C. Pianta. 2009. "Teacher-Child Relationships from Kindergarten to Sixth Grade: Early Childhood Predictors of Teacher-perceived Conflict and Closeness." *Social Development* 18 (4): 915–45. doi:10.1111/j.1467-9507.2008.00508.x.

Johnston, Peter H. 2012. *Opening Minds: Using Language to Change Lives*. Portland, ME: Stenhouse.

Kagan, S. L., Moore, E., & Bredekamp, S. (Eds.). 1995. "Reconsidering Children's Early Development and Learning: Toward Shared Beliefs and Vocabulary." Washington, DC: National Education Goals Panel.

Katz, Lilian G., and Sylvia Chard. 2000. *Engaging Children's Minds: The Project Approach* (2nd ed.). Norwood, NJ: Ablex.

Kostelnik, Marjorie J. and Marilyn L. Grady. 2009. *Getting It Right from the Start: The Principals Guide to Early Childhood Education*. Thousand Oaks, CA: Corwin.

Kumar, Revathy, Stuart A. Karabenick, and Jacob N. Burgoon. 2015. "Teachers' Implicit Attitudes, Explicit Beliefs, and the Mediating Role of Respect and Cultural Responsibility on Mastery and Performance-focused Instructional Practices." *Journal of Educational Psychology* 107 (2): 533–45. doi:10.1037/a0037471.

Ladson-Billings, Gloria. 1994. *The Dreamkeepers: Successful Teachers of African American Children*. San Francisco: Jossey-Bass.

——. 2006. "Yes, but How Do We Do It? Practicing Culturally Relevant Pedagogy." In *White Teachers, Diverse Classrooms: A Guide to Building Inclusive Schools, Promoting High Expectations, and Eliminating Racism*, edited by Julie Landsman and Chance W. Lewis, 29–42. Sterling, VA: Stylus.

——. 2014. "Culturally Relevant Pedagogy 2.0: A.k.a. the Remix." *Harvard Educational Review* 84 (1): 74–84. doi:10.17763/haer.84.1.p2rj131485484751.

Langford, Rachel. 2010. "Critiquing Child-Centred Pedagogy to Bring Children and Early Childhood Educators into the Centre of a Democratic Pedagogy." *Contemporary Issues in Early Childhood* 11 (1): 113–27. doi:10.2304/ciec.2010.11.1.113.

Lee, Rosalyn D., Xiangming Fang, and Feijun Luo. 2013. "The Impact of Parental Incarceration on the Physical and Mental Health of Young Adults." *Pediatrics* 131 (4). doi:10.1542/peds.2012-0627d.

Madaus, George F., Jennifer Higgins, and Michael K. Russell. 2009. *The Paradoxes of High Stakes Testing: How They Affect Students, Their Parents, Teachers, Principals, Schools, and Society*. Charlotte, NC: Information Age.

Mavilidi, Myrto-Foteini, Anthony D. Okely, Paul Chandler, Dylan P. Cliff, and Fred Paas. 2015. "Effects of Integrated Physical Exercises and Gestures on Preschool Children's Foreign Language Vocabulary Learning." *Educational Psychology Review* 27 (3): 413–26. doi:10.1007/s10648-015-9337-z.

Maxwell, Lesli A. 2014. "U.S. School Enrollment Hits Majority-Minority Milestone." *Education Week*. Accessed September 19, 2018. www.edweek.org/ew/articles/2014/08/20/01demographics.h34.html.

Meier, Deborah. 2007. "Quick Fixes and Student Potential." *Profession* 2007 (1): 136–40. doi:10.1632/prof.2007.2007.1.136.

Meisels, Samuel J. 1999. "Assessing readiness." In *The Transition to Kindergarten*, edited by Robert C. Pianta and Martha J. Cox, 39–63. Baltimore: Paul H. Brookes.

——. 2007. "No Easy Answers: Accountability in Early Childhood." In *School Readiness and the Transition to Kindergarten in the Era of Accountability*, edited by Robert C. Pianta, Martha J. Cox, and Kyle L. Snow, 31–47. Baltimore: Paul H. Brookes.

Metz, Kathleen E. 2004. "Children's Understanding of Scientific Inquiry: Their Conceptualization of Uncertainty in Investigations of Their Own Design." *Cognition and Instruction* 22 (2): 219–90. https://doi.org/10.1207/s1532690xci2202_3.

Mindes Gayle. 2005. "Social Studies in Today's Early Childhood Curricula." *YC Young Children* 60 (5): 2–18. https://works.bepress.com/gayle_mindes/11.

Miyake, Akira, Naomi P. Friedman, Michael J. Emerson, Alexander H. Witzki, Amy Howerter, and Tor D. Wager. 2000. "The Unity and Diversity of Executive Functions and Their Contributions to Complex "Frontal Lobe" Tasks: A Latent Variable Analysis." *Cognitive Psychology* 41 (1): 49–100. https://doi.org/10.1006/cogp.1999.0734.

Moll, Luis C. and Norma González. 1994. "Lessons from Research with Language-Minority Children." *Journal of Reading Behavior* 26 (4): 439–56. doi:10.1080/10862969409547862.

National Research Council. 2000. *How People Learn: Brain, Mind, Experience, and School.* Expanded Edition. Washington, DC: The National Academies Press.

——. 2012. *A Framework for K-12 Science Education: Practices, Crosscutting Concepts, and Core Ideas.* Washington, DC: National Academies Press.

National Science Teachers Association. 2014. "NSTA Position Statement: Early Childhood Science Education." Accessed July 31. www.nsta.org/docs/PositionStatement_EarlyChildhood.pdf.

Nieto, Sonia. 2002. *Language, Culture, and Teaching: Critical Perspectives for a New Century.* Mahwah, NJ: Lawrence Erlbaum Associates.

Ottolenghi Carol. 2002. *Jack and the Beanstalk.* Greensboro, NC: Carson-Dellosa.

Paley, Vivian Gussin. 1992. *You Can't Say You Can't Play.* Cambridge, MA: Harvard University Press.

Paris, Django. 2012. "Culturally Sustaining Pedagogy: A Needed Change in Stance, Terminology, and Practice." *Educational Researcher* 41 (3): 93–97. https://doi.org/10.3102/0013189X12441244.

——. 2016. "On Educating Culturally Sustaining Teachers." Ann Arbor, MI: TeachingWorks Working Papers. www.teachingworks.org/images/files/TeachingWorks_Paris.pdf.

Parker, Audra, and Stacey Neuharth-Pritchett. 2006. "Developmentally Appropriate Practice in Kindergarten: Factors Shaping Teacher Beliefs and Practice." *Journal of Research in Childhood Education* 21 (1): 65–78. doi:10.1080/02568540609594579.

Parks, Amy Noelle, and Sarah Bridges-Rhoads. 2012. "Overly Scripted: Exploring the Impact of a Scripted Literacy Curriculum on a Preschool Teacher's Instructional Practices in Mathematics." *Journal of Research in Childhood Education* 26 (3): 308–24. https://doi.org/10.1080/02568543.2012.684422.

Poppe, Lisa M., LaDonna A. Werth, Jacqueline M. Guzman, Gail L. Brand, Marilyn S. Fox, Leslie Crandall, Tonia Renee Durden, and RaSheema Pi. 2011. "Ages and Stages: 3-, 4- and 5-Year-Olds.G2106." *Faculty Publications om CYFS* 76. https://digitalcommons.unl.edu/cyfsfacpub/76.

Polakow, Valerie. 2007. *Who Cares for Our Children? The Child Care Crisis in the Other America.* New York: Teachers College Press.

Purvis, Karyn B., David R. Cross, Donald F. Dansereau, and Sheri R. Parris. 2013. "Trust-Based Relational Intervention (TBRI): A Systemic Approach to Complex Developmental Trauma." *Child & Youth Services* 34 (4): 360–86.

Ramírez, Naja Ferjan, Rey R. Ramírez, Maggie Clarke, Samu Taulu, and Patricia K. Kuhl. 2016. "Speech Discrimination in 11-month-old Bilingual and Monolingual Infants: A Magnetoencephalography Study." *Developmental Science* 20 (1). doi:10.1111/desc.12427.

Raver, Cybele C., Clancy Blair, and Michael Willoughby. 2013. "Poverty as a Predictor of 4-Year-Olds' Executive Function: New Perspectives on Models of Differential Susceptibility." *Developmental Psychology* 49 (2): 292–304. http://dx.doi.org/10.1037/a0028343.

Resnick, Lauren B. 1995. "From Aptitude to Effort: A New Foundation for Our Schools." *Daedalus* 124 (4): 55–62. www.jstor.org/stable/20027327.

Reynolds Arthur J., Judy A. Temple, Dylan L. Robertson, Emily A. Mann. 2001. "Long-Term Effects of an Early Childhood Intervention on Educational Achievement and Juvenile Arrest: A 15-Year Follow-Up of Low-Income Children in Public Schools." *JAMA* 285 (18): 2339–346. https://doi.org/10.1001/jama.285.18.2339.

Rinaldi, Carlina. 2006. *In Dialogue with Reggio Emilia: Listening, Researching and Learning.* London: Routledge, 2010.

Rogoff, Barbara. 2003. *The Cultural Nature of Human Development.* New York: Oxford University Press.

Santos, R. M., and M. M. Ostrosky. 2002. *Understanding the impact of language differences on classroom behavior: What Works Briefs.* Champaign, IL: University of Illinois at Urbana-Champaign, Center on the Social and Emotional Foundations for Early Learning.

Schwartz, Sydney L., and Sherry M. Copeland. 2010. *Connecting Emergent Curriculum and Standards in the Early Childhood Classroom: Strengthening Content and Teaching Practice.* New York: Teachers College Press.

Seefeldt, Carol, Sharon Castle, and Renee C. Falconer. 2013. *Social Studies for the Preschool/Primary Child.* 9th ed. Boston: Pearson.

Sherfinski, Melissa. 2013. "Class and Parents' Agency in West Virginia: Between Choices and Rights." *Education Policy Analysis Archives* 21 (78). Retrieved September 19, 2018, from http://epaa.asu.edu/ojs/article/view/1268.

Sleeter, Christine E. 2011. *The Academic and Social Value of Ethnic Studies: A Research Review.* Washington, DC: National Education Association. www.nea.org/assets/docs/NBI-2010-3-value-of-ethnic-studies.pdf.

Smutny, Joan F. and Sarah E. von Fremd, eds. 2010. *Differentiating for the Young Child: Teaching Strategies Across the Content Areas (PreK–3).* 2nd ed. Thousand Oaks, CA: Corwin.

Souto-Manning, Mariana. 2013. *Multicultural Teaching in the Early Childhood Classroom: Approaches, Strategies, and Tools, Preschool-2nd Grade.* New York, NY: Teachers College Press.

Stacey, Susan. 2009. *Emergent Curriculum in Early Childhood Settings: From Theory to Practice.* St. Paul, MN: Redleaf Press.

Stipek, Deborah. 2006. "No Child Left Behind Comes to Preschool." *The Elementary School Journal* 106 (5): 455–66. doi:10.1086/505440.

Uggen, Christopher and Suzy McElrath. 2014. "Parental Incarceration: What We Know and Where We Need to Go." *Journal of Criminal Law and Criminology* 104 (3): 597–604.

US Census Bureau. 2010.

U.S. Department of Education. 2016. "The State of Racial Diversity in the Educator Workforce." Washington, DC: Office of Planning, Evaluation and Policy Development, U.S. Department of Education. www2.ed.gov/rschstat/eval/highered/racial-diversity/state-racial-diversity-workforce.pdf.

U.S. National Education Goals Panel. Goal 1 Technical Planning Group et al. 1995. *Reconsidering Children's Early Development and Learning: Toward Common Views and Vocabulary.* Washington, D.C.: National Education Goals Panel.

Vinovskis, Maris. 2005. *The Birth of Head Start: Preschool Education Policies in the Kennedy and Johnson Administrations.* Chicago: The University of Chicago Press.

Vygotsky, L. S. 1978. *Mind in Society: The Development of Higher Psychological Processes.* Edited by Michael Cole, Vera John-Steiner, Sylvia Scribner, and Ellen Souberman. Cambridge, MA: Harvard University Press.

Weiss, Joanne. 2007. "Conditions for Student Success: The Cycle of Continuous Instructional Improvement." School Finance Redesign Project.

Wiggins, Grant, and Jay McTighe. 1998. *Understanding by Design.* Alexandria, VA: Association for Supervision and Curriculum Development.

Willingham, Daniel T. 2009. *Why Don't Students Like School?: A Cognitive Scientist Answers Questions About How the Mind Works and What it Means for the Classroom.* San Francisco, CA: Jossey-Bass.

Wittbold, Maureen. 1997. *Let's Talk About When Your Parent Is in Jail.* NewYork: PowerKids Press.

Wood, David, Jerome S. Bruner, and Gail Ross. 1976. "The Role of Tutoring in Problem Solving." *Journal of Child Psychology and Psychiatry* 17 (2): 89–100. doi:10.1111/j.1469-7610.1976.tb00381.x.

Zigler, Edward, Katherine Marsland, K., and Heather Lord. 2009. *The Tragedy of Child Care in America.* New Haven, CT: Yale University Press.

Index

Page numbers followed by (f) indicate figures.
Page numbers followed by (t) indicate tables.